Taste Berries™ for Teens #3

Taste Berries™ for Teens

#3

Inspirational
stories and
encouragement
on life, love,
friends and the
face in the mirror

With contributions
from teens for teens

Bettie B. Youngs, Ph.D., Ed.D.
Jennifer Leigh Youngs

Authors of the bestselling series
Taste Berries™ for Teens

Health Communications, Inc.
Deerfield Beach, Florida

www.hci-online.com

We would like to acknowledge the following publishers and individuals for permission to reprint the following material. (Note: The stories that were penned anonymously, that are public domain or were previously unpublished stories written by Bettie B. Youngs or Jennifer Leigh Youngs are not included in this listing. Also not included in this listing but credited within the text are those stories contributed or based upon stories by teens.)

Brown Hair, Green Eyes, Big Feet by Amber Mendoza and *Have You Ever Been to Juvenile Hall—Even to Visit Someone?* by Victoria Moore. Reprinted with permission by publisher Health Communications, Inc., Deerfield Beach, Florida, from *A Taste-Berry Teen's Guide to Managing the Stress and Pressures of Life* by Bettie B. Youngs, Ph.D., Ed.D. and Jennifer Leigh Youngs. ©2000 Bettie B. Youngs, Ph.D., Ed.D. and Jennifer Leigh Youngs.

A Letter to My Child (formerly titled *And a Child Shall Lead*) by Bettie B. Youngs, Ph.D., Ed.D. Reprinted with permission by publisher Health Communications, Inc., Deerfield Beach, Florida, from *Values from the Heartland* by Bettie B. Youngs, Ph.D., Ed.D. ©1995 Bettie B. Youngs, Ph.D., Ed.D.

September 11, 2001. Excerpt by Lisa Drucker reprinted with permission from the author.

Library of Congress Cataloging-in-Publication Data

Taste berries for teens #3 : inspirational stories and encouragement on life, love, friends and the face in the mirror / [compiled by] Bettie B. Youngs, Jennifer Leigh Youngs.

    p.   cm.

  ISBN 1-55874-961-6 (pbk.)

    1. Teenagers—Conduct of life. I. Title: Taste berries for teens number 3. II. Title: Taste berries for teens number three. III. Youngs, Bettie B. IV. Youngs, Jennifer Leigh, date.

BJ1661 .T36 2002

248.8'3—dc21

2001051763

Publisher: Health Communications, Inc.
       3201 S.W. 15th Street
       Deerfield Beach, FL 33442-8190

R-06-02

Cover illustration and design by Andrea Perrine Brower
Inside book typesetting by Lawna Patterson Oldfield

When I approach a young person,
I am inspired by two sentiments:
tenderness for what he is, and respect
for what he may become.

—Louis Pasteur

To: _____

. . . . a definite "taste berry"!

From: _____

Also by Bettie B. Youngs

A Taste-Berry Teen's Guide to Managing the Stress and Pressures of Life (Health Communications, Inc.)

More Taste Berries for Teens: A Second Collection of Inspirational Short Stories and Encouragement on Life, Love, Friendship and Tough Issues (Health Communications, Inc.)

Taste Berries for Teens Journal: My Thoughts on Life, Love and Making a Difference (Health Communications, Inc.)

Taste Berries for Teens: Inspirational Short Stories and Encouragement on Life, Love, Friendship and Tough Issues (Health Communications, Inc.)

Taste-Berry Tales: Stories to Lift the Spirit, Fill the Heart and Feed the Soul (Health Communications, Inc.)

A String of Pearls: Inspirational Stories Celebrating the Resiliency of the Human Spirit (Adams Media)

Gifts of the Heart: Stories That Celebrate Life's Defining Moments (Health Communications, Inc.)

Values from the Heartland: Stories of an American Farmgirl (Health Communications, Inc.)

Stress and Your Child: Helping Kids Cope with the Strains and Pressures of Life (Random House)

You and Self-Esteem: A Book for Young People—Grades 5–12 (Jalmar Press)

Safeguarding Your Teenager from the Dragons of Life: A Parent's Guide to the Adolescent Years (Health Communications, Inc.)

How to Develop Self-Esteem in Your Child: 6 Vital Ingredients (Macmillan/Ballantine)

Self-Esteem for Educators: It's Job Criteria #1 (Jalmar Press)

Keeping Our Children Safe: A Guide to Emotional, Physical, Intellectual and Spiritual Wellness (John Knox/Westminster Press)

Developing Self-Esteem in Your Students: A K–12 Curriculum (Jalmar Press)

Getting Back Together: Repairing the Love in Your Life (Adams Media)

Is Your Net-Working? A Complete Guide to Building Contacts and Career Visibility (John Wiley)

Managing Your Response to Stress: A Guide for Administrators (Jalmar Press)

Stress Management Skills for Educators (Jalmar Press)

Problem Solving Skills for Children (Jalmar Press)

Also by Jennifer Leigh Youngs

A Taste-Berry Teen's Guide to Managing the Stress and Pressures of Life (Health Communications, Inc.)

More Taste Berries for Teens: A Second Collection of Inspirational Short Stories and Encouragement on Life, Love, Friendship and Tough Issues (Health Communications, Inc.)

Feeling Great, Looking Hot and Loving Yourself: Health, Fitness and Beauty for Teens (Health Communications, Inc.)

Taste Berries for Teens Journal: My Thoughts on Life, Love and Making a Difference (Health Communications, Inc.)

Taste Berries for Teens: Inspirational Short Stories and Encouragement on Life, Love, Friendship and Tough Issues (Health Communications, Inc.)

Getting What You Want Out of Life: Goal-Setting Skills for Young Adults (Learning Tools, Inc.)

Contents

PART 1: GROWING PAINS: UNDERSTANDING—AND LIKING —THE FACE IN THE MIRROR

PART 2: MAKING, KEEPING AND
COPING WITH FRIENDS

PART 3: XOXO: FEELINGS OF LOVE

PART 4: TEENS TALK ABOUT
"THE PARENTS"—
"PILLARS" TO "POTHOLES"

PART 5: MOMENTS THAT CHANGED
THE WAY I LOOK AT LIFE

PART 6: VOICES FROM "BEHIND THE WALLS"

PART 7: COPING WITH PRIVATE PAIN

PART 8: DEAR DR. YOUNGS: WHAT SHOULD I DO?

PART 9: WHO IS "BINKY POODLECLIP"?
AND OTHER TANTALIZING
TRIVIA TIDBITS

Acknowledgments

We would like to thank the "taste berries" in the development of this book. First, to the many teens who were a part of this new addition to our *Taste Berries for Teens* series: Thank you for so generously opening your hearts and sharing your experiences so that other teens might better understand theirs. As always, you teach us the importance of living close to your heart, and of greeting each day with anticipated wonder—and without attachment to outcome. It's the last part that's most difficult, but you know it's what brings value and meaning to life. May we all be inspired to learn what you intuitively know and find so easy to live.

As always, we extend a heartfelt gratitude to our publisher, Peter Vegso, and the talented staff at Health Communications—most especially those with whom we work most closely: Christine Belleris, Lisa Drucker, Susan Tobias, Erica Orloff, Maria Dinoia, Kim Weiss, Randee Feldman, Lori Golden and to the others who are intricately woven into transporting our works into the hands and hearts of our readers. As always, a special thanks to Andrea Perrine Brower for her beautiful and fun cover designs on our books. We also extend a very special thanks to the taste berries in our office who worked closely on this project; most especially a staff of teens whose valuable input in this book is evident throughout.

And to the many important taste berries in our personal lives.

Bettie: Thank you Dad and guardian angel Mom and husband David Kirk, and to my brothers and sisters and their families. And to my "little chicken," Jennifer. You sweeten my life "just because." Always I honor the tenderness of who you are and deeply respect the privilege of watching your mission in life unfold year by year.

Jennifer: From the bottom of my heart, Mom (Bettie Youngs), thank you. I so appreciate the time we share in working together almost as much as I honor the love we have for each other. Every year I learn how special it is that in life we have one another. Thank you, Dad, Dic Youngs. You are my hero. And thank you, Jan Roff, for being such a support to our team. And to the love of my life, Clayt Ratzlaff, for all the ways you love me, and have shown me the truest and deepest meaning of being a taste berry. I so love you.

Also to the many friends in Chico: To Chad and Rhonda— your witnessing has been a testimony to the importance of my own, and your friendship has been a true blessing. And to Laura Lucht, a most dear friend and one who changed my life. To Glenn, for all the inspiration you've been. And to "Peanut" for the "attitude"!

And from both of us, to our many *brothers* and *sisters everywhere in the world,* thank you for sharing the journey and holding our hearts in such a touchingly human way. As always, we give all glory to God from whom all blessings flow.

Introduction

Welcome to *Taste Berries for Teens #3: Inspirational Stories and Encouragement on Life, Love, Friends and the Face in the Mirror*. If this is your first introduction to one of our books in the *Taste Berries for Teens* series, you're no doubt asking, *"What is a taste berry?"* A taste berry is a little fruit that, when eaten, mysteriously convinces the taste buds that all food—even something as bitter as a lemon—is delicious! This bright little berry has been used around the world for countless years to make the sometimes necessary eating of bitter foods, such as roots, tolerable.

The taste berry is a good metaphor for people helping, inspiring and encouraging each other: Has someone reached out when you were suffering a disappointment, nursing a broken heart, or feeling overwhelmed or "down-and-out"? If so, that person was acting as your "taste berry."

On some days we could all use a taste berry! No one knows this better than today's teens coping with the ups and downs of life—which is one reason you value your friends as much as you do. Good friends cheer each other on, laugh and cry together, and commiserate and listen to each other. They allow a "safe place" for you to share your deepest thoughts, lofty and noble goals, and your hopes and fears—without worry of being judged, criticized or made to feel silly for feeling the way you do. In short, good friends are taste berries: They sweeten life's joys and ease the bitterness of life's downtimes.

That teens readily understand the importance of "being there" for others is another reason we so enjoy working with teens and writing books that deal with real-life teen issues. In doing this book, *Taste Berries for Teens #3*, once again we've worked with hundreds of teens between the ages of eleven and twenty, from different backgrounds and from all over the country. Based on our work with teens, we've included units on themes you teens tell us are the staple of life—making, keeping and coping with friends, finding a special someone and then coping with breakups and makeups, and sorting through control issues with your parents. And, in each new book in the *Taste Berries for Teens* series, we include units that we find to be of growing interest or concern. For example, more and more teens are deeply concerned about friends and classmates who are facing a health crisis such as being diagnosed with bipolar disease, personality disorders or AIDS (frighteningly, 50 percent of new AIDS cases are found in the fourteen to twenty-four age group), or who have a serious alcohol or drug problem. Or you may want to know how to best encourage a parent to get help for a problem you feel he or she is having (such as drinking too much, or being too stressed-out much of the time). We hear you. So in this book, we've included several units of your stories expressing your concerns and your thoughts and advice for teens.

This book, like several others in the series, is divided into nine units. Each unit stands alone, so you can move around in the book as you see titles that are of interest to you. Each unit opens with "A Word from the Authors," which is our chance to introduce the subject and to sum up what you can expect to find within it. Then, we've included ten to twenty stories expressing the many sides to that theme. Note that the views expressed within stories are those of the teens writing them, and as such, do not necessarily represent our view. A story may represent how you see things, but maybe not. So read each story with an open mind and know that other teens come to their views just as you come to yours: through experience—what they've seen or heard to date. Perhaps this is another reason teens enjoy the *Taste Berries for Teens* series: You get to read about what other teens are going through, and how they've approached or are working through these experiences. From this, you can get an idea about how you're doing with similar issues, and also see how much you've grown—matured—or wish to.

As always, we hope you will be inspired and encouraged by reading about other teens. To that end, we also invite you to send us your stories or experiences that have touched your life and shaped your views of life and living. You may send a story for publication in an upcoming *Taste Berries for Teens* by writing to:

Taste-Berry Teen Team
3060 Racetrack View Drive
Del Mar, CA 92014

❤ *Taste berries to you, Bettie and Jennifer Youngs*

Part 1

Growing Pains: Understanding— and Liking—the Face in the Mirror

There is no greater gift you can give the people you love than to be healthy and happy.

—Ann Richards, former governor of Texas

The worst loneliness is not to be comfortable with yourself.

—Mark Twain

The influence of a beautiful, helpful, hopeful character is contagious and may revolutionize a whole town.

—Eleanor H. Porter

A Word from the Authors

Just as you strive to have a good relationship with your family, teachers and friends, you also want to be on friendly terms with the face in the mirror. "Liking the face in the mirror" is about *knowing* and *understanding* yourself. It's the *work* of coming to terms with "who you are"—identifying your values and being willing to stand up for them. It's discovering your interests, talents and gifts—and being willing to develop them to the point where they bring you great joy. It's about learning your likes and dislikes—and understanding how those can change as you mature and change. Self-understanding, then, is about discovering who you are. Just as when you were an infant, then a toddler and a pre-teen, being a teen means you are still in a state of growing and changing. So, who you were at thirteen is different from who you will be at nineteen.

In short, discovering "who you are" is about discovering yourself year by year by year. In a recent workshop, seventeen-year-old Heather MacNaughton from Edmonton, Canada, told us, "When I was fourteen, I just knew I was cool. But then one day last year (when I was sixteen) as I was cleaning out a drawer with old papers and things, I found an old two-page letter I'd written to a friend. This was a person who was my friend primarily because she 'used' me to help do her homework—or to copy mine. The letter was my response to her telling me she didn't want to be friends anymore. The reason she and I were in an argument in the first place was because I spoke up and told her I didn't want to turn over my homework to her as much as she asked me to. I informed her that I was tired of doing that, and basically served her notice that I wasn't about to continue. But when she threatened to kiss our friendship good-bye if I didn't continue to meet her demands, I promised her in the letter that I'd continue helping her with her algebra homework every night, and that she could copy my homework whenever she needed. I promised this girl the use of my coveted school jacket, and I promised her other things, too. I couldn't believe it. If something like that happened to me today, I'd say, 'Gosh, I'll help you with homework if I have the time, but as for copying my papers on a regular basis, no way!' And if a friend threatened to end our friendship based on my saying this, I'd use it as a sign we had no friendship in the first place. So, finding and reading the letter was interesting in that I realized how much I'd changed in just the barely two years since I'd written the letter."

Good for Heather: We like her "new and improved" commitment to assert herself! And we agree with her that the letter was a good measure of how she'd changed. *Change* is a key word in learning to like and accept yourself. The many teens we worked with on this unit described working toward self-understanding as both a "painful and loving experience." Perhaps sixteen-year-old Sabrina McGraw summed it up best when she said, "Liking the face in the mirror is a simple enough concept, but it's not without its challenges. The person I see looking back in the mirror has a changing face. One day everything is just the best, and I'm very sure of myself, but on some days, the face looking back is upset with me over something I've said or done or because of the way I've handled things in a given situation. And sometimes the person looking at me in the mirror is a total stranger, a 'new me'—or at least a new part of myself I'd not recognized before. I do try to be patient, still, it's not always easy to be on completely great terms with the face in the mirror." Sabrina makes a good point. New experiences, along with the constant emotional ups and downs of teen life, can leave you feeling confused about knowing who you *really* are.

"Mom, I can relate to Sabrina. There were times when, as a teen, I didn't know how I'd respond to a given situation until I was actually face-to-face with it. While I prided myself on 'being together,' and 'being cool to cope,' the truth is, I 'winged' a lot of moments. One that comes to mind right now is when I had a job I really liked at a hotel gift shop. Every day I worked there, I did a good job, and I knew the manager knew it. Then one day, the manager decided I would be an asset working at the front desk, in reception. So I was given a pay raise and moved to the front desk.

"It sounded like a good idea at the time, but the truth is, it was more than I could handle—particularly the first day. I found it totally overwhelming! I wasn't familiar with how to check in guests and there was a line a mile long. Not only was I unfamiliar with the computer program used to check them in, but also all three million of the phone lines were ringing, and guests were staring at me as if I were incompetent—which is exactly how I felt. When I left for my two o'clock break, I just breathed a huge sigh of relief and thought, 'I'm out of here!' The thing is, I didn't come back. Nor did I tell anyone I wasn't going to come back after break. I know I didn't handle this situation very well, but I was so overwhelmed at the time. Not returning seemed like an option to me, even though it was out of character for me to react in that way.

"Being a teen is much like that: You don't always know what you're going to do or how you're going to respond. Each new obstacle and challenge is a matter of trial and error. It's this trial and error that can fill you with a great deal of uncertainty about who you really are. Prior to that day for me at the reception desk, if someone had posed that scenario and then asked me what I would do to handle it, I'd have the 'right' answer. But when faced with the situation, I didn't know what to do (so I left and didn't return). Personally, I was surprised there was a part of me that felt so overwhelmed! Not knowing exactly how you're going to respond in all situations (which can make you feel as though you don't have it 'all together') can make it difficult to always like the face in the mirror. And of course, on many days you feel like the most cool person on the planet, but again, being a teen is to constantly move between these two feelings—so you're certain you don't know yourself."

From meeting the expectations of family, friends, teachers and classmates, to meeting those of your own; from being sized up by your friends and classmates, to sizing up peer pressure with solid resolve, being a teen provides ample opportunities for meeting different faces in the mirror. As seventeen-year-old Sean McDonald suggested, "If you're going to get to know the face in the mirror, you'd better eat your Wheaties daily!"

Here are five suggestions from teens on how to *get on a first-name basis with yourself:*

- **Spend time with yourself, alone.** Just as you spend time with your friends to get to know and enjoy them, spend time alone with yourself. Whether listening to music while relaxing or going for a bike ride, or enjoying your hobby, take the *time* to be in a relationship with yourself.

- **Talk to yourself and call yourself by your name: It "personalizes" the face in the mirror.** For example, if you're faced with a big decision, you might say, "Bobby, you're going to have to think about this so you really know what you'd like to do here. Your friends think you should do X, your parents suggest you should do Y, but what do you think you should do? How do you really feel about this and what outcome are you hoping to achieve?" Try it. You'll find that talking to yourself cements a personal, friendly relationship with the face in the mirror.

- **Be as positive as you can.** Start with the words you tell yourself. Forgo any negative self-statements ("I'm so stupid"), and do not "dog" on yourself (get in a funk or have a bad attitude). Such things only serve to make you feel bad about yourself. Doing so is not productive, and doesn't help you be your best or do your personal best. Seeing yourself in the most positive light is a good way to have a good reputation with yourself.

- **Forgive yourself for goof-ups.** No one can be cool all of the time. When you're not at your best, say, "I'm sorry" or "I thought that was a good decision, but I can see now that it wasn't the best choice" and then move on. Doing this doesn't mean you have a ready-made excuse, but rather, that you are looking closely to see for yourself if the choices and decisions you made are the best possible ones—and know the difference. It sets you up for having a good reputation with the face in the mirror. It shows that you understand that on one day you are a superhero, and the next, simply human. That you are capable of greatness—and doing stupid and goofy things, too—is a healthy and realistic image.

- **Pep talks are always welcome!** Know that it's normal to sometimes feel like a yo-yo—bouncing around from one feeling to another. Adolescence is a time of hormone changes, some of which can account for one moment feeling pulled this way, and the next moment feeling pulled in a different direction. Be patient with yourself as you renew your day-by-day goal to do and be your personal best. When you look in the mirror, *encourage* yourself: Pep talks are always welcome!

We love that advice, and wish we had room to print all of your many suggestions. As the stories in this unit show, not only are today's teens deeply involved in self-exploration, but they are aware when they unearth new understandings. And while you teens find that the work of self-discovery is sometimes "an uphill battle," you also know the effort is worth the gain. As Sir Edmund Hillary's famous quote suggests: "It's not just the mountain we conquer, but *ourselves.*"

❤ *Taste berries to you, Bettie and Jennifer Youngs*

Two Sides of "Me"

When I was young,
life was easy,
Summers were then,
slow and breezy.

Now I'm a teen,
No more solitary voice,
It's a complicated life
Everything's a choice.

Once just Mandy,
Now me and she,
I'd like to say "I,"
But it's really "we."

There's a me on the inside
And me on the out,
It's confusing us both,
And keeps me in doubt.

When I look on the inside,
I see a girl who
Feels quite secure
And isn't demure.

She's sure of herself,
Refreshingly cool,
She can handle it all
And is so smart in school.

She's friendly and witty,
Commits to writing in ink,
And she doesn't much care
What anyone thinks.

But on the outside
Is a shy, timid girl,
Who feels insecure
And not all that sure.

A girl not in control
Or gutsy,
Or cool,
And merely average in school.

Not pretty enough
Quite often a klutz
Not graceful nor witty,
And thinks no one really likes her that much.

Inside and out
How long will it be
Before I'm together
And there's just one of me?

Mandy Flaspeter, 18

Cantaloupe, Hampa,
Letters and Balloons

My mother always does the family's big grocery shopping on Saturday. Usually I go along, but yesterday I was feeling sort of down and asked if I could just hang out in my room, listen to music and clean my closet. Mom said okay. I put on some music and laid down, just thinking about things: my friends, things going on at school and Hampa—who seemed to be the person most on my mind.

Ever since I was a little girl, I remember our family going to my grandparents' house every Sunday afternoon. When I look through my grandmother's pictures, I realize I've been going to her house even before I had memories of it—so really, I'd been going there *all* of my life.

Unfortunately, my grandmother no longer lives in the house I recall with such fondness. Now she lives in a smaller house. She said she moved because after my grandpa died, the house "was too big for me to handle!" I think it was because the house gave her too many memories of my grandpa. Her new house is a nice enough house, but it isn't the same. I look at the walls where pictures hang, and I remember exactly where they used to hang at the old house. I think they looked better on the walls of her old house; they seemed to be more at home there than here.

But I can see how Grandma could feel that the memories of the two of them in that old house were just too much to deal with every single day. I know I'd want to move away from things that reminded me on a daily basis—maybe even every minute of every waking hour—of having someone as awesome as my grandpa in my life, but no longer.

Grandpa—we used to call him "Hampa"—was worth remembering. I have so many fond memories of him. One of my favorites was how he used to hoist me up on a really tall kitchen stool to sit next to him at the kitchen table. He had a "sweet tooth" as he called it for eating cantaloupe and sweet pickles—together. He had a little routine for doing this. Carefully, he pared the cantaloupe, and cut it in slices. Then, he opened a jar of pickles canned by my grandma. Then, he'd look at the cantaloupe and sweet pickles, rub his hands together—like he couldn't wait to begin eating—roll his eyes, lick his lips and say, "Ready, set, go!" Then handing me a fork, with a slice of cantaloupe in one hand, we'd stab the fork into a sweet pickle—right from the jar—and alternate eating the pickle and cantaloupe. Grandma would look at us and make faces and say, "Oh, I don't know how you can stand to eat that!" But she was used to our doing it. "Those two!" she'd say, shaking her head and laughing as she brought us a wet cloth to wipe our hands and faces. The first words out of my grandfather's mouth the moment he had finished his first bites were always the same: He'd close his eyes and with his head swaying from side to side say, "Oh, Lordy! Nothin' like cantaloupe and pickles!"

I never did get used to the taste of cantaloupe and sweet pickles, but I ate them anyway. I just loved being with Hampa. He was so sweet, so affectionate. And I liked the way he smelled, sort of like that muscle rub Ben Gay, a kind of minty smell.

The older I get, the more I remember our times together. Maybe it's because when I was small and Grandpa was alive, I didn't have to "remember" him; he was right there. But now that he's gone, the memories just keep flowing, like all the affectionate nicknames he had for me. If my parents went out of town or if they were going to have a late night out with friends, I got to stay overnight with my grandparents—who would let me sleep in their bed with them. Sometimes I would lay there—in my red footy pajamas—unable to get to sleep. My grandma had no problem going fast asleep, and I'd hear Hampa snoring, so I knew he was asleep, too. So I'd slip out of bed and try to sneak out of the room. Never once did I make it! Just as I got to the door Hampa would say, "You get back here and get into bed you 'little monster'!" I loved it when he called me that!

A couple of years later, Hampa had a heart attack.

I have memories of that, too.

I was eating chicken-noodle soup when the call came to our house. "A coma?" my mother asked, nearly whispering the words. I didn't know what it meant, but the way she put her hands to her face, my sister and I knew it couldn't be good. Then, nearly slamming the phone back on the hook, she yelled, "We have to go to Grandpa's house, kids. Get your coats. Now!" I remember thinking, "Well, I guess Grandpa and I will have cantaloupe and some sweet pickles then." When we got to my grandparents' home, my grandfather had already been taken to the hospital.

Hampa died.

I have memories of that, too.

I was sitting (on a very hard wooden bench) at the funeral with my family. Everybody was sad and crying, and I really didn't understand what a funeral was about. People cried when they got hurt or when they fell down—but everyone here was dressed up. It didn't seem a lot different from church. So to keep from looking at everyone crying, I just played with the zipper of my pink jacket. Finally, I asked, "Why is everyone crying?" No one answered me, although later that day my older sister explained to me that "Hampa died."

"What is 'died'?" I asked.

"Well," she explained, "it's where you lie down and are very quiet for a long time."

"Okay," I said, thinking it was fine for Hampa to lie down for a while. I figured that when he woke up, everyone would stop being so sad. Being so young at the time, I didn't understand that when someone died, it wasn't like they were going to get up any time soon. But about a week after Hampa had gone away (died), my mother explained "died" a little more and said that Hampa was now in heaven, and that we should be happy for him.

Happy or not, I missed him. So I began writing Hampa letters telling him that I missed him and that wherever he was, to please come back because everyone missed him, especially Grandma—who now cried all the time. I wrote my letters and gave them to my mother, who worked for the post office.

I was positive I'd get immediate replies from Hampa, because with my mom working for the post office, I knew she'd see to it that my letters got delivered. She knew how much I missed Hampa and wanted to hear from him, so I assumed she would make sure my letters got delivered even before anyone else's letters to their grandpa.

Sadly, it didn't work that way. Months and months went by, and still, no reply from Grandpa. Then one day as I was watching TV, I saw a show where a little girl was in the same predicament as I—only it was her father, not her grandfather, who had died. Instead of mailing letters to her father—who was also in heaven—she attached a letter to a balloon, took it outside, and then released it. Sure enough, the balloon took the letter soaring heavenward.

Her approach worked much better than my sending letters through the post office: She got letters back from her father! Well, this seemed like proof-positive that sending letters to heaven in a balloon was far more effective than going through the post office. Immediately, I wrote Hampa a letter, attached it to a bright red balloon and let it go.

The next day I checked the mail. No letter. I checked the next day. No letter. But I knew Grandpa was old and forgetful, so I thought he probably forgot to write back—but it didn't mean he didn't miss me. So I was patient. For almost a month, each and every day I'd check the mailbox. Still, no return mail from Hampa—even though on every envelope, and at the end of my letter, I'd printed in bold letters, "Write Back Hampa!"

That's when I decided that "died" was more permanent than I had imagined.

I'm sixteen now, and sometimes I have this need to just sit quietly and think of the times I spent with my grandfather. I'm surprised at how the memories of him are so important to me. And I'm amazed at how vivid the images of him are—like it was only yesterday that we sat together eating cantaloupe and sweet pickles, laughing while watching *David the Gnome* or *Inspector Gadget*. Always these memories put a huge smile on my face.

I think memories may be important not just to the times we've spent with others, but also to our own understanding of ourselves in those times. I know this is true for me. When I "see" myself as that little girl sitting with her grandpa eating cantaloupe and pickles, I love her: I love that little girl and the way she loved her grandpa. And I think memories have other benefits as well. When I recall times with my family and grandparents, I feel "safe," like I won't fall apart at those times when my life seems like it's breaking apart. I also think memories are a way to compare who I was then and who I am now and see all the ways I've changed, and that it's okay to change so much.

And maybe memories have an even deeper significance: Maybe they are one of God's ways of letting those who love each other "talk" to each other. I know that whenever I get this feeling of really missing Hampa, I feel it's because he's reading one of my letters. So I smile and know that it's at these times when Hampa is *writing* me back!

Mandy Martinez, 16

Monkey Bars

I know who I am.

I'm a fifteen-year-old in my "formative teens,"
Living the "best years," me and my raging hormones and genes.

I dream of getting my license and driving a fast red car,
But I'm not yet ready to give up playing on the monkey bars.

I'm a bookworm with purple hair and a daredevil "do,"
I'm on the fastest ride and a couch potato, too.

I have a song for every one of my ups and downs, good and bad,
Rave, reggae, jazz, and love songs for when I'm lonely or sad.

I'm a little afraid of what the future may hold,
But ready to soar high, wide and bold.

So full of "do-or-die" emotions, both highs and lows,
Some days it's tough to know whether to come, stay or go.

I'm ranting one minute and raving the next,
Then quiet and reflective and very perplexed.

Calmly walking to class—then bouncing off the walls,
Am I going crazy—or just to the mall?

I tackle life with the speed of a sonic boom,
But can't get out of bed, wanting to stay in my room.

I'm cool and confident and lonely, too,
And willing to trust—if you promise to be true.

Thousands of emotions, I'm all over the map,
Like love songs, then hip hop, then disco, then rap.

Oh, yes, I know who I am,
The question is, "Who do you think I am?"

Margaret Garza, 15

"Mr. Personality Plus"

Joel Kneely was one of the "cool" kids at school. He and I had sat next to each other in Spanish class. Everyone liked him. He seemed to have it all: He was good in academics, terrific in sports and one of the friendliest students at school. He had a great personality, and a special knack for making others feel good about themselves, no matter what. Like, whenever he saw anyone down in the dumps, it was his nature to want to help that person turn around what we students referred to as a "suck-attitude." We all appreciated his way of looking at the "up" side of things. He was our "Mr. Personality Plus."

Image our shock when he committed suicide!

We learned this horrendous news through our teachers and counselors at school one day, when a special assembly was called and everyone in the entire school was mandated to attend. We didn't know why a special assembly had been called, but we figured it was for something special—like perhaps someone at our school had won some mega contest or something. We're a big school, and someone is always doing something awesome. But nothing of the sort had happened. Instead, we learned that our friend had taken his life. The assembly was called by the school counselors to tell us how we could "come to terms" with our friend's suicide.

I don't think I can, or that I ever will.

It's been several months now since our friend took his life. I'm still as numb as the day when I sat there having just heard the words, "Your classmate, Joel Kneely, has died . . . suicide . . . funeral on . . ." Obviously, though we thought of Joel as "Mr. Personality Plus," he didn't feel that he was.

I think about him, and I can't imagine why he would want to end his life. Every time the classroom door opens and a student comes in late or returns from the restroom or something, I still find myself looking up, and for a few seconds, see him walking in, his big crooked grin in place. It's never him, of course. I miss him, and I'm sad, too.

It's been a while since the funeral, and still, I'm having a hard time understanding why he wanted to die. I tell myself that things happen for a reason, and Joel's in a better place—heaven. Still, I don't understand it: Joel had friends. He was cool. He was liked. So what didn't he have that he needed to hang in there? If he had personal problems at home or was in a lot of inner pain, why didn't he reach out for help? I mean, if he needed more love and attention than he was getting, why didn't he do what he needed to get it from us? You'd think that given his considerable skills in helping others feel good about things, he would have known how to illicit that from us. You'd think he would have allowed us to help him through whatever it was that was making his life so obviously unbearable.

This whole thing has left me doubting a lot of things. I especially doubt myself now. *Why didn't I see warning signs that he was hurting in some way?* The grief counselor at school told us students not to feel guilty about Joel's death, but how can we not? Every time I hear in the news that a kid has shot a classmate or teacher, they say there *are* warning signs and that most anyone should be able to pick up on them. So I keep thinking back on things to see if there were signs—behaviors out of the ordinary— with Joel, but I can't find any. I saw nothing that would lead me to believe Joel was unhappy—most especially to the point of ending his life. I especially think about those times when he was cheering me up—did it mean anything? Was it meant for me, or was he reassuring himself? I'm practically driving myself crazy wondering what I could have missed—and what I could or should have been looking for. That I didn't notice his sadness disturbs me.

The good news is that I've become more aware of how even the little things I do or say affect others. And I'm probably going to take the school counselor up on getting some counseling for myself. I've been feeling *really* guilty about turning to Joel when I was down, but I'm uncertain if I ever gave it back—or at least in ways that might have made a difference to Joel so that he'd still be alive. I don't think I trust my ability to see the little hurts or pains in others, and that worries me. If a friend or classmate of mine is hurting, will it have to look like a flashing marquee before I see it? And, should I trust myself to know my own feelings? What if I don't know myself as well as I thought, or if, when I'm feeling down, it's a worse sign than I imagine it to be?

I'd say this whole thing has made me feel insecure right now and that my self-esteem is a little shaky. I'm finding myself a little more quiet and withdrawn, which is because (I think) I'm still in shock, not only because a classmate committed suicide, but also because I had no clue he was feeling so distraught. You always hear the words, "Know yourself." For the first time, those words have meaning to me. I'm feeling like I need and want to know more about what makes people "tick" and why. My goal is to begin with me. I think that may be the best way to know and understand others.

Melissa Jean Wiley, 16

Daily Personal Pep Talk

Today's a new day!
You can do it!
Hop to it!
Start now!
Stand tall!
Chin up!
Look smart!
Think big!
The sky's the limit!
Smile!
Bear down!
Get to it!
Just do it!
You're doing great!
Keep it up!
Good work!
Wonderful!
Awesome!
Alllllllright!
Good job!
Way to go!
Excellent!
You did it!
I am proud of me!
I knew I could do it!
Cool!

Jennifer Leigh Youngs

A Seat in the Back

I've always been the sort of person who detested being called upon in class, not because I didn't want to look silly or stupid if I didn't know the answer (because I'm pretty smart, and usually do have the right answers), but mainly because I didn't like attention drawn to myself. And, unless otherwise assigned a seat by the teacher, I have always been a person who sits at the back of the classroom. There are other things about me, too: I don't have a lot of friends. I get teased a lot. And I've always been a chubby kid—which is also what I've been teased most about in my life.

I've found a way to change all that.

It began when a teacher suggested I try out for the basketball team. At first I thought it was an absolutely crazy idea because I wasn't a good athlete at all. Being chubby and all, not only was I not the most coordinated person in the world, but I had asthma to boot, so I get winded easily. I just knew that I'd never be able to keep pace with the others on the team, and everyone in the entire world at school would make fun of me. I'd only embarrass myself. I had other fears and doubts, too, but because the teacher—a favorite with me—kept insisting I "go for it," I decided to give it a try.

You can't believe how many times I nearly backed out of going. I mean, I truly was petrified, especially as the day of basketball tryouts got closer. But I did go!

Getting up the courage to go to the tryouts was only the half of it! When I first started attending the practice sessions, I really didn't have a good handle on the game of basketball. To be honest with you, I didn't even know the rules of the game, much less what I was doing. Sometimes I'd get confused and take a shot at the wrong hoop—which made me feel really stupid. Then, when I saw two other girls do the same dumb thing, I decided to take it in stride and just focus on learning the game. So I made sure I understood which hoop was the one where my side racked up the points: Obviously, that was the one to aim for. Luckily, I wasn't the only one "new" at the game, so I decided to do my best at each practice session, and not be too hard on myself for the things I didn't know "just yet." This was something I had to tell myself over and over, because most of the girls were more experienced than me, and some were really good players. That some girls made it seem so easy made me a little frustrated at times. But I was learning, and I was getting better—even if it was little by little.

And then it became more fun. Soon I knew the rules, and the "moves"—even if I never really did get good at the shooting hoops part. Being part of a team was also really fun. And motivating. I practiced and practiced. And practiced. Pretty soon the competitive part of me was winning over my chubby-kid complex. I began to forget that I was chubby—and because I was, I thought I couldn't be a good player. This was "liberating"—a word I soon learned (and liked). With time, I learned the rules of the game, learned how to play and was making friends in the process—friends who respected my efforts to work hard and be a team player. I also discovered that my "size" wasn't such a disadvantage at all; I could make a basket from right under the net and block at the same time! I never had so much fun!

Now here's the thing: Gaining self-confidence in playing gave me the incentive to try out for other sports. Now, two years after I first tried out for basketball, I've tried out for volleyball and track and field. I like volleyball, but do not like track. I'm getting good at volleyball, and since that time, I even began a little weight training (we have a really great gym at our school, which helps because in our physical-education course, we get to choose our fitness activities). I'm still a little overweight for my height, but I'm in the best condition I've ever been in, and I'm really proud of that.

I wanted to share my story with you because I've changed my life—and it feels good. I have gone from "hiding" in the back of the classroom and not wanting to call attention to myself, to raising my hand—even when I sometimes wasn't 100 percent sure I had the right answer. And I have a better appreciation for my athletic abilities. I've learned that while I can't change everything (like I probably always will be a large-boned person—which makes me appear a little heavier than if I had small bones), I'm healthier, and that's a positive thing, too. And I have more self-confidence in myself, which is really useful. I'm less annoyed when others still find it their God-given duty to say something snide. I can do this not because I can ignore their comments or "consider the source," but because my life is a little "bigger" now. And I have better self-esteem.

With my "new and improved" self-confidence comes more compliments, and with more compliments comes more self-confidence. Sometimes those compliments come from teachers, and sometimes teammates and classmates. But these days, they also come from the face in the mirror—which is the person whose comments I value most. Best of all, I'm learning to really believe in me. It's such a good feeling. And a personally satisfying one.

Marie Nadyne Hersey, 16

The Most Incredible Kiss

I was in a relaxed pose, just leaning against his locker. Seeing me, he smiled. It *wasn't* one of those smiles that said nothing more than, "Okay, so you're person number three-trillion-and-one on the planet, but what the heck, here's a 'Hi person' smile for you." No. His smile was a genuine "Wow, where have you been all my life?" smile—or at least that's the way my heart took it.

That smile was packed with meaning for every cell in my body—especially those that know exactly who is to become the love of your life. I mean to tell you, when my eyes saw that smile, my heart leaped; cannons exploded in my head, and my entire being was simply rocked.

"Hi!" he said, still smiling that smile, and then, "I'm Roger. It's my second day here. My family just moved to town. What's your name?"

What's your name? One smile had made me feel giddy, but now he wanted to know my name! Suddenly, not one thing was wrong with my life. I loved the world and everyone in it. In fact, I loved the whole universe, the galaxy—extraterrestrials included. I believed in heaven, no questions asked.

"Celine," I answered shyly, yet coolly—knowing the two of us would have a love to rival Romeo and Juliet.

"Where are you going? I'll walk you there," he volunteered.

"Class. Sure . . ." I said, aglow with feelings I couldn't even name.

The next morning he was waiting for me at my locker and walked me to my first-period class. We sat together at lunch. He walked me to the bus after school. Finally, I had a real life.

On day three (Friday), I wanted to yell out my feelings for him but instead I decided to ask him if he'd like to come hang out at my house on Saturday afternoon. He apologized and said that he was needed at home to help his family unpack the rest of the boxes from the move. So we agreed to talk with each other by phone and meet up again first thing on Monday.

Monday was even better than the five other days we'd known each other: It was that day, as I was putting books in my locker, that he kissed me! We celebrated with a second kiss! The following day brought kiss number three, and by the end of the week, we'd shared seven more. I just knew my life couldn't get any better. Even though the school year was about to end, I was looking forward to the summer—and dates with Roger.

But tragedy struck. With eight days remaining in the school year, just five weeks and two days since I'd met him, Roger told me that on the last day of school, he would be leaving town to live with relatives in the town from which he and his family had just moved. When I asked him why, he said it was to work in the same summer job he'd held the year before and to spend time with his aging grandparents before he went off to college in the fall.

Wouldn't you know it, the summer was here and my Romeo was there, one thousand miles away—which might as well be Mars. Though we e-mailed each other almost every day, there's no comparison between reading "kisses and hugs" and receiving them in person.

That was my first experience with "love." What can I say except that it was awesome, and tragic, too. At least I can say that love has come and gone and no one wronged the other. Even though I miss Roger, and my heart hurts because he's gone, it's not like I've been jilted, so probably it's a different sort of heartache than when that happens—though I don't know that for sure. But what I do know for sure is that because of my feelings for Roger, I met a new part of me—and it was so good and so positive. I found myself walking around with a smile on my face—just because. If I had to nail down how my feelings toward Roger—and his feelings towards me—changed me, I'd say that

I've become a more "generous" person. I use that word because feeling as I did about him, I felt more alive, and I found myself more willing to listen to others and to want to do good things. I was more helpful at home, and I paid more attention to my little sister and was kinder to her, like when she wanted to spend time with me or go along with me when I ran errands and things. I was always like, "Okay!" and she loved it. I just felt more loving overall. Things seemed better, brighter.

Learning that loving another person is also about becoming a bigger and better and more loving person *yourself* is a most amazing discovery. What a remarkable thing! So Roger, if you're reading this right now, thank you for that smile. I will always remember it—and the way I felt when I was with you. And I most definitely love the ways it's changed me.

Celine Roarke, 17

Nasty Words

Taking my usual route to geometry class, I stopped in the bathroom. As I walked in, I heard hysterical laughter and saw three girls huddled together near the towel dispenser. I'd seen them around, and while they weren't girls I hung out with, I was nice and cheerfully said hello. They sort of looked at me, scowled, and made it clear I wasn't about to be let in on what was so funny. I washed my hands and reached for a paper towel. That's when I finally saw what they were laughing about. They'd scribbled vulgar messages about a girl named "Jessica K." all over the dispenser.

Jessica K. goes to our school and is one grade older than me. I thought about her seeing these terrible things written about her and how bad it would make her feel. I know I should have said something, but at the time, I was intimidated. I mean, they are mean-spirited girls: What if they then used my name as the target of their "fun"? And if I did say something, what would I have said? But then, looking around the bathroom, I suddenly saw all the different graffiti in the room: On the walls, near the mirrors, on the sinks, even on the floor—it was everywhere. The funny thing is that it had always been there; I'd just never noticed it before. Still roaring, the girls picked up their notebooks and backpacks and left the bathroom, all but stumbling with laughter.

I don't know whether it was their laugher or that I knew how wrong these terrible words were, but suddenly I had sort of a "I'm-sick-of-humanity" feeling. I looked at the vulgar words again and thought about it. I mean, marking up school property is an act of vandalism. But it is more than that. It is a hate crime. Hate crimes can lead others to feel that it's acceptable to express their hurt and rage openly, and to inflict it whenever and wherever and on whomever they wish. And that leads to violence, something that is a growing concern for everyone. It sure is in my community. Even the girls' bathroom in my school was filled with hatred!

I thought about how other students would have to see these ugly words whenever they used the towel dispenser. And that's when I decided to do something. I knew I didn't want Jessica, or anyone else, seeing these terrible and ugly words. So I spent the next minute smudging out the messages on the towel dispenser. I felt good about erasing the negative words—and the spirit of hatred or anger that had been written in the bathroom that day. And Jessica would never know what had been written about her.

It was the first time I saw myself as being a "social activist." Thinking of myself that way makes me feel proud of myself. It makes me feel taller and stronger—like I can be counted on to do my part in the world to create and keep the peace. What an amazingly simple concept: Peace begins inside each person. I'll never be silent again. I like this in me.

Shannon Tucker, 17

The Optimist Creed

Promise Yourself—

To be so strong that nothing can disturb your peace of mind.

To talk health, happiness and prosperity to every person you meet.

To make all your friends feel that there is something in them.

To look at the sunny side of everything and make your optimism come true.

To think only of the best, to work only for the best and to expect only the best.

To be just as enthusiastic about the success of others as you are about your own.

To forget the mistakes of the past and press on to the greater achievements of the future.

To wear a cheerful countenance at all times and give every living creature you meet a smile.

To give so much time to the improvement of yourself that you have no time to criticize others.

To be too large for worry, too noble for anger, too strong for fear and too happy to permit the presence of trouble.

Authored by Christian D. Larson in 1912, and adopted
as Optimist International's Creed in 1922

Getting It "Write"

My thoughts
are all gibberish
inside of my head
swirling and twirling,
fumbling and tumbling
end over end.

Emotions meet
and retreat
all rushing at once
clarity then confusion—
my head's in a spin.

Finally I sit
a pen in my hand
I scribble, then write,
oh yeah, comes the light!
words flowing so free
until finally
and totally
without any doubt
I understand me.

Kayleigh Sherman, 14

Dear Crystal . . .

Dear Crystal,

It's over. I'm done believing in you.

For so long I looked to you to make me feel better than I was. You offered me the chance to feel like I was covering all the bases, able to accomplish anything I wanted, including flying without a parachute. I said you were the solution to staying trim, being cool, being up and on. You worked your magic for a while. But you were wrong in assuming I'd be your friend forever.

I'm writing this letter to you because I am now making my own choice to go on without you.

Truth is, I feel better without you. I can be myself, and people still like me. The truth has set me free. I now realize how cunning you were to have made me believe so many lies about you—and about myself. All the things you brought to our friendship have crumbled. Worse, it almost killed the hope I could ever be myself. I've since learned that I depended on you to do what I can do for myself; the only difference is I have only myself to credit.

My old friend Pot, I thought you could make me happy, but honestly, I have to say good-bye to you also. The idea that your tar will linger in the fat cells of my body and brain totally grosses me out. I had no idea you, too, were as destructive as Crystal. You made me lazy and I forgot that life is fun without you. You made me lose my ambition, my drive, made me moody and live in a fog—one that lost me countless productive days, not to mention friends—and who knows what else.

Crystal and Pot, it's like this: Essentially, you both prevented me from being the person I was before I met you, and that's sad. I wish to find that girl again, apologize and reclaim her. You have not added to my life in positive ways, and in fact, have kept me from the life I should have, could have, and now intend to reclaim for myself. You see, today, I am a person in recovery, taking the time to learn all about myself and to deal with the shame and guilt because you were in my life. It's going to be tough—real tough—but I know I can do it. I've already begun.

My life today is new and exciting in so many ways. I see the world around me, and it's amazing to know that anything is possible—as long as I stay clean and sober. As long as I commit to bidding you good-bye. And yes, I can do it; I am that committed to me.

Paige Olds, 16

Nights Alone

My little brother, Nicky, is the most self-confident person I know. Courageous, too. Every day he has to struggle just to stay alive. He has cancer, and he's only eight years old. Every day Nicky has to take so many different kinds of medications, so many times, with so many different side effects—all without knowing if they'll even help. Some of them haven't even been proven completely safe—or effective. He boldly takes them anyway, even though some of them make him feel tired and more sick than he already is.

So far this year, he's spent ninety-six days in the hospital. For someone so young, that's a lot of time to spend alone. He's had more shots and been poked for blood tests more times than you can count. He's had chemotherapy and lost all his hair. He's had pneumonia three times.

Yet, for all he goes through, he hardly ever complains. And, even more amazing, he never gives up on believing he's going to be well someday. "When I'm an astronaut, I'll bring you a rock from the moon," he promised me just last week. That's Nicky's big dream, to be an astronaut when he grows up. He never doubts that he'll get better and become just that someday. You should've seen how excited he was when a team of three astronauts took an eight-hour space walk to repair the Hubble Space Telescope on Christmas Eve. Steven Smith was one of them. Astronaut Steven Smith is Nicky's hero. "I can hardly wait to meet him!" Nicky said, when we were watching the space walk on the news. "I'll bet someday he and I will go on a mission together! Maybe I'll even share an office with him at NASA."

I am so inspired. When I see all my little brother goes through, and in spite of it all, holds onto his dreams—and watch how that helps him get through his ordeal—I better understand the importance of truly believing in oneself. Even the doctors (and very early on in my brother's diagnosis) told us how important *believing in yourself* is to health. So I'm already a believer in the importance of a good self-concept. But it is watching one incredible little boy—my brother—who has shown me the magic of loving the face in the mirror.

Roma Leitty, 15

Of Greatness—And Goof-Ups!

A while ago
I was feeling lonely and lost
Living in a frenetic and impersonal world
Never quite feeling like I belonged.
Something was missing
But what could it be?
It couldn't be God, friends, boyfriend or family—
I had all that.

Then one day I figured it out.
The emptiness was inside; I was missing the *full* sense of me.
A self too narrowly defined,
Limiting—because there are so many sides to me.
I have my share of tears and fears, even doubts and insecurities.
I'm capable of greatness—and goof-ups, too.
I am a princess wishing for a big stone castle,
I am an Olympic champion, with silver, bronze and gold;
I am a daughter, sister, cousin, student and friend.
I've claimed all once missing parts of me.

Danyalle Williams, 16

Part 2

Making, Keeping and Coping with Friends

To have a friend,
be a friend.

—Proverb

All that matters is what we do
for each other.

—Lewis Carroll

Be a lamp, or a lifeboat, or a ladder.
Help someone's soul heal.
Walk out of your house like a shepherd.

—Rumi

A Word from the Authors

In each of the other books in our *Taste Berries for Teens* series, we did a unit on "friends," specifically how teens feel about their friends, and ways friends help make each other's lives more fun and exciting—and as teens everywhere said, "more bearable, too." We printed stories on how teens related to each other as they shared great times and helped each other cope through difficult times, as well. We shared with you stories on lessons teens learned, such as when they discovered that sometimes being a friend meant just "being there" (listening, comforting), yet at other times, being a good friend meant actively getting involved in problem-resolution or giving advice. And, sometimes, especially in the realization that a problem was more serious than a friend could get out from under on his or her own, it meant finding (or telling) someone who could help the friend—even if that meant breaking a promise not to tell anyone—which, as teens discovered, brought on lessons as well.

Understandably, harboring a friend's secret is a difficult thing to do, especially when you know it's not wise—or safe—to do. While teens learned that in the end, seeking help for a friend most always turned out to be the right decision, often he or she worried that doing so would (because the friend might feel betrayed) "break the back" of their friendship. This was most often not the case, and, in fact, because the friend did get help and did get better (sometimes one friend's reaching out actually saved the other friend's life), there was a great appreciation— and so it made the relationship even stronger than before.

Because we covered so much ground on the issue of friends in *Taste Berries for Teens* and *More Taste Berries for Teens*, we considered not having a "Friends" unit in this book. You convinced us otherwise. When we polled teens to find out what topics they would like to see covered in this book, *Taste Berries for Teens #3*, once again, issues surrounding "friends" settled among the top three. You told us that just as having friends is the "salvation" of teen life, and without friends life would be "boring" and "tough to get through," even so, being a friend and having a friend are big parts of the stress and *drama* in your lives.

Here's an overview of what teens said they would like to hear more about from their "peers"—and why:

Making: Making friends is tougher than most people think it is. Many grown-ups think that making friends is as easy as "going to school." Probably they think this way because teens are surrounded by many other students (which they automatically assume—and call—"your friends"). It doesn't necessarily work that way. Classmates are more like "peers" than they are "friends." Sixteen-year-old LaToya Ross summed it up this way, "I have 465 classmates. Of those, I'd say I have two or three friends, and I really don't have a *best friend*—though I'd like to."

Keeping: Keeping friends is tougher than most people think it is. A friend isn't necessarily a friend for life. Friends move away or transfer to other schools. The best part of having friends is seeing them every day and doing things together, so when someone moves away, mostly, you lose the bond. And of course, sometimes a friend decides you're no longer the person to fill the role of "Top Friend." Sometimes a friend finds someone else with whom he or she has more in common or gets a boyfriend (or girlfriend). When that happens, it's almost a certainty that your friend will then spend more time with that person than with you—and you'll be left walking to class or eating lunch alone—so that's no fun. When it happens, you have to find "new ground" with your friend or find new friends.

Coping: Friends can be difficult to put up with. When Sara McLaughlin discovered her "fun friend of four years" had suddenly developed a habit of spreading what Sara called "seedy rumors" around school about several classmates, she found herself in a "good days–bad days" struggle with her friend. Hoping her friend would stop spreading rumors, but not wanting to tell her friend "good-bye," Sara went from having a smooth relationship with her friend to one that was on-again, off-again—depending on how the rumor mill was going. Once, Sara even found herself the target of a rumor—one started by her supposedly "best friend"—an incident that produced some "rough" times for the friends to work through.

In working with teens nationwide, we discovered another issue in "coping" with friends: Sometimes, you outgrow the friendship. Being a teen, you're busy learning, growing and changing. With growth, comes change. Many teens suggested that whereas they were once more willing to "tolerate" another person at times when they "needed" the friendship—when a "new identity" emerged (feeling more secure and "grown up"), sometimes it meant one friend needed the other less and so the friendship changed. In many cases, it ended.

Even so, with as much "coping" with friends as you do, what we heard strong and clear was that even though sometimes friends can be difficult, it doesn't mean you'd rather be without them! So here, once again, is a unit on one of your favorite subjects: Friends—finding, keeping and coping with them—and the lessons they bring into your life. Enjoy these stories, and as you do, consider all the ways each of your friends is a taste berry to you—and all the ways you are a taste berry to each one of them!

♥ *Taste berries to you, Bettie and Jennifer Youngs*

Great Inspiration

Sometimes I wonder
What it's like to be you,
To bring so much joy
The way that you do.

To make people smile
Day after day,
To speak kind words of wisdom
Others trust what you say.

When someone's upset
In a funk, or a pout,
You soothe and you comfort
They no longer worry or doubt.

You're a great personality
You have your own style,
It's real and it's genuine—
What an awesome profile.

You never give up
You always succeed,
You do not follow
You have your own lead.

It's amazing to think
How many lives you've touched—
And mine is one of them!
Thank you so much!

You're a great inspiration
And a person who's kind,
A friend like you
Is a really good find.

Ashley Kuiken, 14

The Difference Between a Friend and a Best Friend

I have a couple of good friends. Of them, Berneice Long is my *best* friend. Last Tuesday was her last day at school. Berneice said that she had to move away because her father didn't make enough money at his job, so he took a better-paying job in another town.

I don't think I'll ever see my friend again, and that is such a sad feeling.

My two other friends and I live only a couple of blocks from school, so every day we walk home together. Usually we talk about some of the things that happened in school that day, like if someone in our class got called on and they didn't know the right answer or said something really weird or stupid. My friends and I always talk about who wore what (especially if that person got something new) and how she looked in it. We tell each other if we've heard a new rumor (and who started it, or, who we think started it), and we go over the current status of an old rumor. There's so much to talk about that we barely cover everything before we part ways to go to our own homes. Then we call each other when we get home and talk some more. It's great to have friends!

On the way home from school yesterday we didn't talk about the things we usually do. Yesterday, all we talked about was our friend Berneice, and how sad we were about her leaving, and how much we were going to miss her. And we all cried. We were so sad that we actually just stopped walking because we needed to wipe away our tears. Seeing how sad each of us was, we just stood there for a couple of minutes, held hands, hugged, and then cried some more. Finally, because all we could manage was to cry, dry our eyes, cry and then wipe away some more tears— and seeing how each of us was doing that—we all started to laugh. That made us feel much better, so then we started walking again. The rest of the way we just talked about how nice Berneice was, and how we hoped we would all get to see her again. We all agreed she was a good friend.

I guess that when you're feeling as much hurt over one particular person as we are over our friend moving away, you know that the person was really a good friend—and a very special person. I mean, I've had other friends move away but I didn't cry over them. My older sister's friend once told me that if you break up with a boyfriend and you don't cry, then it means that it really wasn't love—that the boy was more of a friend than a boyfriend. So, if crying over a friend is proof that that person is a best friend and not just a friend, then for sure Berneice was a best friend (and probably to all three of us).

That day, as we parted ways, the three of us promised each other that if any one of us were ever to move away, we'd all feel this very same way toward the one who left. We agreed on something else, too. We were all now more than just friends. We had become "best" friends.

Meghan Smith, 12

Alopecia Areata, a.k.a. Aunt Fester

I started getting bald spots—and it wasn't from old age! My parents took me to see a dermatologist, and I've been diagnosed with alopecia areata. Alopecia means that you are allergic to your own hair! It sounds really strange, but basically, the hair follicles tell your brain that they're dead, and when that happens, your hair falls out! Is that the perfect way to make a teenager feel like a "reject" or what!

Within one year from the time I'd been diagnosed, I went from having a few bald spots to having more bald spots than patches of hair. It was totally terrible and incredibly embarrassing. The kids at school looked at me like I was a weirdo—and some called me that (among other things).

When even more hair fell out, my parents took me to a different specialist. This one recommended steroid shots injected directly into my head. The doctor said he thought it might slow down hair loss, and maybe even put my head condition—the alopecia thing—in remission. So then I started getting the shots injected into my scalp. It was so painful that I'd cry on the way to the doctor's office and not want to go in at all—even though I badly wanted to have hair.

Within two months, the shots worked! My hair began to grow back in. I was so relieved. But then I found out that I couldn't take the shots for very long, because your body can take only so many steroids—or else you injure your liver and other internal organs.

So then my hair fell out again.

It was really embarrassing to go to school with my scattered patches of shaggy hair—especially because the other kids made fun of the way I looked. So Mom bought me a wig. Wearing a wig is really awful because you never know when it's going to fall off—or get *pulled* off by some kid who thinks it's a "cute" thing to do.

I can tell you, having alopecia areata is the absolute pits. But just when I thought things couldn't get any worse, they did. We moved to Washington. At first, I considered the move a good thing because I left behind schoolmates who watched me go from hair to scattered patches of hair, to bald, and then wearing wigs. But I was wrong. At the new school, kids hadn't seen my slow "demise," and so thought I was just weird looking. Without knowing anything about me (or what I was going through), I was instantly rejected. Most just stared and didn't even say "hi." In front of everyone, one boy yelled, "Hey weirdo, what member of the Addams family are you?" After that, some of the kids called me "Aunt Fester" (as in Uncle Fester, a character from the TV sitcom, *The Addams Family*).

Maybe because I was already down on myself, their teasing and taunting were more than I could handle. I got really depressed. So then my mother took me to see a therapist. That's when things began to turn around for me. I was seeing a counselor and attending group sessions with other teens (some with problems worse than mine). In "group" (where, with the therapist present, teens share with each other the things going on in their lives), I met teens who were not at all down on me. In fact, they were kind and really understanding of my condition. They were so nice to me. It was like they truly understood how difficult it was to deal with a condition like alopecia—and weren't about to make me feel even worse than I already did.

So that has been the best thing of all. In group I've found a bunch of really nice friends. And I have other news to report, too. One year after finding friends in group, I started high school. I love it, especially since teens at this level are more mature and understanding. Now I feel that I'm beginning to be accepted for who I am—and not for the condition of my hair—at least in the friends department. In the hair department, I am completely bald.

Having alopecia areata has taught me a thing or two about

having friends: Because it's been such a nightmare of an experience, I've learned to accept people for who they are. I don't judge them, and I don't criticize. I accept people based on heart and personality. As I do this, I'm learning something else about having friends. Friends can help you feel less self-conscious about the hardships you face. I was so embarrassed about my appearance that I'd spend a lot of time being defensive, feeling the need to always defend my appearance. And now, I'm able to lighten up about it a little.

I've thrown my wig away. Now that I have friends who are understanding and accept me as I am, I'm learning to stop thinking that when people see me, they can't get past my bald head. Now I focus on who I am on the inside and let my personality shine. So the news on my current condition is that I finally have good friends. *Really* good friends—some of whom I even let call me Aunt Fester. Isn't it amazing what you'll let your *real friends* get away with—and feel okay about it!

Katie Philipsen, 15

The Way It Is

Friends . . .

Laughing
Talking
Sharing

Blaming
Shouting
Crying

Explaining
Apologizing
Giggling

Laughing
Talking
Sharing

Blaming
Shouting
Crying

Explaining
Apologizing
Giggling

Laughing
Talking
Sharing

Friends. It's just the way it is.

Jeanna Renee Withers, 14

"With Ears Like That, You Must Have to Hide During Rabbit-Hunting Season!"

"Look at the way she walks with that ugly brown backpack! She looks like a camel!" my friend Kim said loudly as we strolled into the girls' bathroom. Kim was talking about Tamara Bailey, one of our classmates, who was walking into the bathroom in front of us. I don't know why she said it. I mean, she doesn't even know Tamara all that well. But comparing the brown backpack to a camel was sort of funny to me, so I laughed right along with Kim. But I also laughed for another reason: Kim is my best friend, and she expects me to be loyal.

Then, Kim made yet another snide remark, this one directly to a girl new to our school (whose name is Nina Nguyen) who happened to be with Tamara. As Nina looked in the mirror at her hair, which she was wearing up, Kim met my eyes in the mirror and said, "With big ears like those, can you believe she'd wear her hair up like that?" Frankly, I thought the style was kind of cute on her, and the truth is, Nina's ears aren't all that big. I couldn't believe Kim made this remark—and so loud—so I held my breath, wondering what would happen next. What happened was, Kim looked straight at Nina in the mirror and said, "You must have to hide during rabbit-hunting season!"

I glanced at Nina's stricken face and then glanced away real quick. I knew the comment hurt Nina's feelings. I knew I should've said something right away so she wouldn't feel so bad, but I didn't.

I was really in a bind. It's not a good feeling when you know a remark has hurt someone—even if the remark is a funny one. The thing is, what's a friend supposed to do? I mean, Kim makes smart remarks all the time, and sometimes what she says is really funny. But when she says it in front of the person—and when you know it hurt that person's feelings—that's when I think it's just mean.

This time, I just stood there being silent—which obviously upset Kim. "Hey!" she called out, elbowing me so as to remind me I was supposed to say something in support of her. I know she was waiting for me to join her in her laughter, like I usually did, but I didn't do it this time. Instead, I looked from Kim to Nina and said loud enough for both of them to hear, "Yeah, I heard you, but it's not even true." My heart was pounding because it's hard to stand up to a friend who might dump on you—and maybe even dump you as a friend.

See that's the hard part about having friends. Sometimes they do and say stupid things, and you're just supposed to back them up. Sometimes when we have class discussions in Life-Skills class, we talk about things like this. And everyone has all the "right" answers; they say all the words that sound right and, in reality, are. But the truth is, when you don't back up your friend, she's going to get back at you. There will be a time when YOU are going to be the butt of her joke, the person who gets made a fool of in front of the whole world. That would be so embarrassing.

Anyway, Kim was upset that I hadn't backed her up. She rolled her eyes and shook her head and said snidely, "Whatever!" She never commented on the incident again. But Nina Nguyen did. The first time she saw me alone, without Kim, she thanked me—which was a very nice feeling.

Friends! From the moment you enter kindergarten, you think that friends are the most important things in the entire world. But the moment you have friends, things get complicated. Right now, I'd say that having friends really keeps you busy guessing what they'll do next. Don't get me wrong; I don't want to be without friends. That would be awful; it's just that having friends is, well, like being a rabbit in rabbit-hunting season— there are times when you'd like to find a good place to hide!

Janice Langsworth, 16

"Just Slap Me!"

A couple of months ago, a classmate, Gary Martin, came up to me at school and told me a really mean "fat girl" joke. Well, I'm a little overweight, and while it's not like I let a few pounds upset my life, I'm not about to have someone think he has the right to make such a comment to me. Plus, I knew the joke was told purposely to make me feel bad about my weight, so I doubly didn't appreciate it.

I was surprised that Gary Martin told it to me. He's shy and, basically, a nice guy. I'm pretty sure someone put Gary up to it, because I don't really think he would have done it without being egged on.

It all happened when I took my seat in a class Gary and I are in together. As Gary was heading for his seat, he stopped and nervously blurted out the joke. I was so upset about the personal nature of the mean-spirited joke—because when telling it, you obviously insert the name of the person you're intending to insult—that without even going to the teacher and getting a hall pass, I got up and ran out of the room. I kept running until I reached the girls' bathroom, and then I just cried and cried. I was there for about five minutes when the school counselor came looking for me. She took me to her office, talked to me for a while, and then told me to wait in her office until my next class.

The next day in the same class, Gary Martin dropped a note on my desk as he walked by me. I couldn't believe it! My first thought was, *Oh, great! I'm going to get another nasty joke—this time written out!* I was about to toss the paper back at him, but knew if I did, the teacher would see me and then I would have to stay after school! So I read it. It said:

Dear Chelsea,

I'm really really really really really sorry for saying that joke to you. I didn't stop to think that it would hurt your feelings. I can see now that it did. I'm not apologizing just because the counselor said I should. I'm apologizing because if I had used my head, I wouldn't have told you that joke. You should have just slapped me.

Gary Martin

I've never slapped a boy, and I certainly wouldn't have thought to slap Gary Martin, or anybody for that matter. But, it was inconsiderate of Gary Martin to tell the joke—even if someone put him up to it. I also thought it was nice that Gary apologized.

The next day after school, Gary Martin called me at my house, asking me if I would explain a homework assignment. He called the next day after school, too. For an entire week, five days in a row, Gary Martin called me every day after school about a homework question. And then, on the following Monday of the second week from when he had told me the fat-girl joke, I went to my locker and there was a note from him. He'd wedged it into my locker so that I'd see it, but so that it wouldn't fall out unless the locker door was opened (you have to do the combination first). His note read:

Dear Chelsea,

I sure missed not talking to you on Saturday and Sunday. Would you like it if I called you on the weekend? I don't know what we would talk about since I get all my homework done on the weekdays after school and never have any to do over the weekend. But maybe we could think of something. Would that be okay with you, and would your parents be cool with it? I really really really really really hope so.

Gary Martin

I asked my parents, and they said it was okay with them as long as he called before 7:30. So now Gary and I talk on the phone—even on the weekends. And just yesterday, Gary Martin walked me to my locker after the class we take together. So that means that everyone knows that Gary and I have become friends, good friends.

Who knows, some day, he just might become my boyfriend. (My parents say I'm too young to have a boyfriend just yet. They said I had to wait until I was thirteen, so I'm really anxious to be thirteen as soon as possible—which won't be for about six months.)

So it just goes to show you that some classmates can be mean to others. And they sometimes talk others into doing things for them—especially when it comes to taking cheap shots like telling nasty jokes. So, you have to get wise to these things and not just go along with them absentmindedly. I say this because Gary told me that Scott Bobrow put him up to telling the joke, and that Jenna Colt informed me that Danny Lane put Scott Bobrow up to getting Gary Martin to do it.

Even thinking about that joke makes me upset all over again. Believe me, I'd like to slap the person whose idea it was in the first place, except that I'm not that kind of person. For sure, I'm glad I didn't slap Gary Martin, because now I really really really really like him!

Chelsea Bamber, 12½

The Spoils of War

My younger brother is really fun to be with. I'd say he's my very best friend. I'd say that I have a better time with him than anyone I know. Take four weeks ago, when my aunt and uncle came to visit our family. For nearly a month before their arrival, everything was, "When Aunt Mary and Uncle Ted get here. . . ." We even made a list of some of the many things they could do to make their time here in San Diego really special, and even went to the San Diego Convention Center and got brochures of some of the places they could visit. From checking out some of the new zoo exhibits, like "Polar Bears on Ice," "Penguin Village" and the "Reptiles Den" to going to the beach, from taking the trolley to Tijuana to visiting the San Diego Wild Animal Park or touring the Space Museum, we planned on making sure my aunt and uncle had the perfect vacation.

My parents even painted the guest bedroom to, as my dad said, "spruce things up." But the guestroom isn't all that was cleaned up. The week prior to their visit, Mom cleaned the house from top to bottom. She wanted everything to be "immaculate."

My aunt and uncle were scheduled to arrive in the early evening. My parents went to pick them up at the airport, which is about forty miles from where we live. The four of them planned to stop for dinner before they came home, and they put me in charge of taking care of my little brother, Frankie, who is eleven.

Both my brother and I love spaghetti sauce and noodles so when my parents go out to dinner, Mom makes it for us as a special treat. As usual, my mother had prepared spaghetti sauce and noodles, and all we had to do was heat it up in the microwave. On this special day of the arrival of my aunt and uncle, this dinner came with the lecture: "Be very careful, do not spill, and clean up after yourselves." Then, for added assurance, looking me right in the eyes, Mom reminded me that one of my privileges for showing I could "assume responsibility" was "just around the corner." She was referring to my being able to use the family car when I turned sixteen—which at this moment was three months, fourteen days and eight hours away. She and Dad had ingeniously figured out a way to make the family car an incentive for my good behavior "in advance."

"When you turn sixteen" became a date when days for good or bad behavior could be added or subtracted. (This plan started about my fifteenth birthday, when I had asked if I could get a job and work toward saving for a car, and they said, "No. You just concentrate on getting good grades, being responsible and playing sports, and if you do that well. . . . ") For example, when I got a C-minus in math two semesters ago, they deducted one month from using the car. And when I got a progress report that said my geometry homework wasn't always turned in on time, they deducted three weeks. Then when I failed to do my chores on Saturday morning before I went skateboarding with friends, they took off another two weeks. Luckily for me, my brother—who is just as anxious for me to get my license so we can go places together—did my chores a couple of times so I wouldn't get even more deductions. See, I told you he was a great friend! So that means that rather than being able to drive on the day I actually turn sixteen, because I screwed up those couple of times, I actually won't get to use the car until I'm sixteen, two months and five days. So, you can only imagine how important it was to me to do all I could to make sure everything went according to plans.

"Don't worry about a thing, Mom," I assured her. "We'll make sure things are 'immaculate'!"

Like the responsible big brother I was, I heated up the spaghetti sauce and noodles, set the table and warned Frankie not to make a mess. We heaped spaghetti on our plates, and then reached for the bowl of spaghetti sauce—at the same time. Playfully, we kind of struggled over it, and then I decided to just let go of my side of the bowl. Well, it happened so suddenly that my little brother lost his grip and the spaghetti sauce splashed up and out of the bowl and onto his face and lap—and everywhere else, too!

"Hey!" he screeched, staring at the splattered sauce covering him. It must have sort of irritated him, because he picked up the spoon in the bowl and flicked it at me, getting droplets of spaghetti sauce on my face. So I decided to get him back! I scooped some noodles and flung them at him. They landed right in his hair. It was so funny. By this time, Frankie and I were no longer at war; now we were having fun and howling with laughter. But then things got really out of hand. Frankie scooped up a really big handful of noodles and threw them at me. Well, that was all it took for a wild food fight to be in full swing.

Then our dog, Petey, not wanting to be left out of the fun, came bounding into the room. Landing on some noodles, his front legs skidded one way, his back legs another as he scampered about for balance. We were both practically crying with laughter, and I don't know what possessed me, but I picked up the bowl of remaining spaghetti and turned it over on Petey's head, and for good measure, squished it down. Happy as can be, Petey, his head draped in noodles, his body stained red with flecks of spaghetti sauce, barked, wagged his tail, and then promptly sat down at our feet in the spaghetti sauce! What a mess! We laughed so hard we had to hold our stomachs because they hurt from laughing. Then terror set in: Our parents were coming home from the airport—soon!

Terrified that all four of them would walk in and see the positively awful mess we'd made, we got to work. Luckily, the floor was tile and the chairs were wooden and not covered with fabric. Still, we had our work cut out for us. I gave Frankie kitchen spray cleaner, a sponge and instructions, but it seemed like whatever he wiped down was so streaked, I had to go over it a second and third time. In fact, we discovered that we were making things worse—and we were, until I figured out that we weren't using the right cleaners to cut the grease of spaghetti sauce. I was sweating it: If we didn't get things back to "immaculate" before my parents arrived home, I wouldn't earn the right to use the car until I was seventeen.

Between the entire kitchen cleanup and bathing Petey—which is always a big job—it took us more than a full hour to return the kitchen to normal. Fortunately, we managed to get everything cleaned before they got home. When I saw my parents pull in the driveway, I looked forward to greeting my aunt and uncle—and to my driving the car in five months, nineteen days and four and a half hours!

Or at least until the next morning when, from across the kitchen table, Frankie's eyes silently motioned for me to look up at the ceiling. To my horror, there were several strands of dried spaghetti hanging off the light fixture, and red specks of sauce splattered on the ceiling—evidence we hadn't spotted the night before. Though we both managed not to laugh until we left the room, (and labeled the spots "the spoils of war") we quickly worked out a plan to wash them off as soon as we could before anyone else discovered them. The moment our parents left the house to go to the grocery store, we stormed the kitchen to wash off "the spoils of war." To our great amazement, everything was spotless! I mean, really spotless!

Still, to this day, my brother and I find it impossible to look at the ceiling and not laugh. My parents have never brought it up, though the next time they went out for dinner, my mother prepared grilled cheese sandwiches and told me to heat them up for Frankie and I to eat! And here's the really good news: My parents never deducted one minute of time from my date for getting to use the family car!

Anyway, this incident, along with so many others, is yet another of the many memories and good times between my brother and me. So I'd say that not only is my brother a good friend now, but I can see us being the best of buddies for all our lives. I've thought about it and it's a very good feeling, because we will always have each other. No matter where we live or how our lives change over the years, he will be a best friend for life. I do have good friends at school, and I really enjoy being with them, but it's my brother's friendship that is the deepest. Probably, it will be the most long-lasting, too.

Gerard Foch, almost 16!

Are You a Friend or Foe?

Wondering as I sit here alone in my room
My feelings so sad, all doom and gloom.
I think about us, the bond between me and you—
How you're my friend, but very often, a real foe, too.

Your "on-again, off-again" confuses me to no end,
You say you're sorry, and you'll make amends.
When I share with others how perplexed I feel,
They say, "Maybe your friendship just isn't for real."

Maybe they're right: It's a double-lane road,
Your being two-faced is such a burdensome load.
Mostly I can't stand the way you gossip around,
Always loving the mean-spirited news you've just found.

I'm afraid if I tell you I've had my fill,
You'll give me that look, and a silence to kill,
Then there'll be consequences to pay,
And I'll be compromising; oh, I hate feeling this way!

I'd like to tell you, have the truth be known,
About my feelings—an interest you've never shown.
Giving wings to my words is a big help
What a relief to give in to the things that I've felt.

I know you've noticed we've grown apart,
More foes than friends, so we've got to start
To talk about us, about you and me
I think you'll see, this is no way to be.

So how about it, when can we start,
To find a new way to talk heart-to-heart,
To bring back the warmth we used to share?
'Cause deep down inside, I know we both care.

Elizabeth Martone, 16

"Think Team"

I knew that my mom and dad were serious about moving from Chicago to Houston when, the moment school let out for spring vacation, we all piled in the car and left for Houston. Probably so that we wouldn't feel so bad over having to leave behind our friends—and basically, give up our lives as we knew them—our parents asked my brother and me if there was one "special requirement" each of us would like our new house to have. I have always wanted a bay window, and my brother wanted a yard big enough to kick around a soccer ball. My parents thought that sounded good, too, and said we'd try to find a house with a "little personality"—hopefully one with a bay window and a big yard.

My brother was upset that we were leaving Chicago. He had a lot of friends and played sports. I was happy to leave Chicago! I didn't really have a lot of friends at all and, in fact, was sure that the kids at school didn't like me. I was constantly called a "teacher's pet" and a "suck-up." The only explanation I could think of for the other kids calling me these names was that they must be jealous of the good grades I got. I've always been a straight-A student. And I am polite and have good manners; I'm also quiet and shy. So I was looking forward to going to school somewhere else. Moving didn't seem like a losing proposition to me: I was glad to say good-bye!

Once in Houston, we stayed with my aunt. Each and every day we got up early and along with my aunt and cousins, we'd drive around to see all different types of houses. My brother was bored to tears, but I didn't think of it as all that bad because I got to hang out with my older cousin, Ashley, who is very cool. Besides, inside the model and open house homes we looked through, there were free sodas, donuts and cookies (and sometimes bowls of mixed candies). Since we were told we could help ourselves, that was good, too.

By the second weekend of June, my family had found the house we were going to live in. It was brand-new—and yes, with a big yard and a bay window in the living room! But since our house wasn't going to be completed for a couple of months, it meant we had to stay with my aunt for longer than we had planned.

When school time rolled around, we were still living with my aunt and uncle so my mom signed my brother and me up to go to school where my cousins went to school. I was happy to be going back because I've always liked school.

Unlike my school in Chicago, this school had a "Cooperative Learning" curriculum—which is basically a philosophy of "think team" (the teachers' words)—which means that the learning and studying is done in groups of three to five students. This also means that there's no such thing as an individual grade: You get a "group grade," and everyone in the group receives the same grade. It's a fun way to learn—and a great way to know other students, so I was having a good time.

Then, about two months later, my family learned that our house was ready. Our new house was on the other side of town so after the move we'd be going to a school closer to our new home. I was really disappointed to have to leave this school, because I liked it so much. Nevertheless, the next week I enrolled in my new school.

While my goal was still to be a good student, I hoped to make friends. I decided to try out what I'd learned from the head teacher of the Cooperative Learning curriculum who had said, "It's not just about you; think team." I'd say "think team" is a good approach to making friends—or at least it's working for me. Basically, that means I remember that other people count, and I should do my part to reach out and be friendly.

When I think back to my having friends in Chicago, I think it's fair to say that I expected to have friends simply "because." Then, when no one really knew me, I blamed it on their being jealous because I got good grades. Now I know that had nothing to do with it. Here at this school, I'm still smart, still a good student, the teachers like me—*and* I have friends!

Lindsay Moody, 15

Alexandra Sinclair

Alexandra Sinclair. The name kind of just floated off your tongue like an exotic character in a romance novel. She was my best friend. Nothing came between us. "You're more than a friend," she once told me. "You're a best sister."

We met in the second grade and just sort of gravitated to each other. From then on, we were always together, two peas in a pod—friends who had so much fun together. Like the times we'd put on our favorite CDs and then, pretending to be rock stars, we'd sing at full throttle and dance like wild women!

Even our classmates knew we had something special. We'd catch them staring—and smiling—especially when we would do things like eat each other's food—without having to ask—or sticking pretzels up each other's noses. She called me "Becca," short for Rebecca. I called her "Alex"—although she never allowed anyone else to shorten her name; "Alex" was reserved for me.

With her, hours passed like minutes. We could talk about everything and everybody—and didn't have to say ". . . but don't tell anyone" because it was understood that we would keep each other's secrets as if they were our very own. Our words were golden. Even our silence was meaningful. Being in her presence just felt good.

It was like our friendship was bigger than our hearts could hold, and so it spilled over in our rooms. From pictures of the two of us to each other's clothes in our closets, it was clear we were first in each other's lives. In school, we tried to always be in the same classes, and we lived on the phone at home. And weekends were always spent with either me at her house, or her at mine. In summertime, we would lie in her hammock and point out our favorite stars; we even renamed a few, sometimes after ourselves. We'd talk about our lives and plans for our futures. We talked seriously, and about "nothingness," too. When either of us had a date, the next day we called each other to discuss how things went—and sometimes, we called each other the same night when we got in. We cried over some things. And laughed until our sides hurt. We disclosed deep-down feelings off-limits to others, even our parents. There was no emotion that wasn't safe between us. We rarely disagreed, but when we did, we weren't afraid to "fight it out." And we also found it impossible to stay upset with the other for too long—because it was too much of a hardship. So we sort of "got to it" and said what we were going to say so we could get over the "mad" and get on with the good times.

Once, when I'd been in a minor car accident and ended up in the hospital, Alex was there in a heartbeat. It was a relief to have her there. I've heard that sometimes the doctors don't tell you everything that's wrong with you all at once—and I was a bit worried because my body was so stiff and sore I could hardly move. But, looking into my friend's eyes, I could tell that the broken arm was the extent of my injuries. I trusted her that much.

Some months later, while taking a load of clothes from her room to the laundry room, my friend took a pretty bad fall down the stairwell. It was the first of a spell of blackouts; then, the blackout spells seemed to be a regular occurrence. The doctors ran one test after another to try to determine what was causing them. One day, they discovered what it was.

I found out when I arrived home from my job at a deli. I worked every Monday, Wednesday and Friday from 4:00 to 6:00 P.M., and all day Saturday. Making my usual swing by the answering machine—my first priority when I walked in the door—I saw only a red zero staring back at me. Alex hadn't called? Of course, she'd called. She always called, always. She expected to check in. And I expected her to ask if I'd brought some dark pink "Extra" gum from work. "Extra" was her favorite, and the deli where I worked carried it.

I dialed her up. "Hey snot," I teased. "What's going on?" My friend breathed a long sigh and replied quietly, "Not much."

The response was just something that wasn't true—she always had a million things going on, and she was always excited about them, too. I knew something was up. "Hey girlie, you okay?" I asked.

"No," she replied, matter-of-factly.

"No?" I teased. "What do you mean '*no*'?"

"Becca," she said quietly, "I've got some really terrible news."

I didn't know what to say except, "What? Tell me," and "Do you need me to come over?"

"Yes," she replied and then hung up.

With her hanging up like that—so abruptly—I knew something was really wrong.

When she answered the door, the look on her face made my heart drop to the floor. I thought something drastic must be wrong with her mom or dad—maybe one of them had been hurt—fatally even.

"I'm really, really sick," she blurted out, and then began to cry. She looked so scared. We just stood there holding each other. I searched her eyes for a clue that this wasn't really happening, that it was only a joke and that she was just upset because her parents were having a bad argument, splitting up or something. But it was true. Alex was very ill—and the doctors knew of no treatment that could make her healthy again.

Because her illness was, as the doctors termed it, "full-blown," and because Alex quickly became even more ill, she could no longer attend school. She was tired and spent a lot of time sleeping. Within a month, her condition was really bad, and she wasn't allowed to see friends for long periods of time. One month later, she was so ill that she couldn't comprehend things going on around her, including my visits.

I was still in shock that Alex, a young person with her whole life to live, could be dying. My friend, who cried with me when

Seinfeld went off the air, who likes coffee ice cream . . . with pickles, who lied about her first kiss because she wanted to have hers before me, but didn't!

On one visit, she seemed a little more alert. When she understood that I was in the room, a tear rolled down her face. My heart just broke. I lay on the bed with her, frantically lecturing her on how she must not give up, how she must fight to win over this thing that wanted to claim her life. Only when I could think of nothing more to say did I shut up.

"Yeah, sure," she whispered softly.

So I knew she wasn't going to win over it. And I knew that she knew it, too.

"I'm really scared, Becca," she said. "Please hold my hand."

I fell asleep holding her hand.

A week later, I sat at her funeral—except that I couldn't stay. I had to leave because the pain was overwhelming, my body bursting with emotions I couldn't put into words. I am so lost without her. I feel so numb. Everything reminds me of her. Nothing is the same. Like at work when I see "Extra" gum. My stomach sinks. If only my "best sister" was there so I could buy some for her.

Jillian Sanderson, 17

If You'll Wear Blue Lipstick for Me . . .

Marsha Thomas would do anything to hang out with me. "Marsha, put some of this on," I instructed one day, handing her a tube of blue lipstick.

"But it's freaky-looking," she said. But I knew she would wear it. Marsha Thomas would do practically anything I'd ask her to. Like when my speech teacher, Ms. Cline (who was also the head of the drama department and Thespian Club), gave me a B minus instead of the A that I thought I deserved. Upset, I decided a boycott was in order. "I'm really ticked off about this," I said. "And we're going to get even. *We* are not going to attend any more of the plays."

"But Scott, my boyfriend, is in the play," Marsha moaned. "I have to go!"

But I wasn't about to back down on my decision.

"Oh, okay," she finally sighed, giving in.

Like I said, my word goes. Say I wanted to walk by Shawn Harrington's class during fifth hour so that he would see me— but not let Shawn think that I was walking by deliberately to see him. I'd tell Marsha to get a restroom pass from her fifth-hour teacher and meet me at a certain time, so that we could walk by Shawn's class together. Marsha would go along with whatever I wanted. Lori Kallem was a different matter.

Lori happens to be "the star" of the school's baseball team, so I told Marsha she *had* to try out with me. Not that I was all that serious about playing baseball. I just thought it would be a great way to get to know (and be around) Lori.

"Sure hope we win our game against Lincoln High," I said when I saw Lori coming my way the second week of practice. It was small talk, but at least I would get her attention, and she'd have to say something back. Well, she did.

"Those of us who come to practice on time intend to!" she quipped and then walked away.

Her words stung, because I knew she was referring to my getting to practice late—which I had twice last week, and once this week. As a result of my getting there late, the coach had added fifteen minutes onto each day, saying, "Practice is sixty minutes long each day. Hopefully, each of you will learn to be a team-player."

I know I shouldn't have been late, but the next day, I was late—at least it was only five minutes late. But that didn't deter Lori from saying something.

"You're late—again," she said matter-of-factly. "If you don't want to be here, why don't you quit and let someone have your spot?"

My reaction was to make an excuse. "I needed to talk to my friends about something, and it took me a little longer than I expected," I explained.

Lori didn't buy it. "The rest of us have friends, too. Your coming to practice late means the whole team has to stay later, and I for one do not appreciate it. Get to practice on time. End of story."

Lori taking me on like she did was embarrassing—especially with Marsha standing right there listening—but at the same time, I knew Lori had a right to be upset. I knew that for a girl like Lori Kallem to take me seriously—or even consider me as a potential friend—I was going to have to get serious about being prompt for baseball practice. So that's how I began my "about-face."

I wasn't late again.

I wasn't the only person affected by Lori Kallem's style of being direct. About two weeks after Lori's words to me on the practice field, I learned that Marsha had resumed going to school plays. Of course, I jumped on her about *our* agreement to boycott them. To my surprise, Marsha stood her ground. "What's with the 'we'?" she asked, and then informed me, "From now on, boycott plays if you want, but I'm not going to. And by the way, here's your blue lipstick back; it's putrid. End of story."

So, these days, I'm not only getting to practice on time, but I no longer ask Marsha to meet any "demands," including asking her to wear a shade of lipstick I personally wouldn't be caught dead wearing.

Patty Chase, 16

It Only Takes One

I was that girl you would see alone. *Always* alone.

I'd sit alone on the bus, at a table in the lunchroom, alone at a big table in the library. I was "that girl who is always alone. You know, the one who's always reading." I loved to read, but I also knew that it was my cover, a way to look busy and not like I was miserable being alone. I didn't want to appear as though I had no friends—which was basically true. I mean, who can find fault when you're reading a book? Reading is a good thing, right?

One morning, as usual, I got my backpack and went to the bus stop. I got on and, as usual, found a seat and sat down. As I always do, I got out my book and put my head down. A few minutes later, I heard someone ask if I minded if he sat in the seat next to me. I looked up, and there stood a boy I didn't know. Sitting down, he looked nervous as he introduced himself. His name was Chad. As it turned out, he was new to the neighborhood, and this was his first day at school. That day at lunch, when he spotted me at a table in the lunchroom, he hurried over and sat down. And that's the way it happened. I stopped being alone.

For the next few weeks, it wasn't just the new boy who looked to see if he could sit next to me—I looked for him, too. Little by little, we began to talk about school and other things, like our families and, eventually, ourselves. We soon became friends, and then, best of friends.

Isn't it amazing how overnight your life can change? Mine did. I feel so different now—less alone, less like a loner, less "left out." And you know what, it only takes one other person to make you feel as though you are no longer alone in the world—because, of course, you no longer are.

So I no longer hide behind books—although I am still an avid reader. Chad loves books as much as I do, so now we go to the library together, check out books, and trade back and forth when we finish reading them. Then we take them back to the library and check out new ones. Even when one of us reads something in our school texts that we think is really interesting or fun or weird or hard to believe, we always read it to the other person and talk about it. Amazing, just one other person is all it takes to make you feel like you are really important. I am so lucky—and come to think of it, so is Chad.

Shire Feingold, 14

Part 3

XOXO: Feelings of Love

*When somebody just loves you,
and when your presence alone makes someone
happy, you suddenly feel like the most important
and beautiful person in the world.*

—Angelina Jolie

*To love and be loved is to feel
the sun from both sides.*

—David Viscott

*The heart is forever inexperienced
in matters of love.*

—Henry David Thoreau

A Word from the Authors

"You know, Mom, as a teen, I was absolutely, positively, unequivocally and totally certain—and I do mean beyond a shadow of a doubt completely sure—that having a special someone in my life was as essential to my being happy as was air to my lungs. All of my friends felt this way: those who had a special someone, and those who didn't—but were hopeful they would soon. As a teen, not only does having a special someone give meaning to your total existence, but it makes you feel alive, energized and 'with it.' On a personal level, it was the best reason I knew of to get my homework completed without letting it pile up for the weekend, and it made me look forward to each day. And, of course, it was why certain dates on my calendar were encased with a heart in red ink—which always was cause for excitement right there!

"Every teen knows the importance of having a special someone: You have someone with whom to hold hands, to attend school functions—without the dread of wondering if anyone is going to ask you, and if so, WHEN!—and, you're one of the privileged because you're getting kissed."

As we found out in working with teens for this unit, love is the motivation for a lot of things, from staying on the good side of your parents to being certain to brush your teeth *every* morning! Certainly the poets on sixteen-year-old Calista Doane's Day-Timer agree about its importance:

> *There is only one happiness in life,*
> *to love and be loved.*
>
> —George Sand

> *Love conquers all things.*
>
> —Virgil

> *One hour of right down love is worth*
> *an age of dully living on.*
>
> —Aphra Behn

But famous poets and lyricists have nothing on teens. Perhaps Plato, the famous philosopher, was right: "At the touch of love everyone becomes a poet." Certainly teens are among the best poets in the world when it comes to writing about love, whether it be a desire to call it to their lives, to cope with the demands and challenges of love, or to speak to its many lessons—from make-ups to breakups. But while most teens can speak to its importance and acceptance amongst themselves, they are also fairly unanimous in their assessment of how we adults view having a special someone in their lives. "What I don't understand," commented seventeen-year-old Dianna Leland from Charlotte, South Carolina, "is that everyone knows how motivating and exciting life is when you have someone special in your life. Why, then, are adults so quick to give you all the 'warnings'? It's like they're trying to scare you off or something. 'What you need to do right now is concentrate on your studies. There'll be plenty of time for love (later).' Or someone asks (thoughtlessly): 'Can't you find someone *better?*' Or, should you break up—even if your heart is hurting—teen love is trivialized. People say insensitive things like, 'Oh, don't worry! There'll be others!'"

"You know Mom, Dianna's comments really hit a nerve with teens—hundreds and hundreds of them who feel that adults have a conspiracy against their having a special someone. As I said earlier, as a teen, love was an important ingredient to my happiness. The thing is, it still is—and I'm hoping that's never going to change. But like Dianna, even now as an adult with love in my life, I still have to defend myself. As an example, just the other day I went to the local deli (one I've been going to since high-school days) to get a sandwich for lunch. The moment I walked in, the owner—a guy I really like and someone I've known for a long time—greeted me. A jubilant, happy-go-lucky person with an 'I love the world and everybody in it' kind of personality commented, 'Jennifer, you look *different* than when I last saw you!' Then, stopping what he was doing, he looked me over, walked out from behind his counter, looked me over even closer and commented, 'I'll say! Let's see what it is: Is it that sparkle and gleam in your pretty green eyes? Or, that bigger and brighter smile than usual? Hmmmm. I'm not sure. Something's going on; what is it?' He pretended to think on this for a moment and then said, 'Oh, don't tell me!' He reached for my hand, searched my ring finger, asking, 'You didn't get married, did you?'

"'No,' I laughed. 'But I do think I might be falling in love!' With these words, the deli owner looked alarmed, and then warned, 'Oh, Jennifer, Jennifer! No! No! You're too, too young to get married! I got married very young, and if I could do it all over again I would never do that.'

"'Well,' I said, quickly defending myself—and perhaps the art of love, too—'I said I thought I might be falling in love! I didn't say anything at all about marriage . . . though . . . you never know! And besides, even if you decided to never get married as young as you did, or even never chose to get married at all for that matter, surely you would want to be in love, wouldn't you?' Personally, I was rallying for love—and everything that had to do with it. I mean what's the point of life if it's not about love?

"Looking at me a bit more cautiously now, the man softened, and then offered, 'You know, I was so in love, I couldn't wait to be married—which is why I did. Practically everyone I knew tried to talk the two young lovers out of it, but no one could! And by the time I was your age, I had a couple of kids. So who am I to warn you that you're too young to get married? I guess everyone says that to young people, but love is love! It's got a mind of its own. Besides, if *everyone* were in love, it'd make for a better, kinder world!'

"Now beaming from ear to ear, he then informed me, 'I've been married for just over thirty years now, and I'm still very much in love with my wife.' Then, turning to the wall behind him—one totally covered from wall to wall and floor to ceiling with photos of infants, teens, families and portraits—he said, 'Just look what our love turned in to: thirty-two in all—our children, their spouses and children, and our grandchildren.' With these words he momentarily scanned the entire wall of photos. Then, his eyes welled over and with a great amount of love in his voice he said, 'There's so much love hanging there on that wall. I don't know what I'd do without them. Guess I'd be just another watermelon in a watermelon patch!'

"I thought it cute that he compared himself to a watermelon in a watermelon patch, but meaningful, too. Here was a man surrounded by love and who understood its importance to his life. 'You're a lucky man,' I told him, and thanking him for preparing my food, I left. I thought about his first having cautioned me about love—and then how he had fondly acknowledged how loving and being loved by so many people made his heart swoon."

Swoon. What a great word. Love can make our world swoon, if we let it. And teens certainly want it to do just that. In the words of sixteen-year-old Miranda Cally from Davenport, Iowa: "When you see a 'couple' walk down the hall together, sit together during lunch or going to the library, walk each other to and from classes, and most especially, should you see them holding hands and kissing—well, if you don't have a special someone of your own, you know you definitely want to! When everyone else is going with someone, you're sort of left out."

"First you have to get love in your life," cautioned fifteen-year-old Jessica Mallory, also from Davenport, Iowa. "And that's not as easy as it sounds. I've wanted a boyfriend all year long, and I still haven't found 'Mr. Right'!"

"I think just finding someone is the easy part," said Cherish Stevens, sixteen, from Moline, Illinois. "It's a lot of work to have a really good relationship. I've been going with a guy for two months now, but he's a very jealous person. Truthfully, I don't know how long my relationship with him will last, because it seems like we're always doing the 'We've got to talk' thing."

"Oh, I know what you mean!" seventeen-year-old Brad Conrad (from Minneapolis, Minnesota) said. "I'm going steady with a girl and what is most steady about our relationship is the breakups and makeups. It's great one day, and the next, we're supposedly fighting over something. Sometimes I don't know what caused the rift in the first place—something I find maddening. Love is great, but a lot of work, too."

Love. So important and central to our lives. What can be said about it that hasn't already been said? Probably nothing, but that won't stop this magnificent emotion from being one of the most passionately debated, much discussed and diced subjects in the universe! For young, old and in-between, love is, quite simply, everywhere you go. It is, as Lou Rawls' famous ballad implies, "simply in the air."

Ever inspirational, it makes us happy, and happy for others, or as Ralph Waldo Emerson said, "All the world loves a lover!" As teens discovered, from seeing other teens "in love" to finding someone special of your own; from setting the tone for the relationship to discovering if the relationship will work out—or is even right for you; from breakups to makeups, there's a lot to learn about the emotion termed, "love." In this unit, you'll meet teens who, through experience, learn about love. What is particularly remarkable about teens and their sense of love is that they simply believe in it—and its ability to change the world and their lives. May we always be listening to their taste-berry wisdom!

♥ *Taste berries to you, Bettie and Jennifer Youngs*

What Time Did You Say You'd Call?

A page from my diary:

5:01 P.M.

It is one full minute past the time he said he'd call. He DID say he'd call. Why hasn't he called?

Be patient. He'll call. I'm SURE he'll call. He's a nice guy. . . .

5:05 P.M.

Still, no call. He said he'd call. SO call! He'll call—he IS a nice guy.

5:11 P.M.

Maybe he only *seems* like a really nice guy. No, things will be fine. He'll call. I can tell when a guy is only pretending.

5:17 P.M.

Maybe he's going to wait a couple of more minutes so that he doesn't seem too desperate to call me. Guys have to keep that cool image, right?

5:30 P.M.

Reasons Why He Hasn't Called Me Yet

1. His house is on fire.
2. He's on restriction with his parents and can't use the phone.
3. He's having a wisdom tooth pulled.

4. The phone lines are down in his neighborhood.
5. He lost my number.
6. While walking his dog, he was struck dead by lightning.
7. He doesn't like me.

5:32 P.M.

Obviously, he doesn't think I'm cool. Besides, he's probably dating someone else.

5:34 P.M.

WHO NEEDS GUYS ANYWAY!!!

5:36 P.M.

(Ring)
Oh my gosh! The phone is ringing!
(Ring)
(Ring)
Should I answer it? Of course I should. It's him apologizing profusely for not being able to call because he was late getting home from having a wisdom tooth removed, and then, since he was on restriction with his parents and couldn't use the phone, he had to sneak over to a friend's house to use his phone. Then, when he got to his friend's house, he discovered that the power was out in the neighborhood and by the time it was restored, he discovered he hadn't brought along the piece of paper I'd given him with my phone number on it! Thank goodness he wasn't hurt by that lightning bolt when walking his dog—and that there wasn't a fire at his house.
(Ring)
I'll answer on ring six so he doesn't think I'm sitting by the phone waiting for his call. Four, five . . .

(Ring)

"Hello."

"Hi. It's Mark."

"Mark?"

"Mark Burres. We met at the Tri-City All-Schools Fair. You gave me your number. I told you I'd call tonight."

"Oh, yes. Mark. How are you?"

"Great! How about you?"

"Fine."

"Sorry I'm a little late in calling. I was walking my dog."

"I was right!"

"Excuse me?"

"Nothing."

"Are you upset I'm late in calling?"

"Actually, I'd forgotten you said you'd call."

Mark's thoughts:

I shouldn't have called. She obviously has second thoughts about wanting to go out with me. She probably thinks I'm not cool. . . . She's probably seeing someone else. . . .

Nicole D. Burgan, 17

Twelve Ways to Say "I Love You"

Love may be its own language, but each language has its own way of saying those three special words! How many ways can you say, "I love you"? Go ahead, match them up—and play cupid in as many languages as you can!

Ways to Say "I Love You"	Languages
Eu amo-te	French
Tha gradh agam ort	Spanish
Te amo	English
Wo ai ni	German
Jeg elsker deg	Italian
Je t'aime	Chinese
Ko cham Cie	Dutch
Ik hou van jou	Gaelic
Ich liebe dich	Polish
Jag alsk ar dig	Norwegian
I love you	Portuguese
Ti amo	Swedish

Correct Match-Ups:

Eu amo-te ....Portuguese
Tha gradh agam ort ....Gaelic
Te amo ....Spanish
Wo ai ni ....Chinese
Jeg elsker deg ....Norwegian
Je t'aime ....French
Ko cham Cie ....Polish
Ik hou van jou ....Dutch
Ich liebe dich ....German
Jag alsk ar dig..Swedish
I love you...English
Ti amo..Italian

Have You Ever Dated
Your Sister's Ex-Boyfriend?

Never, and I mean *never*, go out with your sister's ex-boyfriend! I did, and it turned out to be a big mess.

Here's what happened: On July 7 at 6:30 in the evening, my sister Sherrie broke up with her boyfriend, Colin. She broke up with him because she wanted to date Denny Lott, instead. So, she told Colin it was over between them, called Denny Lott and started dating him as of seven o'clock that same evening.

I never expected to hook up with Colin, now her ex. What happened was that about two weeks after my sister had broken off with Colin, a group of us friends (five total) spent the afternoon at Sea World. Because Colin was friends with a bunch of my friends, he was one of the five of us that day at Sea World. Though Colin didn't arrive until almost four o'clock (the rest of us got there at two o'clock), when he did, he walked mostly alongside me. And when two of the friends in the group went to see the Otter Exhibit, but two others didn't want to see it (because they'd seen it on a recent trip), even though Colin had also seen it, he came along with the two of us who wanted to see it.

Then, when all five of us sat down to watch the porpoise show, Colin wedged in between my girlfriend, Tara, and me. I really didn't mind. He's a nice guy, and because I knew him from being at my house and dating my sister, I was cool with it.

All of us were riding rides together, seeing the shows, joking around with each other, and just having a great time. It was a lot of fun. But then, when we were walking along a path to see the whale exhibit, Colin reached for my hand. I was really surprised—but not as much as when he picked up my hand and slipped his class ring on my finger. That shocked me. "Be my girl," he said, and then put my hand to his lips and kissed it. It was very sweet, but startling, too. But even more surprising was that I said, "Okay." I couldn't believe I'd said it—it just sort of slipped out of my mouth. For the next ten minutes, Colin and I walked in silence—even though some of our friends were running and laughing, grabbing Tom Lintel's cap and starting a game of toss it around the group. I don't know what was going on in Colin's mind, but I was too stunned (and happy, too) to speak. And all I could think of was how I would explain this to my sister.

I told her the very next morning. To my great relief, she said, "It's okay with me. I'm done with him, and I've got Denny." But even though she said this, I could tell that she was not all that cool about my wearing Colin's ring because after being silent for a while she commented, "Don't you think it's a bit early to be getting his ring?"

Then, an hour later, when she passed me in the hall on the way to her room, she said, "You'd think you'd have a little more common sense than to accept a boy's ring on the first date." I could hear the sarcasm in her voice so decided to say nothing in response, because my sister had gone out with Colin for seven weeks, and he hadn't offered his class ring to her, so I could see where she had a right to be jealous.

Just then the phone rang. We both made a mad dash for the phone, but my sister reached it first.

"Really?" my sister commented after listening for what seemed like five minutes. Then, "Really. Oh, really?" So about this time I figured it was one of her friends and was just about to go back to my room when I heard her say, "So is Colin with her now? Like right now, this minute? He is . . ."

That got my attention. What Colin? Who is Colin with? "Who?" I shouted at my sister.

Putting her hand over the mouthpiece on the phone, she answered, "Seems like your Colin is with that Linda girl from your English class. They're across the street at Siam's house."

Taking her hand away from the receiver she said to her friend, "Gotta go!" and then hung up.

Turning to me, she said, "C'mon. That traitor. What a cheat. Let's check it out."

My heart was pounding against the walls of my head. I didn't know what to think or how to feel. Then I started crying. On a full run, my sister ran into her room and quickly returned, stuffing something in her pocket. She grabbed my hand and off we went—my sister cussing and yelling as we crossed the street.

Then, even before we got to Siam's house, my sister started yelling to Linda about how she could possibly be with someone who was going steady with someone else, someone he'd even given his class ring to. Then, my sister started yelling at Colin—but not just on my behalf! She yelled at him because *she* was still mad at him about something in their own relationship. "Just how many girls do you think you can wrap around your little finger?" she demanded, her voice shrieking.

Then the scene got ugly.

The door to Siam's house opened and Linda came flying out, yelling profanities. Then my sister started screaming at her and calling her names like "cheat" and "scumbag"—which made Linda so mad she reached for my sister's hair. So my sister started pulling on her hair. About this time, Colin came out of the house and just stood there saying, "Stop. Stop. I said, stop." Finally, Linda pulled loose of my sister's grip on her hair and ran into her house, yelling and cussing out Colin. Now turning to Colin, she started yelling at him. Then, my sister reached in her back pocket and took out several photos. As dramatically as she could, she held them high in the air and tore each one into tiny little pieces—and threw them. Like the tiniest particles from the fallout of a gigantic fireworks display, a million and one tiny scraps of photos came sprinkling down, covering the ground all around us. Then looking fiery-eyed at Colin, she said, "And that's what's left of us! So there!" But she'd saved the best of her revenge for last. She reached into her pocket and pulled out a tiny fragile glass unicorn—and hurled it at his feet. Hitting the sidewalk, the little glass ornament shattered into a thousand pieces. Colin kneeled down, trying to gather up the pieces. Tears were streaming down his face.

Satisfied—or else really hurting—my sister walked slowly back across the street to our house. "So, do you want your ring back?" I asked him.

"I suppose so," he said, looking sad. I handed it to him and went home. And that was that. My thing with Colin was over.

My sister, obviously very upset about the whole thing—and, I guessed, still in love with Colin—had gone into her room and put a sign on the door that said, "Go away." She didn't come out of her room all afternoon.

I'd like to think that Colin gave me his class ring because he wanted me to be his girl, but I don't believe it. Giving a girl your class ring when you hadn't even declared your love for her is probably not a wise thing to do. Besides, my guess is that Colin gave me his ring and wanted me to be his girl because it was a way to stay close to my sister.

But even if my sister and Colin didn't still have feelings for each other, I'm thinking it's not a smart thing to go out with your sister's ex. Probably that's good advice for guys, too—that it's not smart to go out with your brother's ex. I say this because I don't think it's real easy to tell when someone is completely done liking another person—even if that person says he or she is. I think you should just find someone on your own. That way that person is sure to be just yours. And, should you get in an argument over something, at least you only have that one person who's upset with you and things won't get so messy and be as complicated when you're trying to work things out.

Terrie Hall, 15

Our Secret Place

Meeting in our secret place
Just you and me,
Here with each other
In a world of our own
Discovering our feelings
Sharing our thoughts
Learning about each other
Noticing that love changes things:
We're happy!
Days seem brighter!
Everything is possible!
Shooting stars hold promises
We're sure will come true!
We speak a thousand words
About everything
And yet, nothing in particular
All hold meaning
As does our silence.
Let's both agree
To come here often
Together,
To be alone
Our secret place
In a world of our own.

Jean Burres, 17

He's Yours to Dance With Now!

In the ninth grade I had a big crush on Anthony Mortola, a smart and very cool upperclassman who was a smart aleck around the girls. As far as I knew, he'd never had a serious girl-friend—and I really wanted to be his first. I'm sure every girl in my school felt the same way! It wasn't that Anthony Mortola didn't notice me. He did and commented "What's up, fatso?" or "Hey, chubs!" I liked him anyway. Besides, Anthony Mortola called a lot of people names—some names worse than he called me.

It was summer vacation, and I was hopeful of playing on the school soccer team the next school year, so that summer, I went to soccer camp. The camp was tough with a capital T. We started our days with fitness training, practiced nearly all day long, and the food was "high-carb, low-cal"; it was terrible! Not once did they serve French fries or double cheeseburgers. Sodas were nonexistent. Without these staples, I practically starved to death—which is the truth. At the end of ten weeks there, I lost nearly ten pounds! I was feeling good and buffed, too.

The new school year began and, as planned, I went out for soccer. The summer camp had paid off. Other than Lesha Williams, I was probably the best player. I was sure happy about that, because at our school, athletes are the "in" crowd! So I was moving up the popularity ranks for the first time in my life. If only Anthony Mortola could see me now!

He couldn't. During the summer, his family had moved from town, and no one knew where he was. Wouldn't you know it: I'd become cool and the person I wanted to be cool for was nowhere around. But Kevin Pauls was! Funny I hadn't noticed the year before how cool he was; maybe it was because I was preoccupied swooning over Anthony—or maybe Kevin, like me, had become cool over the summer. Whatever it was, it was turning out to be a great year after all, even without Anthony Mortola around.

I was having a good time being a "star" athlete and all. I had more friends and was feeling really good about myself. Then, three months into the school year—and two months into my relationship with Kevin Pauls—Anthony Mortola moved back to town, which I discovered one day when sitting in the cafeteria eating lunch with my friends.

I looked up, and there he sat, not more than two tables away. He was talking with his friends when he looked up and smiled. Then, with a look of complete shock on his face, he blurted, "Is that Piglet?" ("Piglet" was yet another one of his pet phrases for me.)

I know he timed his leaving the lunch table when my friends and I did, because the moment we got up to put our trays away, he was right there behind me. "Vanessa, wait up!" he called. (It was the first time he'd ever called me by my real name!) Acting like a real gentleman and making small talk, he walked me to my locker, chatting all the way. You'd be proud: I acted as cool as a cucumber! Finally, Anthony Mortola was interested in me!

He didn't waste much time. The next day, he asked me to a school dance being held the next weekend. Less than six months ago, Anthony Mortola was making fun of me; now he was making time with me. You cannot believe how badly I wanted to tell him, "Sorry, Bud. It's my turn to break your heart!" Instead, I thanked him for asking me and then told him that I already had a date. I was looking forward to going to the dance with *my* guy, Kevin Pauls.

Anthony came to the dance alone. About a half-hour into it, he came up and asked Kevin if he minded if he could have just one dance with me.

"I mind!" I said immediately, not letting Kevin be put on the spot. See, I know how these things work. Boys say they "don't mind" when they really do. And I didn't want to get in an argument with Kevin. I really liked him. So instead of dancing with

Anthony, I turned to my best friend, Tara Handley (who had come without a date—and was, I'm sure, thinking she was the last person on Earth Anthony Mortola wanted to be with), and said, "Tara, Anthony was just asking if I would introduce the two of you." Putting him on the spot that way, he had no choice but to dance with Tara. Of course, Tara, who had had a crush on Anthony Mortola for about as long as I did, couldn't believe her good luck when all of a sudden, Anthony Mortola wanted to be introduced to her! With a star-filled gaze, she practically pranced to the middle of the dance floor with Anthony. But I kept an eye out for her, because should Anthony ditch her after just one dance, I wanted to be there for her. When Tara spotted Kevin and I dancing nearby, she came a little closer and whispered to me, "Break in whenever you want."

"No, no," I reassured her. "He's yours to dance with now." She smiled and danced away. I couldn't locate the two until about a half-hour later, when I saw her practically draped over Anthony—who was holding her *very* close. They were so cute together.

That night several things happened. Because Kevin said he was so impressed that I didn't dance with Anthony when he'd asked, Kevin and I officially began "going steady" (although I thought we already were), and Anthony and Tara had a *very* good time together.

Four months later, I'm still Kevin's steady, and Tara and Anthony are boyfriend and girlfriend.

So you see, here's the thing about love: You just can't predict how things will turn out. I mean, if a year ago, drooling whenever Anthony Mortola was around, someone would have told me that within a matter of months he'd be drooling over me—but I wouldn't care less—I wouldn't have believed it. And if someone had said, "Oh, you'll like someone in our class that you don't even give a second thought to now," well, I wouldn't have believed that either. And if someone had said, "Your best friend will be Anthony Mortola's first girlfriend—and you'll be happy for her"—well, I would have found that difficult to believe, as well. But believe it or not, it's all true—things don't always stay the same, and people grow and change—like me and Kevin, and Anthony Mortola. And since people change, feelings can change, too.

Vanessa Andrew, 16

Brown Hair, Green Eyes, Big Feet

I've been waiting and waiting. Patiently waiting for the perfect guy to come into my life. I waited through sixth grade and seventh grade and eighth grade and ninth grade. I've been extremely patient, too, and the reason is because I know that there is that one perfect person for each of us—even though we never know when that person will come along. But I was okay with waiting—because the guy for me had to be just perfect.

I was so sure what I wanted my perfect guy to look like and be like that I made a list of all the qualities he'd need to have. Things like brown hair, green eyes, big feet—and he'd have to pick me up to kiss me because he would be tall, much taller than I.

By the summer after my ninth-grade year, it seemed to me that every one of my friends had found that one perfect guy, while I was still waiting for mine. Mostly I'd pal around with Jenna, Chad, Brian, Kelsey and David, friends who also still had not met their perfect someone. The summer was nearly over, and still that perfect guy for me had not shown up. The fact that all my friends were doing fun things and going to fun events—like concerts, street fairs and state fairs—and each with their perfect someone (well, except for Jenna, Chad, Brian, Kelsey and David—who, along with me, all hung around together) made me very sure that I was more than ready for my perfect guy to show up.

If only he would.

It was one week before school was to begin, and everyone was talking about going back to school. And while I was looking forward to school beginning, it dawned on me that all my friends with their perfect someones would be going back to school, so now I'd really be left out. Then, as a "good-bye" to summer, my friends decided to have a BBQ. That sounded like fun, and I was looking forward to it, even though I knew all my friends would be there with someone, while I'd be there alone.

Of course, I went to the BBQ. They were my friends, and this was a party, of sorts. Just as I'd thought, all my friends came with their dates, and I was pretty much alone—at least that's the way it felt when everyone began to dance. The music was very loud and just great. And I really wanted to dance. So when my friend David, a really nice guy and someone I've known since elementary school, asked me to dance, I thought, *Well, why not? I love this music, and this is a party. And I'm supposed to have fun. David will do.*

David and I danced and danced. And when we took a break from dancing, we went to get food and sodas and sort of just hung out together. This went on for almost an hour, and then something totally unexpected happened. David started flirting with me—and I found myself flirting back. Then our friends teased us, and I felt okay with it. And then something completely out-of-the-blue happened, something that blew me away. When David and I were dancing to a slow song, he kissed me on the forehead. Speechless, I just kept dancing until the song was over, trying to get used to all the feelings going on inside of me. "Let's talk," he said when the music stopped, and steered me over to the corner of the dance area. Holding both of my hands in his, he said, "I've liked you for a long time. And I'd like to ask you if you'd be my girl."

I didn't know what to say, except that my heart was fluttering, and my whole being felt like dancing even though the music had stopped. Then David picked me up and kissed me again. Not one of those little weak kisses. This was an intensive kiss. And that's when I noticed: David has brown hair, green eyes and big feet. And he's so tall he had to pick me up to kiss me.

Amber Mendoza, 15
(reprinted from A Taste-Berry Teen's Guide to
Managing the Stress and Pressures of Life*)*

Counting Petals

We've broken up,
And now you're gone.
I'm sitting here crying,
Thinking of the days we spent together.
Will I treasure our memories?
Yes. Forever.
And ever.

Will I be sad forever?
Oh, I hope not!
You're gone.
And I want love in my life!

Time to move on.
Time to pick another flower
And count the petals—
He loves me; he loves me not; he loves me . . .

He loves me!

The "trick" to love is this:
If you end up on the "loves-me-not" petal,
Then start the count over
Because we're all entitled to love!

Cristal Ortiz, 15

Kathy Was My First Love

Kathy was my first love. I had just moved to a small West Texas town where she lived. Her dad owned the hardware store, and my father had been transferred to the refinery nearby. It was love at first sight, and from the very first moment, we didn't want to be with anyone else. Kathy had been dating a guy named Jimmy, who was on the football team. She purposely broke up with him to be my girl.

Everything about our lives just seemed to fit. We both stayed after school for practice every day: She was in the band, and I played football and ran track. We had lunch together every day at the Dairy Queen. The owner's son played football, so he always gave players extra-large portions for the regular price. Most every Friday night there was a school dance. Kathy and I never danced with anyone else: She was *my* girl. Saturday nights were spent at the movies. The weekends were mostly spent with friends, mostly other classmates who were "couples."

We dated all that summer and couldn't wait for school to start so we could be with each other every single day, all day long. While our worlds seemed perfect, it wasn't an easy time for families in our town. Plants were closing, and a lot of people lost their jobs. It affected all the retail businesses, too. People started to move away. All the school activities lost good students, and the town seemed to be fading away. It brought all the students closer in spirit, especially Kathy and I. It was very reassuring to be with someone who wouldn't be down just because things weren't going the way you wanted them to go. I loved her for it, and she loved me. We loved each other so much.

We had been going together for nearly two years and never even thought of breaking up. Her parents had almost divorced because the plant closing had brought on some really difficult times, not to mention financial hardships. Her parents did get back together. Her mom had told her that she and her father were still in love and just because they were going through some tough times that wasn't reason enough to break up. Somehow that made Kathy and I closer, too, like we could survive anything.

We just knew we'd be together—forever.

If only that were true. Just after Christmas my dad got the news. He was being transferred to New Mexico to another refinery.

I was leaving in two months.

My heart stopped beating. I'd be living nearly six hundred miles away from the love of my life. What would I do without my Kathy?

When I told her, we cried together. After school the next day, we drove to the park and stayed there talking for hours. At first, we were sad, and then we just felt hopeless. At seventeen and sixteen there were no alternatives, no way out and nothing we could do.

The next two months were the saddest of my life. Each day was another heartrending twenty-four hours.

A sixty-day countdown to something unimaginable—being apart. No dances, no lunch-time meals together, not being just a classroom away. Even the thought of not being with each other every day was pure torture. We made promises to call every day, to write every day, to wait for each other and to always be true.

The six-hundred-mile ride out of Texas to the new town in New Mexico took forever. I've never cried so hard and for so long in my life. My heart hurt so badly.

Almost four months after I'd moved to New Mexico, Kathy wrote and asked if I could meet her in Dallas over spring break. She was thinking about attending college there. I had been working after school and was a senior now. I begged my parents to allow me to make the drive, and after two straight weeks of practically driving them crazy, they relented—as long as I would not travel alone. No problem, all of my friends wanted to go. It was spring break! Five of us piled into the car and took off for "Big D." It was a great trip. A lot of sodas, chips, nachos and snoring!

When I finally saw Kathy again, we hugged and held each other and exchanged a lot of salty tears. It was as though we had never been apart. We talked of how we could get back together, go to the same college, get married and have kids. We spent as much time together as we could that week, dreaming, making plans for the future—our future. And then we had to say good-bye again.

Things haven't turned out at all as we thought. As months and months passed, keeping up grades, hanging out with friends and holding down a part-time job soon cut down on time for letters—both to and from Kathy. That same day-to-day life also seemed to ease the pain . . . and eventually, the romance. Now, more than a year later, Kathy is just returning from spending a year abroad as a foreign exchange student. Ironically, I'm in my first semester at SMU in Dallas.

We are both seeing other people. She says she's "in love" with someone new, and I have a girl that I'm crazy about. So I've learned that you can make it through heartache. And that your heart heals. Just as importantly, I've learned that your heart knows how to love again, too.

But Kathy was my first love. I will never, ever forget her and the love we shared together. I've heard there's no love like the first love. That may very well be true. I'm sure we will be good friends for the rest of our lives.

Kirk Alan, 19

Pictures of Us—Together

I look through pictures
Of us being together
Each one reminding me
Of a happy place and time.

I review the life and look
Of such bright
And hopeful moments
Now reduced to a soulful rhyme.

When someone says your name
The pain still overwhelms
Now that you're no longer mine
It will never sound the same.

Tears roll down my cheeks
One for each special memory
Of the two people in the pictures
In, as they say, "Happier times."

It's so very sad
Our hopes—dashed
Our dreams—all bid good-bye
The promises we made—now all put aside.

I think back
On all the loving things we said,
I believed those words
Now bittersweet and yet,

I believed in us,
Took our words to heart
Felt your touch, your kiss
How can I ever forget?

Somewhere love's path parted
And we went our separate ways
I try, but don't forget you
Even dreams have memories.

Still, my only hope is forgetting
So I'll store away our pictures
Along with our happy memories
And bury them with new ones made without you.

Amber Leigh, 17

The Way You Whisper, "Me, Too!"

All the things you do
Are why I love you:

The way you smile,
The way you go the extra mile.
The way you talk,
The way you walk.
The way you hold my hand,
The way you etch our initials in the sand.
The way you look at me,
The way you describe what you see.
The way you stare at me,
The way you stroke my hair.
The way you touch my face,
The way you call me.
The way you whisper, "Me, too!"

Only the tip of the iceberg
In the list of reasons you mean so much to me!

Lexie Reed, 15

Why It's Impossible to Have a Seventh-Grade Boyfriend

If you're a seventh-grade girl and want to have a seventh-grade boyfriend, you might as well forget about it. It's just not going to happen. Since most seventh-grade boys are shorter than most seventh-grade girls, it's difficult—no, make that impossible—to get a seventh-grade boy to dance with you at the school dances. The problem is an even bigger one for girls like me who are taller than the average seventh-grade girl. I mean, schools might as well forget about having dances for seventh-graders and, instead, just do sit-down things—like playing fun games or something.

It's not the seventh-grade boys' fault. There's not much they can do except wait until they grow taller than the girls—which usually isn't until around ninth grade. But I'm only thirteen, and my parents said I couldn't date a ninth-grader until I was at least in the ninth grade. So either I just wait and wait and wait for a seventh-grade boy to get lucky and have a growing spurt, or be stuck with a short boyfriend. The alternative is to have no boy in my life, which is worse than having a really short boyfriend.

Like I said, it's not the boys' fault. They're painfully aware that they're shorter and very self-conscious about it, too. It's one of the reasons seventh-grade boys act so weird to girls, and say and do such dumb things when they're around girls. It's sort of their cover-up for their "short complex." I mean, what are they going to say, "Well, I know I only come up to your shoulder, but would you mind my being your boyfriend—even though we'll look geeky together?" No. At least they're cool enough to not intentionally bring on any more embarrassment for themselves than they're already feeling, and instead, just relate the best they can (which is calling you names like "beanpole").

Even if a seventh-grade girl tells a seventh-grade boy, "Look, I don't care if you are shorter than me. I'd still like you to be my boyfriend," the seventh-grade boy will make a weird face and won't talk to you ever again. At least not until ninth grade—when he's grown a little and you're just too cool for him to resist wanting you to be his girlfriend.

So, I've totally given up on having a seventh-grade boyfriend. But, I've not given up on boys!

La Donna Toepp, 13 (almost)

Can You Stay Awhile?

A knock to the door ever so softly
I stopped a minute to smile
It was love on the other side
Come in, I coaxed,
And please do stay this time!

I've been waiting for you
Wishing, hoping, wanting
Forever and a day
Why did you take so long?
And have you come to stay?

"Love is love!"
Is all love would say
"It's a hand in your hand
A walk in the clouds
A heart so light and gay."

"That's not been true for me!" I cried.
He promised me his heart
Then stole himself away
I don't even know what went wrong
Or what was said that fateful day.

But I'm sad and brokenhearted
Feeling that if he doesn't come back, I'll just die!
If he doesn't have enough love for two,
I do!
Please *make* him want another try!

"It was never meant to be," said love
"The chapter's closed, so turn the page
That space is a place no more.
But if you'll be patient, I'll bring a gift
Please believe, I've better things in store!"

A knock to the door ever so softly
I stopped a minute to smile
It was love on the other side,
So now I know that what they say is true:
Time heals all hurts
And brings new love to you.

Ayla Amon, 15

"Cute, but Slow"

I woke up to my clock radio playing the song that Billy Barnham and I had danced to just nights before at a school dance. I really liked Billy, but it was so hard to get a read on whether or not he liked me. I mean, it was a great dance we had together; he held me really close, and he was smiling the whole time. So that's a good sign, right? But I was the one who had to do the asking. I'd been wanting to dance with him the entire dance, but he never once asked me—and it wasn't like he couldn't see me. I was standing with my friends not more than ten feet away from him. He could see me all right—and he kept looking in my direction. So finally, after feeling anxious and nervous for practically the entire time—and with my heart thumping an extra beat per second—I went over and asked him.

"Sure!" he said, without any hesitation, and led me to the dance floor.

Wouldn't you know it would be the last dance of the evening? As soon as the song was over, the lights went on and everyone scattered. Most of our parents were waiting for us outside in their cars, so we all just hurried out. So unfortunately, I never got a chance to talk with Billy after that one dance.

Then, at school the next day, my best friend, Alesha, told me she had seen Billy in the library earlier in the morning and told him she'd seen the two of us dancing together. "Oh yeah," he'd said, "your friend is cute, but slow." Now, how am I supposed to take that? The "cute" part got my hopes up, but the "slow" part sounded like a put-down to me—and that can't be a sign of love to come. I quizzed Alesha a hundred times on whether he'd said I was "slow" in a sarcastic way. She said she didn't really know, and then reminded me, "You know how hard it is to figure out guys!"

Then, at noon, feeling somewhere between elated and bummed, I practically crashed into Billy in the hall near my locker. My take on this incident was that it was intentional, because the way I saw it, he didn't make any effort to move out of the way. Of course, that got my heart thumping with joy— then galloping with stress, too, wondering if it meant anything more than we almost bumped into each other. I tell you, it's so hard to know how to read these things.

But the nearly-bumping-into-him incident made me wonder if I should ask him if he'd like to come to my soccer match the next day after school. So for the next entire class period, I wrote, and rewrote again and again, a note to him asking if he'd like to. When I'd written the note in a way I thought was cool but not overly done, I wondered how I should best get it to him. But should I? It's tough to know what's best to do in things like this. I mean, what if the dance and near-miss incident didn't mean anything? Worse, maybe he thought I was a geek. I didn't really know. At the dance he'd had one hour and thirty minutes in which to ask me to dance, and he hadn't. And who knows exactly what the bumping into me in the hall meant, anyway? Should I wedge the note in his locker? Should I just brave it and walk up to him and hand it to him? Finally, I decided on giving the note to my friend Alesha, who knows his sister, so she could give it to her brother—and hope for the best.

To my surprise, the note worked its way to Billy within the hour! And, the moment school was out, Alesha came running up to me with a return note from him! It read, *"What took you so long?"*

So now I know that his "cute" was a good sign, and the "slow" meant he was waiting for ME to ask him! It just goes to show you that you never can be sure how to read things. So I learned it's always best to have the courage to believe in yourself enough to reach out for what really matters to you—which in my case was Billy Barnham.

Leliah Feldman, 15

"I Don't Want You to Have Another Boyfriend, Ever!"

He was my to-die-for "hottie," an older-than-I, already-out-of-college and had-a-great-job guy. We'd dated five months when he said, "I don't want you to have another boyfriend, ever!"

He admitted that *he* wanted to be "the last one"! Could you just die? I wanted to cry! Surprised, happy and nervous, too, I dabbed my eyes with the dinner napkin, and hoped my carefully applied eyeliner and mascara wouldn't streak down my face. I didn't know what to say but knew also that words would get in the way of all these wonderful feelings going on between us.

I was so deeply touched. Was it my destiny to have this lovely person be my "last," or was it just a matter of time and sooner or later, I'd find the perfect person—and my time had come? I knew I was in love, but, well, gosh, I hadn't really thought about "forever."

But he wanted to be my "last." I'd never really heard that phrasing before. Like a novel proposal, it was the right thing for him to have said. Maybe it was the only thing someone could have said to win me over. "I don't ever want you to have another boyfriend, ever. I am your last. Period." Those were his exact words. I never get tired of repeating his words. I'd always dreamed it would be like this. Just not quite so soon.

Clayt is his name. Just plain Clayt. Not Clayton, not Clay. Just Clayt. Now, it's my favorite name in the entire world, maybe even in the universe. He's so wonderful. I suppose that everyone in love has only good things to say about the person they love. I try to think if that's true for me. Am I gushy, or simply stating the obvious? Let me think: For starters, he makes me nervous in a good way. You see, that's not something you always hear. And when I'm with him, I'm the playful and funny girl that I know myself to be. With him, I feel so alive. I want to jump out of my skin and fly sometimes. Being in love is amazing.

The thing is, I've broken my own heart and am sad to say, his, too.

There is no good reason. I feel so awful about what I've done; I was so careless in the way I treated him. I don't quite know what to do. Maybe there is nothing I can do. I mean, how do I go back in time and change the things I said? How do I get him to *believe* that I'm truly sorry for all those times when I stood him up, or showed up so late that his carefully laid plans for a great date for us were ruined? "I'm sorry" doesn't cut it.

His words of love have changed into no words at all.

Our breakup was so terrible. I behaved so badly—and said lots of things that I didn't mean. I guess I was frightened that he called it quits—or was the one to do it. I tried to look in control, but I was anything but. You know the type, "So, leave, I'll live without you." I shouted, threw things and made accusations.

Like a true gentleman, he walked away without incriminations or name-calling, leaving me surrounded by his carefully boxed mementoes of the many little things we'd picked out together—like the gorgeous flower vase we kept at his place, and a million-and-one pictures of us together. As he drove away, I wondered if he was feeling that it was a relief to get away from me, or was he as sick to his stomach as I was? He'd told me I was the "girl of his dreams." How was he feeling now: Had he given up the girl, or the dream? Or both?

Given all my actions, I'm pretty sure he's decided the four-year difference in our ages is too much. We talked about that once, and told each other that the way we felt about each other melted the years, erased them. I wasn't so sure: He'd wanted to settle down. I was soon ready to find an apartment and fly into the arms of a waiting world. I was ready to party. It's just that I wanted him always to be waiting for me—but on my terms, when I was ready to be with him.

I miss the friend that held my hands in his when we talked to

God and gave thanks for our blessing of love. He's the sort of person I'd like to have in my life when I'm ready. Unlike me, he was so resolved about being ready to settle down. He wanted to marry, have kids, buy a house. I wasn't ready for that.

I'll be out of high school in a matter of weeks. Sure, dating when I'm out of school will be different than merely having a date for an upcoming dance or the prom. But to settle down? So soon? I'm just not ready.

But now that he's gone, I realize that I love him more than I felt I did. I guess I'm hoping someday his heart will be mine again. And hoping one day, when I am ready, I'll hear him say, "I'm here because I don't ever want you to have another boyfriend. I want to be your last. Still."

Jennifer Ratzlaff, 18

Part 4

Teens Talk About "the Parents"— "Pillars" to "Potholes"

*When I was a kid my parents moved a lot—
but I always found them.*

—Rodney Dangerfield

*We thought we were running away
from the grown-ups, and now
we are the grown-ups.*

—Margaret Atwood

A Word
from the Authors

"Mom, do you think we each deliver the same lecture to our children as we heard from our parents—even though we promised ourselves we wouldn't?"

"Yes, that's the way it works. As so many of our teens discovered, with each passing year, parents are more right than they'd like to admit. You see, Jennifer, parents get wiser with age (yours). Amazing how that happens! Mark Twain called it the law of periodical repetition: Everything happens again and again and again in its own time!

"I'm reminded of the habit my parents had of going on Sunday family drives. As a teenager, I considered this a very boring activity. But I was required to go along, so I had no choice. The leisurely drives that consisted of flower gazing were the most excruciating. My parents would go on long drives pointing out the colorful flowers as they drove ever-so-slowly past blooming fields and meadows and neighborhood yards. If it wasn't for the ice-cream cone promised at the end of these trips, I'm sure all my brothers and sisters and I would have rioted. We did complain. 'This is boring!' one of us kids would say. 'Yes,' the rest of us would chime in. From the front seat came the reply, 'You may not appreciate the serenity of these drives and the beauty of these lovely flowers now, but when you are older, you will.' I was even more certain that being an adult must be pretty boring: My parents actually took great pleasure in the tranquility of these flower-gazing afternoons! And of course, I promised myself I would never do this sort of thing to my children.

"Alas, I have! As I recall, an incident very similar to that happened when you were thirteen, and we went on a 'Sunday drive.' The sun radiant in the blue sky, we drove along winding roads. 'Oh look,' I said, pointing in the direction of a house whose yard was adorned with colorful beds of roses, 'aren't those beautiful?'

"'Yeah,' you sighed with no enthusiasm. A few miles down the road you announced, 'This is so boring! When are we going to do something?' We hadn't gone much further before I said, 'Look over there at those lovely flowers!' I pointed toward a field in full bloom. 'They look like weeds to me, Mom.' You all but yawned. Then, repeating family history, I said, 'You may not appreciate tranquil drives and the beauty of flowers now, but someday you will.'

"Jennifer, I don't want to tell you 'I told you so,' but I've noticed that there are freshly cut flowers all around your house, and the patio on your apartment is densely populated with potted plants! And, I heard you asked your boyfriend if you could drive by the fields of gladiolas in bloom on the way back from L.A.!"

"Omigosh, Mother! I did, didn't I? To me there is nothing more exquisite than a flower in full bloom—whether it's in the field, garden or in my home! And you're right. We probably imitate our parents more than we imagine. Lea McFadden, a seventeen-year-old teen in our workshop last Friday, made a remark along this line: 'I used to think I never wanted to be like my mother. But with each year, I'm becoming more like her. My handwriting is similar to hers, and I find myself raising my eyebrows like she does. And the other day when I was baby-sitting, I found myself using some of the same phrases she uses on my five-year-old brother. At first, I thought it was disgusting! But I do admire my mother, and one day, I hope to be like her.'"

"Speaking of parents being right, teens said another thing they learned about parents is that 'you have to keep in mind that parents are learning as they go along—so they aren't perfect (hence you need to "cut them some slack" now and then)!'"

"That's funny, Mom, but when you think about it, parents are practitioners of sorts. Last year my dad and I were reminiscing, and I was trying to 'get' him on not letting me do something when I was thirteen, and he admitted he made a decision or two he wished he could take back. But then he added, 'Jennifer, you have to remember that when you were thirteen, I was ten years older than you are right now. If you think about that, it would be like you having a six-year-old right now, and evaluating the decisions and choices you had made for your child when she was one and you were twenty-one. When you think back to each year, I'll bet there would be a few things you did that you wished you had done differently. Well, it's like that every year with parenting children. I'll bet that when I am sixty, I'll think back to this period right now, and wish I had said or done some things differently.' I thought he had a great point. We've heard from so many teens who have babies of their own, and the first thing they say is, 'How did my parents do it? Having a child is tough!' Those teens with toddlers—now finding they have to instill rules and consequences in order to help their kids be safe and learn good behavior—find themselves face-to-face with the same issues as their parents."

"Good point, Jennifer. And I agree with your father. To be a parent is to always wish you had done some things differently. Perhaps it's one of the reasons parents look forward to grandchildren. After raising their own, they're better trained for the job! The good news—and something we heard again and again from teens in working on this unit—was how critically important it is to them that they have a good relationship with their parents."

"Critically important, Mother? Sounds dire! Well, okay—

maybe it is. I have some friends who take their parents for granted, but most all of my friends think their parents are pretty important people in their lives. It's not so different from the relationship you and I share. You're an awesome parent."

"Why thank you, Jennifer. Are you trying to get me to take you shopping?"

"Mom, c'mon! You know I'm not . . . well—now that you brought it up!"

"Shopping aside, Jennifer, you and I have always had a very extraordinary bond between us, one that's made the good times simply spectacular, and the trying times really tough. But you're twenty-seven now, so you have more perspective. When you were fourteen or sixteen would you—and your friends—have said parents are 'awesome'?"

"Absolutely. And by the way, I think the special relationship we have still makes the good times simply spectacular, and the trying times really tough. It's part of the push and pull I feel, and I think one that teens readily feel with their parents. One of the things that makes being a teenager so tough is that teens have one foot in adulthood but the other in adolescence. As a teenager, while you may think you're making independent choices, it's all got to be run by those who grant final permission—*the parents*. Having them on your side is always better than having them against you. You learn that it's a love-hate awakening: You still need your parents—but they're in the way, too! Sometimes you love it that you need them as much as you do, and you resent them because you do, as well. Take the issue of dating, or even your friends. I wasn't free to do as I wanted. Everything had to be run by you and Dad. When you approved of a guy I wanted to date (or a particular friend with whom I was spending a lot of time), you weren't as strict about where we went, and you offered leniency in my curfew. So basically, with your approval came more privileges."

"So it can be useful to get your parents to like the person you like—to see them as a taste berry?"

"Sure! But there's another issue here, too. Many of the teens we work with and hear from express not only their desire to be in a good relationship with their parents, but tell us why and how their relationship is troublesome, causing duress and heartache. What is true for some teens is that pain and stress in life centers not just on the normal growing pains teens face with their own lives, but in coping with parents who themselves face overwhelming chaos and personal problems of their own."

To not have "capable, supportive parents" sounds tragic, and is—for both parents and teens. As teens begin to look to the outer world, hopeful they will measure up as they "test the waters," they're still looking over their shoulders for their parents' approval and respect. Parents are synonymous with love, acceptance and hope.

True enough. And in this chapter you'll meet teens who are:

- Learning a deeper appreciation for how much their parents love them;
- Understanding more fully just how much they appreciate and love their parents;
- Facing some shaky times—because of the lives their parents lead;
- Discovering the "secrets" to having a good relationship with their parents;
- Learning that "parents are learning as they go along so you need to 'cut them some slack'"; and
- Understanding that the older teens get, the smarter their parents get, i.e., with each passing year, parents are more right than teens would like to admit!

"At the end of the day," we learn that teens think of their parents as more special than anyone else in their lives, and precisely because this is so, an argument with them isn't just casually sloughed off; the words "I love you" are spoken often;

and wanting to understand their parents and support them in the things that make their own lives fun and full is not saved for later years, but something they wish to work on now.

As teens grow in awareness of their parents as people and their motives for their children—the sacrifices they make, the love behind their rules, their own life pains or past broken childhoods that have caused inadequacies, vulnerabilities and low self-worth—teens are able to empathize. The result is that teens recognize not only the importance of their parents to their own lives, but appreciate how unbreakable the loving ties to their parents really are—regardless of whether a parent is a good parent, or hoping to become one. As you'll see in the stories, teens are taste berries: They seek connection, and they're committed to resolving the things that might get in its way.

❤ *Taste berries to you, Bettie and Jennifer Youngs*

Daddy-Daughter Days

When I was a little girl, my mother would help me get dressed for bed, and then my father would come in and read me a story and then we'd say bedtime prayers. Sometimes my father would make up a story, and as he was telling it, ask me to add to it. This was always great fun; instead of reading someone else's story, we created our own. Sometimes "story time" was replaced by singing little songs, such as "Twinkle, Twinkle Little Star" or the ABCs. And, every once in a while—since my father would some-times tape these bedtime sessions—our time would be spent lis-tening to a "recorded" bedtime session. (Playing them back was always great fun, too!) As always, after the story and song ritual, we'd say bedtime prayers. Then my father would kiss me good-night and turn out the lights.

Needless to say, I loved bedtime. To this day, it remains one of my favorite family rituals and is an especially loving memory of my parents. My parents are good parents. I'm lucky in that way.

As I got older, other rituals came about. One of my favorites was when on my father's day off from work, the two of us would spend the entire day together. My father was fond of calling this time together, "Daddy-Daughter Days." Mostly these days started with a predictable routine: We would begin with a trip to Dunkin' Donuts, and from there, plan our day. In the summer, we would sometimes play miniature golf or go to the batting cages. In the winter, we'd go snow sledding or build a very crea-tive snowman. We had so much fun together.

As a teen, many of these "family rituals" came to an end. There just didn't seem to be enough time (or desire) to devote to Daddy-Daughter Days—or doing as many things with my par-ents as I once had. Like most teens I knew, I was more interested in being with my friends than spending time with my parents. I'm sure they missed these times; I know my father especially missed Daddy-Daughter Days. I think he thought that time together was an assured thing, and just a matter of finding the interesting activity in which we could both share and have fun. I recall a particular Saturday when I was fifteen. My father asked if I'd like to spend the day playing golf, or catching a movie, one I'd expressed interest in seeing. "No, thanks, Dad," I told him. "I've got plans to be with my friends today."

"I see," he replied and then bargained, "Well, how about spending a couple of hours with me, and a couple of hours with them?"

"Nope. Can't do," I told him. "We've got all-day plans. Maybe another day."

"Sure," he said, looking disheartened, and then added, "If you change your mind, let me know, okay?"

A couple of days later, when I came home from school, I found an old cassette tape on my dresser. Sitting alongside was the old tape recorder (so that I could play the tape). I put it in and listened. It was me, at age four, singing my ABCs, followed by "Twinkle, Twinkle Little Star" and then saying bedtime prayers. In my sweet little child's voice I was saying, "I love my mommy, I love my doggy, I love my grandma, and I love my daddy, and I love all the people in the world." This was followed by my father's soft and gentle voice saying good-night.

Listening to it made me cry, because those were such beautiful and loving times. And I knew the cassette had been placed in my room as my father's way of saying he missed the time with that little girl—his daughter. His leaving the tape, I believe, was his way of saying, "I still want time with you. Please want some time with me, too."

In that moment, I loved him so much and knew that I didn't ever want my dad to think that I was too busy to have time for the two of us. So, I placed the old tape recorder and cassette— along with this note—on the dresser in my parents' bedroom:

Dear Dad,

Thank you for the reminder of the loving times we spent together. Though I have a busy life, I am not too busy to spend time with my parents. When I heard that little four-year-old sing "Twinkle, Twinkle Little Star," I was reminded how in all the years we had Daddy-Daughter Days, you never once won a game of miniature golf—because you let me win! So today, I'm making sure we both win. I promise to set aside a certain time each week just for you and me. I want you always to feel that no matter how old I get, our time together is special—and a memory in the making.

Love, your daughter.

Jessica McDermott, 17

I'm Sick of "Checking In"!

My father and I disagreed about curfew. He'd say I was to be in by 10:30 on weekdays, and 12:30 on weekends, no exceptions without my first asking. I told him, "I'm seventeen and shouldn't have to have a curfew." Then I reminded him that in less than a year I'd be away at college, and I'd be coming in whenever I liked. He told me that what I did in college was my choice, but that while living at home, the rules stood. He said he thought the curfew was fair, especially since, should I give him an acceptable reason for staying out later, all I had to do was ask. I told him that it all amounted to my having to "check in"—which made me feel like a junior-high kid, and that it was time he let me be responsible for myself. To this he explained that while a curfew may sound like a restriction, it's really about people looking out for one another.

We just went around and around on curfew, never seeing eye to eye on it.

The very next Friday after one pretty heated exchange, my dad and I had tickets to see our town's professional football league opening-day game. They were good tickets, and it was the season's opening night, so we were really looking forward to going. On the day of the game, my dad had a really important out-of-town business meeting with some major clients he was meeting for the first time. He was driving to a nearby city to meet with these clients and informed me that his getting home and our leaving for the game would be tight.

That afternoon, to make sure we could take off the second he walked in, I made sure we didn't have to waste one minute. I turned off the radio and TV and necessary lights. I put the tickets in my jacket, and getting the sports jacket from his closet I knew he'd be wearing, placed our jackets on the sofa next to the door. When a half-hour had passed from the time he said he'd be home, I understood that he was a little late.

But then, nearly a whole hour passed. I was getting really irritated. I mean, we were going to miss the kick-off! And why hadn't he phoned me and let me know he was going to be really late? I'd hurried through my homework. Had I known he'd be late, I could have taken my time and been a little more thorough. And, his phoning could have meant that maybe I'd find a ride to the game, and Dad could just meet me there. Anxiously pacing the floor, yet another half-hour passed. That's when my frustration turned to anger. How inconsiderate of my father! Now we were going to miss the whole game! I would rather have had to sit alone at the game, instead of missing the whole thing!

When yet another half-hour passed, my anger turned to fear. What if something terrible had happened to my dad, like he had a heart attack or had been in an accident, or something? I began to really worry. After all, I'd already called his cell phone—about ten times—and there had been no answer. I called Mom (my parents are divorced) to see if she knew my father's whereabouts. But she hadn't talked to my father in a couple of days and knew nothing of my father's schedule. So then I began calling around to a couple of my father's work associates; none of them knew anything about his whereabouts either. One didn't even know he had spent the day away from the office.

I was beside myself with worry, assuming the worst had happened.

Finally, the phone rang, and my dad said breathlessly, "Son, I'm so sorry about the game, but there was a terrible accident on the freeway coming home, and I stopped to help and ended up going to the hospital with one of the family members involved in the accident. I left my cell phone in the car, so I couldn't call until now. I'm calling you from the hospital, and need to let you know that it's likely I'll be another forty-five minutes before I get home. I'm really sorry about the game, Son."

I was so relieved to hear from my father and to learn that he was safe that I actually cried. That was when I "got" the importance of a curfew: Checking in! It's about knowing that someone you love is safe.

Now that I really understand what lies behind a "curfew," I let my father know that I appreciate his love and concern. I no longer come in late just to prove to him that I can and will do what I want. When I need a longer time to be out, I call, because I want him to know that I am safe, just coming in later.

Rather than letting the curfew be a wedge between us, I think of it as one more proof of my father's loving me as much as he does. Now rather than pushing us apart, it's drawn us closer. Something else has become clear to me as well. When I hear other kids say they have no curfew, I don't envy them. I wonder *why* their parents aren't making sure they "check in."

Brent Stephenson, 17

The Epiphany

My father was the youngest of four children. His father died of cancer when he was six. His mother, who had left school in the eleventh grade to raise a family, worked hard to support herself and her four children. Times were tough—really tough. But his mother was tougher. "Even though our lives seem shattered," she told them, "we are not shattered. We will stay together and be a family—and a happy one. We will survive intact. I don't yet know how we will do that, but we can, and we will."

As impossible as the odds seemed, all four children not only graduated from high school but also went on to college. Two graduated with advanced degrees. One was my father—who graduated with honors!

Last year my dad was one of two men honored for their contributions to the community. In his acceptance speech, the first man said, "I owe my success to my company, one that gave me an opportunity to earn a good living, and to my wife for her love and support." My father walked to the podium and said, "I agree with the other gentleman honored here today. Working for good people—a quality company—and having the support of family—these are real keys to success. But I really need to credit my success to a woman with an eleventh-grade education. She worked two jobs in order to keep a family of four children together, staunchly believing that we would persevere. And so we did. Her words, 'You can, and you will' were daily reminders to keep going even when we thought we couldn't endure another day of the near-poverty level in which we existed. This small but mighty woman—my mother—is the backbone of my success." Then, holding up the award, my dad looked directly at his mother and said, "Mom, for your years of hard work, tenacity, perseverance and for loving me enough to help me learn the meaning of the words, 'You can, and you will,' this is for you.

You are my hero, my Cinderella in shining armor."

From her place in the audience next to my mother, my little sister and me, my grandmother smiled proudly, tears running down her cheeks. My mother was crying, too. In that moment, I was so proud of my family.

Sitting there that day, watching the love and respect flash between my father and my grandmother, was sort of an epiphany for me. While I'm sure that my father owes his success to "one small, but mighty, woman," I realized that my dad had been working as hard in his life for the benefit of his family as his mother had been for her family. I mean, for my father to have come as far as he has says a lot about my grandmother, but it says a lot about my father, as well. I have so much more than my father had as a kid. We live in a really nice house and have a comfortable life. And for as long as I can remember, every month my father puts money aside for college for my sister and me. And just as my dad's mother wanted their family to be a "happy" family, my father has worked to see that we are, too. I'd say we're a really happy family.

So I respect my dad a lot. Just as he called his mother his hero, I'd have to say that my dad is a hero, too. Obviously the community giving him the award thinks so. I know he's *my* hero.

When I have a family, I want my kids to love and respect me the way I love and respect my father.

Ricardo Torres, 16

Pierced in a Number of Places

I really like a guy named Lonnie. Not in the boyfriend sense, although I can see why some girls would be very attracted to him! We're in the same honors English and science classes, so I get to be around him quite a lot. He's so smart and creative! For example, in one of our classes, the teacher asked us to write an essay listing six things mankind could do to preserve our environment. I wrote about the obvious things, like water conservation and better methods of waste disposal, stuff like that.

Lonnie's solutions were much more innovative. He wrote that we all needed to focus on things such as mass cloning a certain two species of animals and four families of insects and that doing so would eliminate two of the greatest perils of destruction to our environment. Now, I think that's a brilliant approach. Who knows if his suggestions will work, but until they're considered, we all might be missing out on the solution to some of the problems we face in preserving our environment. The point is, we need creative minds coming up with new solutions. Lonnie is what our creative-writing teacher calls a "possibilities thinker."

I, too, think Lonnie is a possibilities thinker. He loves change and is constantly experimenting. From month to month he will dye his hair a different color—sometimes blue, sometimes deep crimson, sometimes yellow or jet black, sometimes green or orange. And he keeps it in the latest style. Some of the kids think some of his styles are a little weird, but they don't get down on him for it. We all love to look at his changes, and of course, many of us would just love to follow his lead—if only our parents would let us! My parents would never allow me to color my hair.

They also said I shouldn't be friends with Lonnie, which really frustrates me because he's a really good guy, no matter what he looks like. But if my parents don't approve of a certain friend of

mine, then they restrict the places I can go with that person—
which really puts a damper on my fun.

When at first I tried to convince my parents that Lonnie was a
neat guy, they said he looked like the wrong kind of guy to hang
out with, and that just looking at him should make it obvious
why I should shun him. "Just look at the guy's hair!" my mother
shrieked. When I explained that Lonnie wears his hair the way he
does because he's creative, she said, "It's not nearly as creative as
it is strange." I don't see it that way at all. I wish I had the nerve
to wear my hair that way and would if only they'd let me.

My parents also object to body piercing—and Lonnie is
pierced in a number of places! I don't think body piercing is
nearly as outrageous as my parents think it is. When I told them
that just about everyone has friends who have either had their
body pierced—or would like to—my parents said that only
"weird kids" would consider anything more than ear piercing.
But that's not true. It's a big thing now, really "in," especially at
my school. And Lonnie isn't the only one at my school who has
pierced things other than his ears. He's pierced his tongue, but
only in one place. I think it's cool. I mean, if he wants to wear jew-
elry in his tongue (and his parents don't object), why shouldn't
he? Jed, a ninth-grader at my school, has pierced his tongue
twice, and I'm sure he's not the only one who has more than one
hole in his tongue. Lonnie has pierced his ears in a number of
places, as has practically everyone. I like the way Lonnie adds his
own sense of personal style to wearing pierced ears. It's artsy. On
his right ear he wears seven earrings, all of which are in an assort-
ment of shapes and sizes of a star. The reason for seven—rather
than two or eight or some other number—is because his birth
sign is the seventh in the zodiac. I think that's very clever. On his
left ear, he wears a large moon earring. So together you get the
moon and the stars. I think that's quite inventive. And very cool.

Lonnie has also pierced his right eyebrow, but again, he's not
the only one at my school who has done this. And he's also

pierced his navel and both nipples. My parents also have a big problem with this. I don't know why. (And really, I don't know why I told them in the first place.) So I told Mom and Dad that if they'd look around, they'd see it happening everywhere.

They weren't impressed. I told them that if they would take the time to know the Lonnie I know, I'm certain they would like him, but I knew it was going to be an uphill battle. Then, one evening when my dad was reading the paper, his eyes widened, he tapped at a picture above one of the articles and said, "Well, I'll be! Isn't that that Lonnie kid?" He promptly passed the paper to my mom, whose eyes studied the photo, then scanned the article. Nodding, she looked pleasantly surprised and murmured, "Who would've guessed?" She handed the paper to me. The small column announced a local teen's publication of one of his essays in an international science journal, as well as his being awarded a scholarship upon graduation from high school. As I read the details in the article, I proudly confirmed, "Yep! It's my friend Lonnie all right! I told you he was brilliant! It just goes to show you that a little hair color and body piercing doesn't ruin your chances for a great future!"

"Well, I guess you could add him to the list for your birthday next month. It'll give us a chance to meet him," Mom said, obviously deciding Lonnie was not a total write-off. "I'll ask him tomorrow!" I said, jumping at the chance to have him come.

Lonnie did come to my party, and while my parents "looked him over," in the end, his great personality and brilliance won them over! It just goes to show you that sometimes you have to be patient with "the parents." They make mistakes, but they mean well. You have to work with them, but sooner or later, they're bound to come around—like mine did.

Joanna Kameran, 16

Virtual Reality

My mother is an alcoholic. Once she starts drinking, she drinks until there isn't any more alcohol in the house. About two weeks ago, my mother was drunk and fell while searching in an upper cabinet for, of all things, more alcohol. It was a bad fall, one in which she hit her head so hard she was knocked unconscious. I was scared for her. I called 911 to get help. Next, I called my aunt and uncle, who live one hour away, and told them what had happened. Just as they'd done countless times before, they immediately drove over to stay with my little sister and me.

I'm hoping and praying that my mother gets well. I know she wants to, but I'm not holding out much hope. She's been through a number of treatment programs—six, I think. So it frightens me to think she may never win over her addiction. I know she has a lot to do in order to get better (and I do hope this time is the final time), because the thing about advanced stages of alcoholism is that it's possible to drink yourself to death. My mother could die. That terrifies me.

My sister and I are still living with my aunt and uncle. We're doing fine, but I miss my mother and wish I could do more to help her get well. Right now she's in a treatment program again, so that's good. At least I know she's getting the care she needs. I just hope she'll continue to seek help once she gets out.

Alcoholism is a disease, a dreadful one. I pray every day for my mother's recovery. I want so badly to be a family again. But deep down, I fear that my mother will abuse alcohol "one time too many." And I feel so sorry for my little sister, who cries all the time because she misses our mother. I think she feels abandoned. Sometimes she asks me why our mother doesn't love us (my sister sometimes thinks that's the reason our mother is away). So I do the best I can by being a good sister to her and reassuring her that our mother does love us; she's just sick right now. I never tell her that if our mother isn't strong enough to live without alcohol, we may have to find a way to live without her.

Hillary Elwel, 14

Anchor to My Heart

Thank you . . .
For standing by me through thick and thin
For not giving up on me even when I didn't win
For your patience when I kept pushing you away
For caring even when I said I didn't need you anyway!

I'm grateful knowing . . .
I can count on your strength
Ask for support, and know you'll go to any length
When I lose my way, you'll help me get back on track
When in pain, your comfort soothes and brings me back.

I'm lucky because . . .
When I was sad, you gave me faith and hope
When I was confused, you taught me how to cope
When I felt I couldn't go on, you carried me long miles
When I didn't believe, you restored my smiles.

Mom and Dad, thank you . . .
For the guidance and faith you've shown
For giving me a safe place where I have grown
For showing me how to strive
Because of your love, I will survive—and thrive.

Teresa Amos, 18

A Sweetheart's Dream

My father is sixty-seven. Though he was planning on retiring at fifty-five, he found his sweetheart and married her (my mother) when he was fifty (she's seventeen years younger than him). Within a couple of years, they had two kids—my brother and me.

When my parents met, my mom worked as a travel agent. Now she's at home full time. For my father (he has three grown sons from a previous marriage), starting a new family—and especially now that my mother had stopped working and was at home full time—meant he couldn't afford to retire. It also meant he hasn't been able to make good on something he's promised my mother. "Sweetheart," he'd say, "I'm going to take you on a cruise." He still tells her that, only these days he adds, "as soon as the kids are out of college."

I know that putting both of us kids through college probably means it's going to be a while before my father achieves his dream to go away with my mother on a cruise—though it doesn't stop him from clipping out ads about a cruise vacation! It's cute, but it's kind of sad, too. I remember my grandmother always wanted to go to Nova Scotia. My grandfather would always say, "We'll go next year, sweetheart." Then she died. My grandmother never got to see Nova Scotia. I just don't want my parents to wait until it's too late. So I've been saving up my money.

My goal is to be able to send my parents on a cruise some time this year, even if it is a short three-day cruise. My friends say to me, "Get real! Saving up for a cruise is something you'll never be able to do." But I don't believe that. It's not like I can send them around the world or anything, but I don't think my putting together the money for a short trip is an impossible goal. About three years ago, I remember my mother wanting a particular vase she'd seen in a store window next to where we always buy groceries. On the way to the grocery store, she'd stop in to look at the vase, and once again, leave without buying it. "Why don't you just buy it?" I asked one time. "Oh, I intend to!" she said with a big smile. "Just not today. I'm saving up my money, though!" I was sure she was.

Then, when I announced my desire to attend a two-week soccer camp that same summer, my mother stopped looking at the vase—even though we still shopped for groceries near the store that stocked the vase she so wanted. Instead of buying that vase, she used her money to send me to camp. I was happy that I was getting to go to soccer camp but sad that it meant her giving up the vase she wanted so much. So later that same week, I went to the store and put down ten dollars (money I earned working for neighbors doing odd jobs and yard work) on the vase, asking that it be put away. The store didn't have a lay-away plan, but the owner said he'd had the vase for some time and maybe he could do it, just for me. So every two weeks, I'd go in and pay on the vase. While it took me nearly nine months to pay for it, I did!

That was three years ago, and I no longer have to depend on odd jobs from the neighbors to earn money. I have a part-time job at a Postal Annex in a strip mall near my house. Each week, I've been putting a little aside for the three-day cruise. I've got other plans for making money as well. Three weeks ago, I had a party and charged everyone three dollars. After paying for expenses, I made $126, so I'm getting there.

I'm determined that just as my parents have made my dreams come true for all these years—from my first bicycle to my first car three months ago—I'm going to do all I can to make their dream of going on a cruise come true. I'm keeping the trip a secret from them for now, though I can't wait until that day when I say, "Mom and Dad, remember how the two of you always wanted to go on a cruise? Well, here are the tickets. Have a great trip!"

Matt Jenkins, 17

My "Options"—Now

Sometimes, I glance over in my mother's direction and see her watching me with my twenty-two-month-old son, and it'll look like she's just absolutely captivated by the sight of us, as if she's awed by the delight of seeing us together. But then there are other times when I'll see this sad, faraway look in her eyes—like she's thinking about something that hurts her. Knowing my mom, I guess it makes her sad thinking of the dreams she had for me (and the dreams I had for me) that are going to be a lot harder to achieve—if I accomplish them at all.

When I first told my mother I was pregnant, we discussed my "options." She told me it was my decision to make; she couldn't make it for me. She said she would support me in whatever decision I made, but she wanted me to make "an informed decision." She then "informed me" what raising a child at my age would mean, and she also made it really clear that when she said she'd support me in whatever decision I made, she didn't mean she would take care of my baby for me.

Well, one thing I can say about my mother, she follows through on what she says. Raising my son has been up to me. Still, I can see the way she sometimes wants to just jump in and do something she's sure she can do better—like disciplining him when he climbs up on the back of the couch to swing the pictures back and forth from where they hang on the wall. But she lets me do it instead (lucky me). She might glare at me and then look over at him throwing his toys wildly about in a mad effort to get my attention, while I'm leisurely talking to one of my friends on the phone and ignoring him. It must be hard for her to hold her tongue (although those looks she gives me do speak volumes). And I know she finds it hard when she has to say "no" when I ask her to baby-sit, but she has a life of her own and she's determined to live it.

As you've guessed, I do live at home. I do have some help from her: She did baby-sit while I finished high school at night, and she still does now when I take two college classes each semester at night—but that's pretty much it. She says Alex is my son, and he and I are building our life together. It's my responsibility and my honor to raise him, and she doesn't want to interfere or deprive me of that responsibility or honor. I resent it when she says that, but I do know that it is her full right. Actually, I respect her for it; she seems to be able to say "no" better than I do. Not that she hasn't helped me out more than she said she would. Up until my son was a year old, she was carrying a full-time load at work, as well as being the main supporter of the family I had started—and basically heaped upon her. I was a minor, with a minor. It's not like she asked for all this. Once my son's father learned I was pregnant, he was gone, completely removing himself from my life—his baby son's life, too.

Once Alex was a year old, Mom insisted I find a job so I could help support him and myself. Even so, I knew it was tough on her, because she's always worried whether or not the baby-sitter is good to him and how it's affecting him. I know she struggles to support us, and thinks that it's time for me to contribute more than I do.

While she loves me and adores her grandson, my being a teen mother has got to be tough on her. My mother started raising children early herself, and with me being the last child at home, I know she was looking forward to living on her own when I finally turned eighteen. So, my having a baby was a big change of plans for her. It must be hard for her not to resent it. But her patience with us is a sign, I believe, of her love for us.

I'm stuck in two worlds—one being a teenager, and one being a mother. It's incredibly stressful. I know it must be hard for my mother to put up with, too, because I act out both roles. I know it can't be easy when I'm being insistent that since she's home she should baby-sit so I can go out with my friends, or think she should let me spend my paychecks on anything I want, instead of paying bills. Her unending forgiveness also shows me her love. She's taught me patience and tolerance, because I watch her exercise it with both me and my son, even when I've finally realized she can't always be feeling as patient and tolerant as she's acting. Being a mother of a little boy as full of life as Alex helped me wake up to this fact. It dawned on me that you have to act patient and tolerant even when you don't feel it—just like my mom must've been doing and continues to do so often with me, and now my son.

Because she loves both of us and doesn't want to make any mistakes, it must be scary for her to know she's a role model for me and she plays such a big part in Alex's daily life. But she never seems to act as if it scares her. Being a mother now myself, I see how easy it is to feel this sense of guilt when it comes to raising a child—like you're so responsible and you love your child so much, you just can never do enough. Then, I wonder if she feels guilty that I got pregnant and had Alex. Sometimes I think she must feel like she should've done something different—or wonders if maybe she did something wrong. Yet, she doesn't act like she's disappointed in me. That's good. Being a parent, I now see that being a mother means feeling a lot of love, and knowing that you are loved, too. I love this part of being a parent, and the new relationship my mother and I now have. Still, the truth is, I'm disappointed in myself that I've short-changed my years of childhood. As young as I am, it's very stressful being a teenage parent. Getting to this point of understanding has made all the difference to me in understanding and appreciating my mother. I love her, of course, but there is now a respect, a solid respect, solidified by my being a mother myself.

Lena Moreno, 19

The Better Part of Me

My past will always haunt me,
A past that will always be,
But I am a better person now,
Having learned the better part of me.

With my arms open wide,
And a heart full of pride,
I can now express to you,
Just what I feel inside.

You tried to lead the way,
Yet I went astray,
And of course I then became
More stubborn, just the same.

Though you felt I was a rebel,
I know that you could tell,
I was only trying to find where I belong,
Just wanting to sing my very *own* song.

But know that you were always there,
So please put away all despair,
For you always mattered
And always I did care.

Believe me when I say "I love you"
Because it's so very true,
I know how much you love me
I've learned of love because of you.

Juanita Aguilar, 20

Step-Witch

My parents are divorced. I live with my father and see my mom as much as I can. Everyone was happy with this arrangement—until my father married Marsha. I called my stepmother "Step-Witch" (but not to her face) because she made our lives so difficult. Step-Witch was always demanding that I spend time with my mother, so that her and my father could spend more time alone—even though it was not what worked best for my mother, my father or me.

My dad and I are very close, but I'm always in school and he's always working, so sometimes we don't have as much time to be together as we'd like. We especially have football in common. Dad played in high school and in college. He's hoping that I'll play well enough in high school to play for a major college team. That's my goal, too. I hope to be a Heisman Trophy winner, and to play professionally for either the Dallas Cowboys or the San Francisco 49ers—both teams have great lead quarterbacks. That's my dream: to be lead quarterback.

Right now I play on my school's varsity team. Dad makes practically each and every game. When he has the time, he even comes by to watch me practice. He's my biggest fan! Then Step-Witch threw a wrench in our time together: She enrolled my father and her in a ballroom dance class that meets twice a week from 4:00 to 5:30, and so Dad has even less time to come watch me practice. Nice going, Step-Witch!

I told her I thought she was jealous of the time I spent with my father and would go to any lengths to have me go live with my mother. I mean, I was really sure she hated me.

One evening at dinner Step-Witch announced, "We've got exciting news, Tom. We're going on a little vacation!" My first thought was that it would be nice to have her out of the house for a few days, but she crushed that fantasy by adding, "The three of us are going to North Platte, Nebraska!"

"Nebraska?" I groaned. "I mean, what happens in North Platte, Nebraska?"

"Lots," Step-Witch explained, still looking as if this was some awesome adventure she was suggesting. "For one, I have family in Nebraska."

"And," my dad volunteered, "the University of Nebraska has a great football team—and Marsha's arranged for us to go to a game while we're there." Any other time I'd be thrilled to go to any college game, but Nebraska with Step-Witch? She and my dad actually expected us all to go have some kind of bonding experience or something—like I cared about her family. I didn't even want to think about it. Before I could say anything, my dad added, "Think it over. I believe it'll be a great time. We'll talk more about this later on."

So, with the pressure off, I went about my life and secretly decided I'd protest going with them to Nebraska as the time to go grew closer. But, the days flew by so fast, and in no time I was heading off on a weeklong trip to Nebraska.

I was prepared to hate it.

The very good news is that on the day after we arrived, we headed for the football game. We all arrived at the field early and found our seats—which were incredible; they were right on the fifty-yard line. Step-Witch had said she'd meet us at our seats. I assumed she was going to use the restroom, but instead, she returned with a man dressed in a University of Nebraska warm-up suit. "Tom," she said, introducing us, "this is my brother-in-law. He's one of the team's coaches. He works with the quarterbacks."

"Nice to meet you," he said. "Marsha tells me you want to play pro ball." I nodded and stammered, "I sure do!" and he said, "I don't have much time right now, I've got to get back to the team, but come on down to the locker room after the game. We'll talk, and I'll introduce you to some of the players."

I couldn't believe it! Talk about a rush! That I was going to meet the coach made the game intensely interesting to me. I watched my stepmother's brother-in-law working with the quarterbacks throughout the game. And then, true to his word, Marsha's brother-in-law met with us after the game (Nebraska won, by the way). The energy in the locker room was really amped up, and needless to say, so was I. I met the players— including the quarterback. It was one of the coolest days of my life—and it all came true because of Marsha—my father's wife, my stepmother.

So, I've decided to work on my attitude about my stepmother. I can see that she's trying to be a part of the family for real, so I've decided to do my part and be nice to her, too.

Tom Dixson, 16

Hidden Diary

Several months ago my mom and I were cleaning out her bureau. As I was going through one of the drawers, I found her diary. "Oh, look!" I exclaimed. "If you ever threaten to read mine, I can retaliate!" She laughed good-naturedly—and quickly scooped it out of my hands and gently placed it beneath an old photo album.

I was dying with curiosity to have a look at it. So the next day, without her knowing it, I retrieved it. I know I shouldn't have read it. A diary is personal, and I wouldn't want her to read mine, but I couldn't resist. I took it to my room and began reading it.

Over the years, my mother never said much about her high-school years. She said she didn't have a class yearbook because she couldn't afford one. But her diary told the tale of a girl who had gotten mixed up with kids who did drugs, skipped school and even had a baby. I was so incredibly shocked.

The diary was more than facts about her life events. It was also filled with the painful feelings she felt about all the things that had happened to her. In the diary, she talked about her regrets. There were lots of them. Reading her emotions—in words—gave me a completely different sense of her. I was also sad for her, for what she'd gone through. Though I knew it was hers, the diary didn't seem like it could even belong to the person I know my mother to be. She doesn't even drink, so I can't imagine her ever taking drugs. She has some really strict rules for me, too—and they include a curfew. Her life as a teen and my life as a teen are very different. Maybe it's because she didn't want me to repeat her life as a teen. I put the diary back in its place without reading further. That night, I went to her bedroom and told her how much I appreciated all the things she did for me. I also hugged her extra long.

Since reading the diary, I don't feel the same way towards my mom. I sympathize with what her life must have been like—and for all she went through. For sure, I have a new respect for her, most especially for the way she is bringing me up—like her rules and curfew. I see how she is trying to shelter me from the terrible things she went through. Getting straight from doing drugs was a terrible ordeal for her. And the boy who was the father of her baby refused to speak to her or see her once he learned she was pregnant. She named her baby *Cherish*. That's me. I think about my name, and how it came about. I think it's a very beautiful name, and since I've read the diary, I love it all the more.

I never told my mom I read her diary. I'd like to, and maybe one day I will. For now, I've vowed that I'll fulfill my mother's hopes that as a teen, I'll not drink, do drugs or get pregnant. I've come away from this so filled with empathy for my mom. And I'm so very proud of her. She's such a good person and a good mom to me. As shocking as finding out about her past was, in a way, it brought us closer. I listen to her a little more closely now, because I know that she parents me from the standpoint of hoping I never have to go through what she did.

Cherish Sanders, 16

Freaky Friday

"What did we do in school today, Honey?" is the first question Mom asks me every day when we catch up with each other. "We"—like school is somehow a family activity. "I don't know, Mom," I usually respond. "What did we do at the Mayo Clinic?" (She's a nurse there.) She just laughs and says, "Don't be stingy. I want to know."

I've never been able to convince Mom that my life is less fun-filled and carefree than she thinks it is. Just the other day I heard Mom on the telephone with her best friend talking about "us" kids, as usual. She was telling her friend how I was going to go with a school group on Saturday to do volunteer work, and she made it sound like something really exciting. In fact, we're all going to a nearby community to pick up trash! Then she talked about how I get to go to Washington, D.C., over spring break. I'm going with a group from my school, and even though I know I'm going to have a great time, it is a school trip, with teachers for chaperones and homework assignments to complete. Listening to Mom, you'd think I was going to a party thrown by MTV!

Next Mom went on about my playing the clarinet in the band at school and representing the school at the state finals. I'm glad I finished first in the local school competition and all, but Mom definitely has trumped up more fun than it's going to be for me. I see it as having a lot of work in front of me in order to do well in the competition—I mean, I will be competing with the best of the best. And there's no way I want to get home from the competition and announce that I finished dead last! Once at the finals—a six-hour bus ride, no less—we're talking early mornings and stress-filled days. Talk about anxiety. But that's *once* I get there. Between here and there, I have to be at school on the practice field by 6:30, and that is not a perky time of morning for me. Plus, by the time my school day is over, mounds of homework await me; I barely have the energy to get to the dinner table, let alone meeting my obligation to, as Mother says, come to the dinner table ready for the fine art of "conversing."

Mom rented me a video one time called *Freaky Friday*. It was all about how a parent and child somehow got scientifically transferred into each other's bodies. At the time, I thought that would be pretty cool; I'd switch my life for hers in a minute! And there was no doubt in my mind that my mother would love to switch places with me—which made me stop and give it some thought.

But the movie got me to thinking—and watching—everything my mother does—her job, the way she takes care of the house, cooks, shops, drives me places—all those countless things that a mom does. She drives me all over, from one event to the next, cooks my meals for me, buys me the things I think I need, and does things like always taking the burned piece of toast. She works night shifts as a nurse so she can fit her schedule to us kids. She's hardly ever missed softball, soccer or basketball games, and she's always there to take me to school activities. My mom is my number-one fan. Truthfully, I don't know how she does it. I have a five-year-old little brother who is bouncing off the walls. Still she manages to love us and make us feel like we're the most important thing in her life. She's amazing!

Last week I heard a youth pastor speak about love. He said that a person only loves you as much as they are willing to sacrifice. My mom must love us kids an awful lot, because she has sacrificed hours and years of her life for us. She's always on the go—and almost all of what she does looks like work to me. It occurred to me that the things I get to do probably do seem glamorous in comparison. So, I don't let it bother me so much anymore. I answer her questions as best I can (given my mood), and try to remember it makes her feel closer to me—which is important to both of us.

Besides, who knows: Someday I may be the one saying to my daughter, "Tell me what we did in school today, Honey!" The reason I feel this way is because I think it's an old parent's line, passed down "through the ages," and regardless of your thinking you won't say it to your kids, chances are, you will!

Melinda Carey, 16

"But It's Only $100!"

Every weekend my parents give me $100 to spend. I bet you think I'm really spoiled. Think again!

It all started when I wanted this really cool CD player. I asked my parents if they would buy it for me and they said no, it was something I would have to buy with my own money. "But it's only $100!" I complained. An hour later, my parents announced there would be a "family meeting" the next night at dinner.

We'd never had a family meeting before, so my brother and I were worried. Something was up; we just didn't know what. "This has to be really serious," my brother, Gabe, told me when I got him alone in the family room. I sat down on the couch and we talked about the possibilities of what the gathering could be about.

"They're going to make us do more work around the house," I said. "I always see things like that on TV, where the parents make their kids do all sorts of work around the house for their allowance."

My parents opened the family meeting with the words, "We've been thinking about how to give you children more say in our family. . . ." Well, you could say my parents are experts at "creative parenting." They brought up a number of "new ways" my brother and I could "have more say." For me, one of those ways was to allow me to shop for the family. Each Saturday, I was to be given $100—along with a shopping list of groceries for the family. It was up to me to buy everything on the list. Whatever money was left over, whether two dollars or thirty, was mine to keep and spend however I want—whether for gas, going to the movies, or to buy CDs, clothes, even a CD player (if I choose to save up for it).

I've been "having more say" in the family now for nearly two months, and believe me, my parents' $100-a-week plan gives me real incentive to shop for the best bargains. Practically my whole lifestyle depends on it! I compare prices on every single item on my list before I decide what brand I'm going to put in my basket. Now I even use coupons! And if there's a big sale on something my family needs at one store, that's the store where I go to buy it, even if it's not where I usually shop. After all, it's only $100, and I want to make it go as far as possible.

I'm still saving for my CD player—and I'm also taking my cue from my parents and working on creative ways to get it: I've put it on both my Christmas and my birthday list and mention it every time I can see they are in a "spending mood"!

Emma Jennings, 16

Dancing Flowers

I know that you love me. I am so lucky!

If I were writing a book on our lives of wonderful times shared, creating memories to treasure, it would be called *Twin Souls, Kindred Spirits.* I'd have each page of words encased with fields and fields of intricately colored, happy-faced dancing flowers, thereby showing how the spirit behind the words had a life as full and as rich as did the words on each page. I would fill the book with pages of feelings—all based on the ways you love me.

You are so important to me. I especially love the times when we are close—even when it would be easy to be at odds, like earlier today when it was clear there were some hard feelings hovering around from an injustice somewhere. You were more right than me; but you didn't say that. Instead, you patiently listened to me, striving to understand. I know it would have been so easy for you to say, "We've been through this before"; even, "I told you so." You didn't. Thank you so much. Your style of listening and understanding diffused all unconstructive emotions—and potentially hurtful words. I knew the victory was ours! We won out over being at odds; we stayed close, and drew closer. What an awesome knowing: We can dance a dance to the music of our own making, and still come together where, like petals embracing the sun, we open knowingly.

Today we did that. We safely opened ourselves up to the other. It was a moment and memory I shall write down in my heart—one worthy of being in my special book with the bordering field of flowers!

When we work through tough times like that, it produces positive feelings and offers such a sense of security for me. Such times become so all-important to me. They help me make it through the days of my life, which sometimes seem more chaotic than I'd like to admit. I live in a constantly changing world, one that all too often is focused on material achievement, and built on fickle and temporary associations. Knowing that I can share with you my concerns and insecurities—and that you are the safe harbor in which these feelings find a safe port—helps me feel more stable in an impermanent world. As a result, I am more at peace, and complete, within myself.

I'm so grateful to have you in my world. I know at the soul level that you thoroughly love me—something that shows in everything you do: the flowers in my room from your garden that always find their drink in the prettiest of your vases; my favorite foods prepared anytime—a mother hen feeding her chick; the comfort you offer—like love on a plate piled high with comfort food to make me full and content.

Mom, you warm my spirit, feed my soul and make my heart happy. You are such a big part of my world. Twin souls, kindred spirits, in a lifetime together—again. Thanks for being *my* mom.

Jennifer Leigh Youngs

A Letter to My Child

I have so many shortcomings; I can hardly believe that I have been entrusted with your care. To run a business, yes. But to help a child develop into a whole and healthy person? I am so inadequate. You came anyway.

You knew how busy I was. There are so many things for me to do and learn in this lifetime. I have needs of my own. There are so many things I want to do in life. And my work is so interesting; there is so much to do and so little time. I have yet other excuses for not taking more time to show you the way. Are you a lesson? My lesson?

You have done both, my child. Did you come to show me the way? You have done that, too.

I have been fortunate in my life to have so many exemplary teachers—colorful, unforgettable, wonderful people who believed in me, opened doors for me, encouraged me and mentored me. Each has deeply influenced my life in many ways. But it is you, my child, who has been my greatest teacher; you have touched my heart and soul unlike anything or anyone I have known. It is from you that I have learned the most intense and extraordinary lessons. Parenting you has offered some of the most profound insights. It has been an impassioned exercise in perfecting my own nature, and often difficult precisely because of that. It has been joyous, yet arduous; and sometimes painful.

The awesome task of parenthood has helped me focus more clearly on the meaning of my own personal journey; this has kept me from sleepwalking through life. Seeking to understand can sometimes be uncomfortable work. Parenting you forces me to take stock of my values and to clean house on them. By virtue of needing to get organized and prioritize that which gives meaning—or causes turmoil—I live more fully than I might otherwise. Loving you as I do causes me to look beyond my own needs and to care deeply about yours. Caring and doing are different, though, and when I am unable to meet your needs, the pain is a searing one. Pain can be a catalyst for growth.

Caretaking you, dear child, alters my feelings of aloneness. Sometimes this makes me feel burdened with a sense of responsibility; at other times I feel so lucky to be needed. In the process of helping you climb the ladder of childhood and learn skills to surmount the challenges found each step of the way, I discover that teaching you how to pass the test of life quite often presents me with a learning curve, too. I've learned that I don't always have the answer key—but for certain, I wish I did. In living with you, in loving you, in being a helpmate as you learn and grow, you have taught me about:

Love: By loving you, I tapped into a reservoir of love and find it bottomless. I didn't know I could love so much. Nor was I aware just how much this emotion would forever bond me to you, causing me to always be concerned about your well-being. I learn that love can be painful. I hurt when you hurt. Likewise, in those times when life rewards you and finds you worthy of its trophies, loving you as I do makes me cry in joy for your joy. I also find, at times, that the line between caretaking and co-dependency is a fine one.

Joy and happiness: As a result of my efforts, I see you prosper as a healthy, intelligent and compassionate person. Likewise, I am aware that when you fall short, its origin may be of my doing.

Empathy: In seeking to understand you, I have had to put myself in your place and learn the meaning of unconditional caring. Sometimes my heart aches as I watch you struggle with a lesson or learn from a potent consequence. Always I have to hold myself back from intervening, because I want to rush to your side to help you, to prevent you from experiencing hurt, even though I know these lessons are yours from which to learn.

Patience: Even with my guidance, you experience the world through your own eyes, in your own time, at your own pace. You just can't hurry some things. Time, it appears, is the essence of many a lesson. I have had to learn to be more patient than is my nature.

Listening: I am learning to decipher not only the various tones of your voice, but to read your feelings—often disguised in subtle behaviors—and to hear what you are really saying rather than what I want to hear. Many times these are different. Sometimes I am wrong.

Responsibility: Because you are so precious to me, I accept the duties and obligations of being a parent and can be depended upon to fulfill them, even at times when I might prefer to be doing something else. You can count on me.

God: The miracle of life and your birth became the catalyst for renewing and deepening my own faith. Daily challenges teach me to continually search out my heart and turn my eyes heavenward. Praying for the redemption of my soul, and yours, takes priority over asking for abundance.

The fragility of human life: Though this feeling began with my pregnancy, as soon as you were born I knew your life was mine to protect, and that I was committed to it at all costs. As I began to understand and value the fragility of human life, I began to take better care of my own health. Protecting your life is a compelling duty. I am often fearful. Such feelings pave the way to care about others whose lives are in jeopardy anywhere in the world—from evil, oppression, hurt, starvation or war.

Purpose: The value of your life affirms my work and adds a crucial dimension of meaning to it. It sustains me.

Living consciously: Because I am being constantly observed by you, I must be aware of what I say, as well as what my actions convey. Setting a good example is an ever-present challenge. Sometimes this makes me feel caged and I must confront my selfishness; other times I am grateful for caring enough to grow. Confronting my own values up close is sometimes rewarding and at other times a bit unsettling. I am learning as I go and so do not always "practice what I preach." There is much hindsight and learning—"after-the-fact" learning.

Growing and evolving: I know that I am becoming a better, wiser and more loving person than I might otherwise have been. And of course, I also learn what I am not, but wish I were.

Parenting forever: When you were an infant I looked forward to a time when you would be able to play independently, and when you could, you still looked around to see if I was there. When you were in grade school, your intellect was insatiable and the need for instilling rules and guidelines to help you operate safely in the outer world was a must. Your abundant activities in junior high school required multiple bandages and a daily carpool; your quest and need to understand your feelings sometimes made me feel like a clinical psychologist with you as my entire caseload. Now that you are a young adult, you need to know your place in the world and to understand that the dynamics of relationships on an experiential basis occupy a good portion of your waking hours. Just as I worried when you were little that you might stick a finger in a light socket or be treated badly by another child, I worry now that you or another driver will exercise poor judgment while in a two-ton car. I want to protect you from being emotionally devastated in relationships, even though you must learn such lessons firsthand. Perhaps my concerns will go on for some time. Just yesterday my mother called and lovingly expressed her concerns for my safety on my upcoming trip abroad, though I have made the same journey nearly twenty times over the past twenty-five years.

Forgiving my parents: The constancy of parenting, the work, the responsibility, the ever-present concern of wondering if I am bringing out the best in you—helping you find and develop your abilities, talents and goodness—is a lingering one. I often struggle with being true to my own needs, yet being there for you. This duplicity is insightful and helps me to forgive my parents for the ways they didn't know me but I expected them to, and for the experiences they didn't provide me, but I wished they had. Parenthood has taught me that parenting is by design, an exercise in completing one's own unfinished business of childhood. I've come to realize that children are little creatures who come to us with their own spiritual history, and as such, every child-and-parent relationship is unique. While parents can devise a master plan, each child comes with his or her own needs for caretaking, individual in the purpose to be lived out in an earthly lifetime. Understanding this helps me judge less, and honor more, the parental actions of my parents.

Honoring my parents: It has been a serious undertaking to show you that I both love you and respect you, that I accept you for who you are—especially during those times when I disapprove of your actions. Mother was right: Little children step on your feet; big children step on your heart. It has taken many moons to help you prepare to live interdependently in the world; it may take many more. It's been a daily exercise of setting appropriate expectations and consistently encouraging and motivating you in living purposefully; sometimes this is tedious and thankless work. This causes me to value the efforts of my parents, and to honor not only their parenting actions, but the efforts of their intentions as well.

Child of mine, teacher of mine. Always you are on my mind.

Thank you for choosing me to help you find your way in this world. I am so genuinely sorry for all the ways I have let you down, and for not always praying enough for insight and guidance. Though sometimes I thought I knew what to do or could figure it out, in some ways I didn't have a clue; sometimes it wasn't until afterwards that I learned if what I did (or didn't do) was, or wasn't, good for you. Interestingly, I tried to be the parent to you that, while I was growing up, I wanted my parents to be for me. Ironically, just as my parents weren't always the parents I wanted them to be, you, too, have found that I haven't always done what you wanted or been what you needed. Alas, the same snow that covers the ski slopes makes the roads to them impassable.

Thank you for choosing me anyway, for having the courage to take a chance on me. Thank you for loving me because you know me so well; thank you for loving me in spite of knowing me so well.

Though it was I who was your parent, it was you who were my teacher. You are the greatest lesson—and teacher—of all.

Bettie B. Youngs

©1995. Bettie B. Youngs. Excerpted from *Values from the Heartland*. Health Communications, Inc.

Part 5

Moments That Changed the Way I Look at Life

*Universal principles show up in your life
everywhere. Believe them.*

—Wayne Dyer, Ph.D.

*Each day comes bearing its own gifts.
Untie the ribbons.*

—Ruth Ann Schabacker

*The way to see truth is through
your everyday eyes.*

—Zen Saying

A Word from the Authors

There are some moments we never forget: spectacular moments that thrill us; unexpected moments that amaze us; painful moments that sadden us; beautiful and tender moments that are deeply moving. Spectacular or beautiful, heartrending or bewildering, some moments literally *change* us. Whether causing us to catch our breath, or momentarily taking it away, such moments are powerful in that they can change the way we look at the world, or even how we see the purpose of our own lives. The insight gained has the power to put the rest of our lives in focus. As a result, we are never ever the same again.

Such a "radical" or "big-time" change in thinking is called a *paradigm shift*. Have you ever heard someone say that such and such happened and he (or she) "did a 180-degree turn"? A paradigm shift is like that. It's a complete break with a certain way of thinking (or being). It's a turning point, one in which you are able to say, "I once thought that way (or believed that), but not now, because after this happened, I no longer feel that way." You "draw a line in the sand" and step over. You've *changed*.

Sometimes the moment or event that caused us to make this significant shift is a blatant "in-your-face" one, or it can be a subtle one. For many of the teens we worked with on this unit, their shift came about as a result of an unexpected loss, such as the death of a close friend or a beloved family member, or by watching the gripping news coverage of the September 11, 2001, terrorist attacks on America and fearing that their country would now be a nation at war. For some, it was the unexpected blow of defeat, or a hard-won victory. Regardless of the circumstance, all were times that had a profound effect on the teen.

For example, sixteen-year-old Belinda Rhimes of Fort Worth, Texas, said, "Watching the horrific scenes of the aftermath of the hijacked planes flying into the Twin Towers in New York on September 11, 2001, was shocking, and I couldn't believe my eyes. Hearing that the Pentagon was hit made me frightened for our national security, and I realized that my 'American freedoms' were no longer as certain as they had once been—which was a truly frightening idea. All these things made me feel insecure and more than anything else, numb and paralyzed—I mean, it's not like I could do something about all this. Then, two days later watching the news, I saw a young child, her face anguished and tears streaming down her cheeks. She held up a picture of her parents and sobbed, 'Have you seen my mom and dad?' Seeing her, hearing her, the horrific and indefensible attack on America moved me from my complacency about being unclear about what I could do to help. That little girl—and millions and millions around the world—need advocacy, and I thought, *Why not start in my own community?* So, the very next day I called a local agency and became a 'Big Sister' for a young girl in my community."

Seventeen-year-old Tara LeBlanc from Dayton, Ohio, saw changes, as well. Once, she characterized herself as "an extremely shy person" and "without any real career plans." But when she won her school's Science Fair contest—and the statewide competition, and then became a national winner—she decided to put away that "shy girl" image and "don't know what I'll do" stance and instead chose to see herself as someone who "in ten to twelve years would be squaring off with the media" (because she wanted to discover "alternative" cancer cures, which she feels would be controversial—at least when first brought to the public's attention). Others saw the change in Tara, too. When Tara returned to school after her trip to Washington, D.C. (where the national competition was held), her classmates understood the sum of Tara's win as more than the five-thousand-dollar college scholarship she'd received as a result of her winning the competition. Her new outgoing demeanor—which she quickly put to work seeking speaking opportunities with her town's Toastmaster's Club and nearly every men's and women's group in town—has served her well. Tara has gained excellent skills in public speaking, not to mention garnering for herself additional scholarships from a couple of organizations and associations to whom she spoke.

Sometimes the change or shift is a subtle one—but crucial nonetheless—as the dawning that you're not as happy as you'd like to be (and wanting to change that), as was the case for sixteen-year-old Todd Larkin from Jean, Nevada. "I was depressed and basically unhappy, but I really didn't know why," Todd told us. "Everything was okay in my life—nothing exciting, but nothing was wrong either. Then one day, as I was sitting in the doctor's office with my mother—who was there for a six-month follow-up visit following breast cancer surgery (she's completed her treatments and been told she will be fine)—I listened to her doctor tell her that 'being happy and joyful and in a positive frame of mind is an important contribution to your health and to staying healthy.' I thought about the doctor's words and realized that being in a 'positive frame of mind' is in one's head. I mean, my mother can't get up every day and go looking for happiness. She simply has to decide to be a happy person. And so did I. That shift in my thinking—that to be a happy person was a decision I made and not something that was going to happen to me—has made all the difference to my being a happier person."

How about you? Have there been times—"moments"—that changed the way you see yourself or look at life? Be on the look-out for such times! In this unit, we asked teens to tell of a time that changed their "paradigm"—the way they look at life, and/or the world and people around them. The stories you are about to read are from teens who themselves have come face-to-face with moments or events that irrevocably shifted their sense of things. Whether a first kiss, the loss of a loved one, a well-deserved victory, a broken heart, or one day taking one's freedom for granted and the next realizing that your country is at war, such times leave us feeling much the same as the admired Eleanor Roosevelt once said of people, "They leave footprints on our hearts. And we are never the same."

Enjoy these stories and commentary from your peers . . . and may they leave footprints on your heart . . . so that you are never the same!

❤ *Taste berries to you, Bettie and Jennifer Youngs*

Rat Dog and Monster Man

It was an awesome sunny Saturday afternoon in San Diego, California. I was holed up in my room, cramming for mid-semester finals—and totally bummed-out about it. My freckle-faced five-year-old brother (I call him Monster Man) came flying into the house with Rat Dog, our three-pound miniature poodle, following him. Monster Man and Rat Dog were two of a kind: playful, equally mischievous. Dog and boy simply adored each other. It was hard to tell who was the leader of these two: usually it was Monster Man, but today it seemed to be Rat Dog, who was always ready for a good romp. Up to their usual antics, today the two were playing a game of "catch me if you can"—which I assumed took its usual path: In the front door, out the back, and then, still going nearly a hundred miles an hour, they tore around the house and back through the front door, on to Monster Man's room where they'd leap upon the bed, then down from the bed, and out the back door and back through the front door. Around and around they went, switching places as to who was the chaser, and who it was that was being chased. Today, on this beautiful sunny *weekend* afternoon, my little brother was defi-nitely having more fun than I was.

I studied for a while more and then, looking out my window, noticed their ongoing game was now in the backyard: a jump over the flower beds, a leap over the bat left laying in the yard from an earlier game of baseball. Rat Dog was in the lead—but not by much. Mom, ever watchful over her little son, had moved outside to water her plants to keep an eye on Monster Man. And then, three events occurred simultaneously: The phone rang, Mom ran in to answer it, and Rat Dog jumped onto the pool cover.

Seems that the game between Monster Man and Rat Dog had taken them to the edge of the pool, and because the dog weighs only three pounds, and he sensed that he'd be able to walk across the pool cover without sinking it, he did. But to an unsuspecting forty-eight-pound little boy—intent on following his friend—the pool cover caught water, and instantly sank.

And then fate stepped in: At that precise moment, I'd decided I wanted a Coke from the fridge, but first had cruised outside for a breath of fresh air. I'll *never* forget the horrific circumstance that waited. My little brother was drowning!

With terror in his eyes, and gasping for air as he bobbed to the surface in a desperate attempt for air, he then sank out of sight. I leaped into the pool, calling to him to reassure him that I was coming to rescue him. Shouting to my mother to call 911, I grabbed hold of my brother and carefully laid him on the cement. I was virtually screaming at him to cough up the water and breathe in the air I was giving him. It was in these moments of resuscitating my little brother (and waiting for the ambulance) that I understood that my little brother could have died.

With this shocking realization, I suddenly had a new respect for life. For my brother, staying alive was reduced to the simplicity of having fresh air in his lungs: No air, no life. I realized that it doesn't matter how big and strong your muscles, how smart you are or aren't, how brave and confident you are or aren't feeling, or how cool you are or aren't: Life can be extinguished in a heartbeat. It was almost true for my little brother.

I am so thankful to be able to say that my little brother survived. Thank God that my little brother did expel the water from his lungs and begin to breathe on his own. And luckily, within moments, the ambulance arrived and took my brother to the hospital for medical attention.

The incident, for me, was life-changing. I realized that for my little brother, a gulp of air could spell the difference between life and death, so now when I see people smoking (because it's a proven fact that smoking seriously destroys the lungs), I realize that smoking is absurd. Now, I know how important it is that we all look out for one another.

Colin Sinclair, 18

"Would You Like to Dance?"

"Would you like to dance?" Those words just tickled my skin. The beautiful guy with jet-black hair, interesting dark eyes and a gracious, sly smile reached out for my hand. Obviously, it hadn't crossed his mind that I might say "No."

We danced. And danced. His name was Tyler Redding. He was funny and made easy conversation. And though a year younger than me, he was taller than me! By the fourth dance, I learned that Tyler Redding loved soccer, had two younger brothers, and we each knew a couple of the same kids at school. He told me he loved my blue eyes and my smile, that my hair smelled "good," and that even with the "zillions of people on the planet," finding me "was just a matter of time." And that's when it hit me: I really liked this guy. I kept looking down, making sure my feet were on the ground because it felt as though I were floating a foot off the floor. We were inseparable for the rest of the party, and the rest of the summer, too.

When the school year resumed, we took our fun and exciting relationship back to school with us. Though we had no classes together, we were with each other every chance we got. School is different when you have someone in your life; it's so much better. Actually it's not just school that is better; your whole life is. My parents liked Tyler, so he hung out at my house a lot. Whether it was watching movies, Saturday bowling extravaganzas, dinner with my parents or taking a nap on my couch on Sunday afternoons, he was there. It felt as though we were one person.

One clear Saturday night while we were stargazing, I told him I loved him. He said he loved me, too. I already knew it, of course, but it felt life-changing to hear the words.

One month later, my life changed again. It was nearly five o'clock on a Saturday afternoon when Tyler called, talking at first about the baseball game he'd won that afternoon, and then explaining that he needed "a little space"—not from me, but from dating. Because my parents were telling me I was spending a little too much time "being a couple," and they'd like a little more of me—without Tyler present—I thought easing up a bit would be okay—at least for a little while. I just assumed he was getting the same message from his parents. But when the very next day, Monday, he wasn't waiting for me at my locker as he always did, I wondered why he wasn't there. And then, when I saw him in the hallway later and he turned and walked the other way, I knew something was wrong. All day long, he wasn't in any of the usual places we hung out. The moment I got home from school, I called his house. His mother answered, saying he was "tied up and couldn't come to the phone." So then I knew that something was seriously wrong; I just didn't know what.

The next day I didn't see him. And the very next, I saw him walking down the hall—hand in hand with a girl.

Confused, furious and saddened to the point of being sick to my stomach, I cornered him in the hall and said, "I can't believe your feelings for me have changed. Let's kiss. If we kiss and you feel nothing, then I'll let you go without a fight. But if you still have feelings for me, then I'm going to fight for our love."

I kissed him.

He didn't kiss back.

That said it all.

Standing there, having just kissed him, and having him receive it like a mummy, was a stunning blow! Tyler had found someone new. The time—and love—that once belonged to me, to us, now was hers, theirs. That he didn't kiss me back took all my inner-fight away: Trying to win him back would be a waste of time.

Every day I see them in the hallways walking hand in hand. They eat lunch together, and I see them standing by the lockers kissing. It's really hard, and it really hurts. The two of them have a definite chemistry between them. And she has pretty blue eyes and a pretty smile, and probably her hair smells "good." Was it just a matter of time that out of the zillions of people on the planet, she'd be his next in line?

There is no happy ending to my "love story." Tyler didn't come running back to me, and there is no new boyfriend in my life. But life goes on. I've learned firsthand that eventually, you really do run out of tears, and your heart gets tired of aching. It's been a big lesson, and one that's changed my views on love. I'm no longer so naïve to believe that there's one and only one love that's meant for you. I've not given up on love. I'm just more realistic. Truthfully, I'm still more than a little hurt from the whole experience. But I know I'll be okay, too. So for now, I slide my sunglasses on top of my head and face the world, knowing that there are zillions of people on the planet, and it's just a matter of time before, once again, there'll be someone special for me to love.

Aly Hutzel, 15

"American"

It was our school's spring break, and I was with my family on vacation. Out of school, on vacation, and out of town! I was in a great mood.

We'd planned a lot of sightseeing. On this particular day, my family and I were visiting yet another memorial, and now found ourselves just about to enter. The entrance, meticulously land-scaped with rose bushes and other lovely and colorful flowers in bloom, led to lush, manicured grounds, still smelling of freshly cut grass. Added to this serenity were flowing fountains, not to be outdone by the sound of the distant waves crashing to shore from the ocean nearby. Obviously as thrilled to be enjoying this beautiful summer day as I was, birds chirped out their joy. My senses were definitely working.

And soon to be on overload.

Now just steps beyond the entrance and onto the greens, I looked up. What I saw before me literally took my breath away. There, for as far as my eyes could see, were white crosses—each one representing the death of a U.S. soldier—a "Garden of Stones." It was an unimaginable number, literally acres upon acres of white crosses—each one representing a soldier who died in battle. I was spellbound at how many "citizens" had laid down their lives protecting the freedom of our country. Standing there, stricken silent at the sight, it also dawned on me that many of these men and women had been the same age as me when they went off to fight a brutal war. Now they lay buried in the U.S. Military Cemetery.

The vivid picture of the multitude of crosses has never left my memory. It has completely changed my idea of being an "American." Having stood there that day, I now know that our democracy must never be taken for granted, and that it is a grace to us, one that came with a huge and sacrificial price—the loss of life.

While seeing the memorial renewed my appreciation of the freedoms I have in being an American citizen, it also made me sad for those who died, and for all the families that lost loved ones protecting that freedom.

I walked away from the cemetery that day a changed person. For sure, I knew war was real—and savage—and that history is relevant to life today, if for no other reason than to fully grasp the price of freedom. Freedom—like life—is to be treasured and honored. And protected. If we have doubts, we simply need to visit that memorial.

Now I am thankful for the fact that I live in a free nation. And having stood in the cemetery that day, I know that it came with a price that has been paid for with human life. I am proud knowing that I belong to a nation of people so stalwart in their beliefs about freedom that we'll lay down our lives for it.

I am an American. Wow! These words have a meaning they never had before. I am so honored.

Megan Mazzola, 18

Then, I Met You

From the first moment I met you
To now this race with time
We knew we'd pace together
A desire to make the other "mine."

First rays of sunlight
A smile dancing in my eyes
Pausing softly on my lips
Stirring gently with each sigh.

You make the moments sweet
From morning "Hi's" to "Please do call at noon,"
Morning, "I can't wait to see you!"
Later, "Can we get together soon?"

Where will this love take us?
What journeys lie ahead?
Will passion write of fulfilled lives?
Or leave some words unread?

I think of you constantly
Morning, noon and night.
You fill my world with loveliness
Just because you're in my life.

I am so happy and feel so lucky
To have your love my own
You've changed my life—my world—completely,
Knowing in life, we'll be side by side—and I won't be alone.

Jennifer Leigh Youngs

READER/CUSTOMER CARE SURVEY

We care about your opinions. Please take a moment to fill out this Reader Survey card and mail it back to us. As a special **"thank you"** we'll send you exciting news about interesting books and a valuable **Gift Certificate.**

Please PRINT using ALL CAPS

Name |_____| |__| |_____|
First   MI.   Last Name

Address |_____|

City |_____| ST |__| Zip |_____|—|____|

Phone # (|___|) |___|—|_____| **Fax #** (|___|) |___|—|_____|

Email |_____|

(1) Gender:
_____ Female   _____ Male

(2) Age:
_____ 8 or younger   _____ 17-20
_____ 9-12   _____ 21-30
_____ 13-16   _____ 31+

(3) What attracts you most to a book?
(Please rank 1-4 in order of preference.)

       1   2   3   4
3) Title   O   O   O   O
4) Cover Design   O   O   O   O
5) Author   O   O   O   O
6) Content   O   O   O   O

(7) Other than school books, how many books do you read a month?
_____ 1   _____ 3
_____ 2   _____ 4

(8) How did you find out about this book?
Please fill in ONE.
1) _____ Friend
2) _____ School (Teacher, Library, etc.)
3) _____ Parent
4) _____ Store Display
5) _____ Teen Magazine
6) _____ Interview/Review (TV, Radio, Print)

(9) Where do you usually buy books?
Please fill in your top TWO choices.
1) _____ Bookstore
2) _____ Religious Bookstore
3) _____ Online
4) _____ Book Club/Mail Order
5) _____ Price Club (Costco, Sam's Club, etc.)
6) _____ Retail Store (Target, Wal-Mart, etc.)

(11) Did you receive this book as a gift?
_____ Yes   _____ No

(12) What do you like to read? *(Please check all that apply)*

Magazines:
12) _____ Teen People
13) _____ Seventeen
14) _____ YM
15) _____ Cosmo Girl
16) _____ Rolling Stone
17) _____ Teen Ink
18) _____ Christian Magazines

Books:
19) _____ Fiction
20) _____ Self-Help Books
21) _____ Reality Stories/Memoirs
22) _____ Sports
23) _____ Series Books (Chicken Soup, Fearless, etc.)

TAPE IN MIDDLE; DO NOT STAPLE

BUSINESS REPLY MAIL
FIRST-CLASS MAIL PERMIT NO 45 DEERFIELD BEACH, FL

POSTAGE WILL BE PAID BY ADDRESSEE

TASTE BERRIES™ FOR TEENS
3201 SW 15TH STREET
DEERFIELD BEACH FL 33442-9875

FOLD HERE

(24) Do you prefer to read books written by:

1) _____ Teen Authors?

2) _____ Adult Authors?

3) _____ No Preference

Comments:

All the Ways He Loved M

Life for me was normal until April 24, 1999, the day my father killed himself.

It's important to me to know that Dad didn't kill *himself*; the diseases of alcoholism and depression are what killed him. Even with an emphasis on this distinction, his death—and life without him—means my life will never be the same.

Let me first tell you a little about the bright side of my father, a man I loved so much. Dad loved his family and was proud to use the words, "My wife and kids. . . ." I am absolutely positive that he loved me, and I'm sure my brothers would say the same. He had many friends. And he was a very successful business-man. Then, there was that dark side of him, one that felt despondent and hopeless to the point that he used alcohol to drown those feelings out. He drowned himself in the process.

When my father died, my first reaction was relief. I know that sounds shocking, but when you live with an alcoholic, life centers on that person's dysfunction—and the stream of stress it creates. It's a relief, a feeling of freedom, to get out from under the blanket of pain and chaos. I remember when, in the first moments I heard the news that my father was dead, there was an immediate knowing that now our family would no longer be imprisoned by the constant worry about Dad's whereabouts—and worrying whether or not he was alive. As for me personally, now I wouldn't have to experience yet another drinking binge of his, nor worry about when one would occur, or witness and endure his embarrassing behavior in public.

But this sense of relief lasted only for a few moments, when I realized that I'd never see my father again. Never. Not ever. He'd never say, "I love you," again. And I could never tell him to his face that I loved him. Suddenly, there was a deep sadness that my dad would never, ever:

- smile at me
- give me a hug
- kiss my cheek
- help me with homework
- sit in the bleachers at my sport games
- gas up my car (for free) as he always did!
- take pictures of me and my date or ask me if I needed a clean shirt to wear
- see me graduate from high school—or college
- attend my wedding
- be a grandpa to my children
- be my friend—for life

With these realizations a deep sadness set in, knowing how much I'd miss him, and he'd be missed, forever. And I felt sorry for myself, and for my mom and brothers, Dad's parents and everyone who loved him.

Next came a boiling anger. Wanting to know "Why did he do this?" filled my head with the fury of a steaming locomotive. When I wasn't centering this question on the disease that he suffered from, I blamed Dad for abandoning his family and, in particular, me (and at a time in my life when I needed him). My father had made a decision, and I thought it a selfish one. But he "couldn't fix what ailed him"—or at least that's what one of his good friends said at the memorial service.

"The heart heals faster from surgery than it does from the loss of a loved one," a friend of his told me at the memorial service. I could relate: My heart had just undergone emotional triple bypass surgery—without anesthesia. How would I ever heal?

My first attempt was to put on a strong face, even if my insides were as wobbly as Jell-O. I began the facade the day following the funeral: I'd get up, shower, go to school, and after school, go to baseball practice or hang out with my friends, as usual. Why let my father's inability to handle life stop me from mine? Besides, his death was a thing of the past now, and I was going forward.

The strategy pretty much worked—except for the fact that my heart wanted nothing more than to withdraw from the world and cry. None of my friends could relate to what I was going through. How could they? Their fathers were alive. I'm sure some of them thought I was even better off (they had experienced on many occasions my dad's drunkenness).

Then came another wave of self-pity: Life had been unfair to me! And why me? He was the alcoholic! I had been a good son. Why would he want to leave me and miss out on being with me? And why should I get strapped with life without a dad; all my friends had dads. And judging from all the guilt I went through every minute of every day—not to mention the sleepless nights—why should I be suddenly saddled with problems and concerns that none of my friends had to even think about, let alone be the one with the stigma of "the kid whose father committed suicide"?

This was followed by yet another stage of anger, one that collapsed into tears and realization: My dad's gone—no matter what else—Daddy's gone! I cried myself to sleep and awoke knowing that on April 24, 1999, whether I was ready or not, my life was changed. I had to deal with not having a father and the sad circumstances surrounding his death. I had to deal with myself, the pain his death caused me. I had to deal with thinking about my future, without my father in it. I had to deal with a broken heart and put it back together again. I had to take complete responsibility for everything I do and make tough decisions on my own that normally wouldn't have been mine to make until later in life.

I'm doing these things. My father's death totally crushed me, but with the help of my family, friends and faith, I'm rebuilding my life. My family and I have all been so loving and kind to each other, and that's been helpful. And working with counselors and attending youth group has allowed me to freely talk about my feelings. It helped me let go of the anger and be able to forgive myself for feeling anger toward my father, and to forgive him for the fathering I hadn't received from him (including his not being there in my future). I've come to understand that it was not my father who committed such a desperate act, but rather, the disease from which he suffered. It's been a lot. Like I said, it's been something that's changed my life.

The result is that now, when I revisit memories of my father, what comes to mind is how much he loved me and all the ways he showed it:

- the smiles
- the bear hugs
- helping me with homework
- being at my sports games
- gassing up my car (for free!)
- always taking my picture
- loaning me his shirts

The list is a long one, and I will always be grateful for his love. And for the years we had together.

Kyle Ross, 18

Why Is Cheesecake Called Cheesecake
When There Is No Cheese
in Cheesecake?

My family believes in God, but we aren't the kind of people to get up on Sunday mornings and go to church. Personally, I didn't know why attending church was all that important if you already believed in God. So when my best friend invited me to go with her and a group of friends to a weekend youth camp, I was surprised that I said yes. But she'd been to the same camp before and said it was really fun. Judging from the group of cool boys who stood waiting for the bus at the "take-off spot" I decided it probably was going to be a whole lot of fun. At that point, I was glad I'd said I'd go!

The drive was five hours—which wasn't all that fun, but we did get to know each other. Then, once we got to the campsite, dinner was waiting for us, served on picnic tables. I was really hungry, so *everything* tasted good. After dinner, we went off to "Club." Here we all sat around and sang songs, and then listened to someone read scripture from the Bible. The singing part was fun; personally, I found the scripture reading a bit boring. And scary, too. A camp counselor had said, "This weekend will change your life. When you leave here, you will be a totally different person."

After Club, we went to our cabins. I lay for a long while thinking about the camp counselor's words, "When you leave here, you will be a totally different person." I was worried because I didn't want to be "a totally different person." I wondered what was planned. *Why* wouldn't I be the same again? Plus, I liked who I was and didn't want to be "totally different." I had ups and downs like everyone else, but otherwise, I was pretty happy. If I did become "totally different," what would I be like? Would my friends still like me? Would they accept the "totally different" me? What would my parents think? And would the "totally different" person (me) want to redo my room, get different clothes, get a new hairstyle, keep the same friends?

What had I gotten myself into?

The next morning we had Club again, and after that, we were directed to go back to our cabins for what was called "Cabin Time." During this time, the head counselor asked each of us questions, and we were to answer in front of everyone. I didn't like the exercise; I had to do oral reports in front of the class, and I didn't like to do them. These were strangers, and some of the questions we were asked I didn't think were any of their business.

Some of the other girls must have felt the same, because when Cabin Time was over, we all went for food and got into a huge food fight. Then, towards the end of the food fight, something peculiar happened to me, something that I still can't really explain. All I know is that it felt as if someone was holding a sign in front of me saying, "Believe with all your heart." It was a startling feeling, but I tried not to make too much of it. Then, after we ate lunch, we had Club again. Once again, I felt the words, "Believe with all your heart." This time I decided to think about where this was coming from. Had the food fight triggered it? Had smashing oatmeal and other things in other people's faces made me delirious? Or did I get food poisoning and was I now hallucinating?

The next morning we had another Club, where two teens gave testimonials of their faith. Their stories were touching and left everyone in tears. Me, too. Then, once again we were directed to return to our cabins where we were to write down our feelings about the testimonials we'd heard. I felt like I let every girl and leader in that cabin down because everyone was very emotional about what they'd heard, and though I'd been teary while listening to them, I didn't particularly have any thoughts about them now. "They were very good," I said. That made everyone look at me like I was weird to not be gushing my heart out over them.

When that exercise was done, we all walked to Town Hall where we talked about everything from boys to why they call cheesecake "cheesecake"—when there is no cheese in cheesecake. And then we talked about Jesus. We talked for two-and-a-half hours. And that night I cried myself to sleep thinking about my life, all the ups and downs, the times when I was so happy, and the times when I was so depressed. Sunday morning came faster for me than you could say "not enough sleep!"

Sunday we had our last Club. Without prodding from anyone, I openly accepted Christ in my life.

The counselor had been right. The weekend "totally changed" my life.

And I was a totally different person. Like pure magic, it was an instant attitude shift. I was genuinely happy—and a genuinely joyous person. There was the knowing that I didn't have to go through life alone, feeling sadness and depression, feeling insecure about who I am or what my friends think of me. Within me now are a serenity and strength that are solid, that I can count on. When you "believe with all your heart," your heart is lighter, your life is brighter. Things feel less disastrous.

Now as I sit here a year later, I think back. I am so thankful that my friend invited me to youth camp, where I was introduced to God in a way I'd never known before, a God who makes it easy to have simple answers to even life's difficult and fuzzy questions. Well, all except "why is cheesecake called cheesecake when there is no cheese in it?"

Carmen Stork, 16

Gabriella

I was pregnant at fifteen, and at sixteen, a mother with a new-born. I've named my baby Gabriella, a little girl who is now a toddler. I can tell you right off that being pregnant at fifteen is not easy. Yet, I would say that as difficult as it is to be a young mother, being a mother has been the most important—and posi-tive—change in my life.

Before I got pregnant, I didn't really care about doing well in school; it was pretty boring, and I had no clue why it was impor-tant that I do well there. Nor did I concern myself about the worry my parents went through over my being late for curfew, or the many times I simply did not call them to tell them where I was. "Checking in" was not something I wanted to do. My future? Well, how incredibly nebulous! I mean how can a young teen possibly be worried about the future when you're just try-ing to make it through the day? As far as I was concerned, the future was being liked (on a day-by-day basis) by my friends, getting my allowance, and getting out of the house to spend time with the boy I loved. The day my daughter was born, my whole world changed.

First, there was the realization of the miracle of birth—and life. I looked at my tiny, fragile and beautiful newborn baby girl, and suddenly, I was the most important human being in the entire world! For sure, I was important to her. She was fragile, tiny and innocent. She depended on me to take care of her and to give her love to live—from one day to the next. Instantly, it was important to me that I protect her and take care of her. I'm lucky in that my baby's grandparents (on both sides) love her and are helping me be a good mother to her and provide for her. But it's important that I do that, too.

Once I didn't have any goals beyond the weekend. But when I looked into her eyes, I knew I had to return to school to complete my education. I knew I needed to get a job, and that the money from it would go for creating a little family, and buying the things that she needed to be healthy and grow up safely. I promised her, and me, that I would pursue my new goals to get a nursing degree.

While a lot of people thought having a child would "destroy" my life, instead, it saved my life—which is also something that I've had to do for her. When my little girl was only three weeks old, she suddenly stopped breathing. It scared me to death. I had fallen in love with a little girl who had become the single most important reason for me to breathe—and suddenly, she wasn't. That I could lose her jolted me out of any complacency that life is assured. Hospitalized with tubes everywhere to sustain her life, I knew my daughter could die. Luckily, she lived. Gabby (her nickname) still has some health problems, but with proper nutrition and medical care, everything is going to be okay. I won't go into her problem in great detail, only tell you that she was diagnosed with reflux in both her esophagus and bladder. This means my little girl has heartburn and acid indigestion all the time. The reflux in her bladder causes urine to go into her kidneys, which could result in bad kidneys if she has it long enough. My baby has been in pain the majority of her life because of this, and still she hardly cries! She has such strength and courage! How can I not measure up?

Her condition helps me understand how precious time is. Every day counts. Because of her, from now on I have to make my life count. For me, making my life "count" begins with my being responsible for her care. I go to school and then to my part-time job regularly. I don't whine about going, and I'm never late. I need my job; I need my paycheck. I love my little family— which has given me a newfound respect for my parents, as well. Now, I ask them for advice and listen. With my daughter's birth, I realized raising children is tough and exhausting work, and I honestly don't know how my parents did it. But I appreciate that they did. Now I want my parents to know how much I love them. I say "I love you" every chance I get, and show them in any way I can.

Being a mom has changed how I see the world. I don't ever remember "hearing" the news before. Maybe it's because playing my music was all that was important. I still love music and always will, and I play it and sing and dance with my baby, but now, I hear things I've never heard before, like the condition of neighborhoods and things. Sometimes I hear good things, and I think, *I'd like to be a part of that because a safe neighborhood is important to raising and keeping my Gabby safe.* And when I hear about ugly things, like shootings and drunken drivers, I think, *How do I get involved to help make that social problem go away?* I never thought of myself as a social activist—because I wasn't. I still don't have the time to do all of the "advocacy" I'd like to, but I want to.

And, tuning in to the condition of our neighborhoods and streets has changed the way I see my own upbringing. I always thought of my parents as way too strict. They always wanted to know things like where I was and whom I was with. Always they would talk with the parent of whoever's house I was sleeping over. I rebelled against the routine of having to come home right after school to do my homework, or having to ask before going to the home of a friend. I had a curfew. Because of all these "rules," I thought they just never wanted me to have "a life." Now I see that's not the case at all. I check up on my daughter all the time, and I'm positive I will when she's a teen. I'm sure now that the rules my parents had for me are good ones, and good enough for my daughter. Why? Because now, I realize just exactly how much my parents cared about me, and that these rules were to keep me safe. They wanted to know where I was so they could make sure I was all right. I had to come home to do my homework because they cared about my future. I look at my beautiful little daughter, and I just know that I'll be as thorough knowing where she is and who she's hanging out with, because I don't want her to get into trouble by hanging out with the wrong crowd. Believe me, I know how easy that is to do.

On that day when my daughter was born, and ever since, I've been a happy person. Every time my little girl looks up at me and smiles or says "mama," I'm overcome with happiness. When she does something for the first time, she's so pleased with herself that her face lights up and her eyes glitter. A little "snicker" follows this. I praise her, of course, but usually it's done with tears of love in my eyes. Seeing her learn and grow makes me want to be a good parent for her, and to her. There is so much for her to learn and experience, and I am going to be the one to guide her through and give her advice. I want to be the one she brings her first "A" paper home from school to, and I want to be the one to tell her how proud I am. I want to be the one she runs to when she gets her heart broken. I want to be her mom.

When I was pregnant, I felt guilty a lot of the time. Here I was a young teen, a child having a child. But you know, she's saved my life, really. I have no regrets. My life is a lot of work, and I have a lot of things to catch up on—like completing school—and much work ahead. I know it's going to be tough to be a parent and get an education, but I am going to do it.

If I could live my life over again, I would want to be older and more set in terms of having finished my education and having a career underway before getting pregnant, but I can't look back now. When they handed me my daughter for the first time, it was a new me who received her. I am not the girl I was before her birth. I'm a new person. And better—in every way.

Amanda Wilson, 17

One to Another

I was in Cambodia last summer, walking through the city streets jam-packed with people. The humidity was so high I could hardly breathe. The noise—horns honking, police whistles screaming at cars and people, and just the rumbles of people all going about their days—was so loud that my head hurt. I looked around and asked myself, "Why exactly have I come?" I was ready to return home.

With this thought on my mind, I looked down and noticed a small boy at my side, trying as best as he could to keep up with my stride. His shirt was as tattered and as dirty as his shorts. His battered sandals were tied to his feet by frayed chords. But it was his face that looked the most worn: He looked to be a very weary old soul, a boy far older than his years.

I have never known poverty, hunger or despair, but something about this young boy told me he was no stranger to these things. I stopped, and he quickly ran in front of me and began to beg for some food. He was so gaunt and frail, even sickly. I wondered when he had eaten his last meal. With eyes pleading, he offered up a faint smile. My heart went out to him. I wondered if there was anyone who loved him, or if he was homeless as so many children here were. Though there was a small spark of hope in his eyes, I wondered how much—if any—joy or laughter was his. Hoping akin to begging, the small boy put his thin hands together as if to say, "I pray you will help me." It made me wonder if he knew of the "peace that surpasses all understanding."

He was such a young boy, a little boy in desperate need of so much. Surely I could help him. I decided to begin by talking about God's love. After all, it was what I had come here with a group of youth to do—help these children learn of God's love. He walked alongside me until I reached my destination, a large military hospital. From the appearance of this building, one could easily mistake it for a garbage dump. The walls were peeling, and trash was piled high on all sides of the building. I stood in disbelief as my eyes took in more than my heart could handle. Malnourished children, some of them very sick, struggled to keep their place in line so as to receive a small portion of soup for the day.

The boy, his hand in mine, stood looking at this dismal scene of poverty, loss, pain and suffering, and then looked to me as though I would somehow make it all go away. I was overwhelmed. I couldn't make it go away; in fact, I felt paralyzed from just seeing it all. Worse, I wanted to go away. But I had come here with a mission. And in that moment, I wanted more than anything to speak their language and to somehow show the love that compelled me to travel across the world, to share the message of God. But then doubt assailed me: Who was I to come to this abused and strife-filled land with words of hope? Somehow the Gospel takes on new meaning in such a setting. Either the Gospel is everything, truly having the power to heal the brokenhearted, or it can seem like a luxury—which for a fleeting moment crossed my mind as being true for this setting. Here food and water ranked first in terms of dire needs. I felt so helpless. I wanted to talk about God, but how could I? I was so young, and there were so many hungry and sick people who needed food and medicine. I didn't even speak their language. Instead of praying for them, I stood in frustration and prayed for wisdom and understanding for me—which came in the squeeze on my hand. I looked down into the big brown eyes of the little boy whom I had befriended. He pointed to the soup line in the far corner of the hospital where sick children stood patiently waiting for their daily meal. The boy was famished, possibly even starving to death, but the food was for the children who were sick, and not just hungry. I watched as the little boy looked on, longing for a bowl of soup.

I pulled from my bag a sandwich I had brought for my lunch and gave it to him. Then, I sat down and placed him in my lap so he could feel secure. The boy rested his head on my shoulder and began to eat. Then, we noticed a tiny malnourished girl watching us, a little soul too frail to get up and join in the soup line. Instantly, the boy got up out of my lap and went to her, and then, sitting cross-legged in front of her, he fed her his remaining sandwich.

One starving child feeding another.

It was a life-changing moment.

My intention had been to teach of God's love. Instead, I was shown it. I was the student that day, not the teacher. It was on that day that two little children showed me the essence of God's love: serving each other. It wasn't about good deeds, but rather, serving and caring for each other. I was taught this not by an eloquent sermon, but by two little hungry children turned out in the streets of a strife-filled country, children who knew how to be God's love for each other. It was an action I'll never ever forget, one that filled me with humility, serenity and strength, too. Watching the little boy's instinctual sharing gave me a newfound love and respect for all people, and gave me greater courage to have empathy for all people.

I am forever grateful for that trip—for the little boy who tugged at my hand and heart that day showed me a deeper meaning of love than I had ever experienced. For sure, that day changed my concept of love—and how we can best witness to others God's love for *all* his children.

Kate Harmon, 18

September 11, 2001

A SPECIAL WORD FROM THE AUTHORS: *On September 11, 2001, international terrorists hijacked four U.S. commercial airliners, flying two of them to New York City and crashing them into the World Trade Center Twin Towers. These towers collapsed, killing more than 5,000 people and injuring hundreds more. A third plane was then flown to Washington, D.C. and crashed into the Pentagon, destroying part of it and killing hundreds more. The fourth plane crashed into the countryside of Pennsylvania, killing all onboard. With the terrorists' attacks came the response of our country to defend the freedoms for which we stand: We are now, along with our allies, a nation at war.*

Our hearts are with the victims and their loved ones—the world over—and with you teens, who find yourself living in a world that still has much to learn about human rights, and much to do to make the world a safe place, one wherein each of its citizens has adequate food and, as our friends Linda and Millard Fuller (founders of Habitat for Humanity—an outreach that builds houses for those in need) would say, a "decent place to live," and are free to worship. In making that a reality, we must all do our part. And we can; it is not an impossible task. When we help others to see the world as full of hope and less impossible—by helping them overcome hardship and strife; ease the bitterness of life's disappointments and losses; and sweeten life's joys—then we become a "taste berry" for others.

Luckily, today's teens are just that: compassionate, astute and proactive in believing that it is their obligation—as much as it is their honor—to make the world a loving, safe and healthy place. We know, because hundreds and hundreds of teens from nearly every state (and four countries) shared their thoughts and feelings on just how September 11 affected them and changed the way they look at life, themselves and the world around them. Here is a sampling of the thoughts and feelings of your peers on the September 11 terrorist assault on some of our world citizens.

❤ *Taste berries to you, Bettie and Jennifer Youngs*

Lauren, Heller, 16: The murderous attack of September 11, 2001, didn't only happen to "others"—but rather, to everyone in the world. I live in Plano, Texas, and it certainly hit close to home for me. Early that morning, my father had taken a flight to Sacramento, California, so when I heard about the terrorist hijackings, I was really worried about his safety. And, I was especially sad for a good friend of mine (who had recently moved here from New Jersey) because she was frantically upset that her aunt and uncle both worked in the area and her little cousin was among those children whose parents did not return to school to pick them up. Then, later that same afternoon, I was sitting in my mother's car at a gas station. My mother went in to pay for the gas while I stayed in the car. Suddenly—just out of the blue—I felt insecure: Were there terrorists around, waiting to strike at any moment? Instantly, I locked the doors and kept a lookout for my mother. It was a jolting realization: The terrorists' attacks had victimized many, from those who lost their lives on board the hijacked planes or sat at their desks at work in the Pentagon or the Twin Towers, to those like me, who lost the security of feeling safe while sitting in the family car at a gas station. It dawned on me that the terrorists had also "hijacked" even some of the things we take for granted, such as basic daily freedom—which is exactly why we must fight to restore and preserve it (and for everyone in the world). So now, I'm really attuned to the importance of "freedom" and doing all we can to protect it. But, those who attacked us must not scare us into locking our doors forever, nor into looking over our shoulders, suspicious and distrustful of anyone we don't know. Because of September 11, I will forever be an activist to preserve our freedoms so as to live without the threat of fear.

Noe Rios, 14: Several months ago, my father, Juan Rios, became a naturalized U.S. citizen. (My mother, Maria, has been a U.S. citizen for a very long time, and I am a U.S. citizen by birth.) My parents are very proud to be citizens, as am I. But it was watching the September 11 news coverage that best showed me what it means, *really*, to be an *American*. When I heard President Bush say, "It's a privilege to have freedom, and we shouldn't be afraid to be proud to have that freedom," I thought how proud I am to live in a country that values freedom and is so totally resolved never to be without it. And we never ever will be without it because, while the terrorists may strike America, they can *never* destroy it because "America" is more than a nation; it is those ideals and values of freedom that live *within* people. September 11, 2001, crystallized, for me, that I am and will always be an American, just as my parents were before becoming naturalized. Now I understand more fully why my parents worked so long and hard to legitimize what they hold so dear.

Diana Seretis, 14: Several days after the September 11 attack on America, I received an e-mail from a friend of mine. (She said she'd sent the same e-mail to all of her friends, even relatives who lived out of state.) She asked everyone who received the e-mail to go outside that evening (at a designated time), stand in their front yards, light a candle and observe a moment of silence—all in the name of the victims and their families. I thought it would be a wonderful thing to do as a community, so I turned the e-mail into a flyer and took it to every house in my neighborhood. I didn't know how many (if any) neighbors would actually follow the instructions, but I hoped they would. I knew I wanted to. So, when the time came to go outside and light a candle, I did just that. To my surprise, there stood practically every neighbor! They all lit their candles and held them high. It was so touching. I felt so connected to the people in my neighborhood. I knew for sure that this tragedy had touched us all. Standing there holding my candle and looking at the twinkling lights up and down the streets in our neighborhood confirmed, for me, that people are not as self-absorbed as we sometimes think. I learned that "we the people" do care about each other and are willing to show it. Imagine if "we the people" did this everywhere in the country, even the world. Collectively, we could change the plight of the world. Let's do it!

Allison Roberson, 14: My best friend, Kristen, lives in the New York area. From where she lives, she could see the Twin Towers fall when they'd been struck by the hijacked planes. Crying hysterically, she called, saying she and her family were told to evacuate immediately—to where, she didn't know. I felt so panicked for her and helpless. Another friend of mine lost her father (he was in New York on a business trip that day at a meeting that was held in a Twin Towers office). But not only did I personally have friends whose lives changed so dramatically that day, but mine did as well. From watching news surrounding the events, I saw the suffering of so many people, from those searching for their loved ones—holding up pictures to see if anyone had seen them—to those who lost their jobs, their livelihoods. In addition to the devastation here in the United States, this horrific attack has been devastating for so many in the world. The newscasts have been filled with searing images of oppressed, starving refugees who are also victims of the terrorists' attacks (because of the war). How terribly sad—and wrong—that people's lives should be so devastated. What happened on September 11, 2001, is an international tragedy. I can only hope that because of it we take to heart what our eyes have witnessed and see to it that our world changes for the better. As for me, the word "peace" has taken on new meaning. We must never forget the importance of supporting world leaders in doing everything in their power to promote world peace. I know it all begins on a personal level. So I've decided to start with the words I use, the attitudes I share, and with my actions—beginning with family and friends—that teach and promote peace. Please, everyone, do the same. We can accomplish peace. And we simply must!

Montel Whiteside, 17: Before the attack on America, I couldn't really relate to my grandparents telling me about the bombing of Pearl Harbor or my uncle telling me about serving in Vietnam, nor my older cousin's stories about Desert Storm. But that's all changed. I am living in a country "at war." Being at war is more than a history lesson now, and it is more than something that happened in my past. War is happening to my generation—to me—too. I'm from the West Coast and recently heard that four bridges are possible terrorist targets. So now, I'm all ears: I really want to know how we can learn from the past and stop terrorism.

Alexis Bedford, 14: September 11, 2001, is a day no one will ever forget. My first realization of the attack on America was when I looked at my mother as I was getting up and getting dressed for school. She stood in the family room, staring at the television, her wide eyes filled with tears, her hands over her mouth. "What?" I asked, going over to stand beside her to get a look at what she was watching. Instantly, she reached out to hug me. Then we talked about what was going on. At school, everyone was as shocked as my family. All the kids were somber; there was no laughter and romping around in the halls. We skipped our regular studies and the entire student body went to the auditorium to watch the news, staying there all day long. Every hour or so, the teachers would turn down the television and we'd discuss what we'd seen. Everyone had something to say; all of us "felt" this awful incident. We were alarmed, offended and had plenty to say about what we felt should be done to keep terrorist attacks—the world over—from never happening again. Spending the day together, talking about "our" world, unified students in a way we had never known. It was like we had all become friends with each other. Everybody welcomed anyone who sat at their table during lunch. On the way home on the bus, we all sang the national anthem—and then every patriotic song we could think of. It was an incredible experience. I would have to say that it was there, on the bus, that I realized that from that day forward, not one student in our school will do or say inconsiderate things to each other. Watching the news and sharing things together as a group and with our teachers, we understand better now how hatred begins, and we've decided it's not going to happen at our school. As for me, I felt sadness for every soul in the world on September 11. As a result, I've made a vow to always speak up when I see injustice, and to be as kind and considerate as I can. I believe it's the single most important thing I can do to contribute to living in a peaceful world.

Drew Jackson, 17: I've heard that Osama bin Laden is responsible for the cruelty of September 11, 2001. I believe he is. Bin Laden may think of himself and his followers as spiritual leaders, but I think of him as a racist who hides behind religious beliefs (ones he's twisted for his own purposes—and used as an excuse for his murderous ways). Maybe he and his followers should read up on the Islamic religion—which is a peaceful doctrine that doesn't sanction what he's doing. The Islamic faith is one that bin Laden clearly doesn't understand, much less follow. He and those who look to him for leadership should stop hiding behind their warped interpretation of the Islamic faith.

Maylynn Lingh, 16: One of the things that struck me about the ghastly events of September 11, 2001, was how everyone honored the moments of silence (in memory of the victims and their families). I've been to events where this same sort of observing silence took place for someone, but mostly it seemed to me that only a few really participated in a serious way. But as I watched those who took part in "moments of silence" for the victims and their families, I saw that everyone was in total observance. Heads were bowed, hands folded and tears were falling. I was so moved at how truly connected people were in sharing in the aftermath of this tragedy. Before this horrific incident, I didn't know how united we were, but now I'm sure that "we the people" have but one heart. Now, we must work on our world having one united, joyful heart.

Casey Igo, 15: When I watched the aftermath of the murderous plots of September 11, 2001, my first thoughts were, "How is it possible to be so cruel and evil?" But now, after watching everything that is taking place, another "picture" has emerged for me. In the aftermath of the attack on America, countless people rushed to help those whose lives had been touched by this tragedy. And our caring wasn't just for victims and their families in America, but those abroad, too. I can just picture it: Planes, side by side, some loading up with soldiers to fight for our freedoms and stop terrorism, and next to them, other planes loading up with food and relief for the innocent families who have also been victimized as a result of the terrorist attacks (and religious persecution). Seeing the goodness of people, for me, has helped neutralize my view that people can do some pretty ugly and brutal things to each other.

Mina Nishio, 14: I heard that the search dogs digging through the rubble of the World Trade Center (looking for survivors) became so discouraged when they weren't able to find anyone day after day, that they would hardly eat. Finally, the rescue workers buried themselves under blankets and let the dogs sniff them out and rescue them, while the other workers watched and cheered the dogs on. This restored the dogs' spirits and they began to eat again, play with one another, and resume searching for victims. I was touched by this story, realizing that we all need hope—we all need to feel like our efforts matter and we can succeed in making a difference, whether to make it through the day or to change the world. I'm going to remember how important it is to share hope and goodwill with each other.

Brittany Karen, 15: The events of September 11 didn't seem real to me until nearly a week later. I was watching one of the many newscasters as he reviewed the numbers of people killed and played clips of the building falling to pieces, when a young girl appeared on the screen. She held a plain white paper with pictures of a man glued to it. The man was smiling, holding something affectionately in his hands. It was then that I saw the desperate plea. "Have you seen my father?" she cried. Instantly, my heart ached for her. The sorrow that I felt was nothing close to the trauma she was going through, but suddenly, the tragedy of that day took hold in my heart. Looking at the crying girl, hoping someone might have seen her missing father, I too had lost a loved one.

Eric Saline, 16: Only minutes before the September 11 attack, "separation of church and state" existed in this country. Prayer was banned in schools, government and other places. But suddenly, after the great ambush on the country that day, people all over the world (and yes, in schools, government and other places) were urging the nation to turn to God for comfort. Congress opened their first meeting singing "God Bless America." President Bush quoted the Bible on national television, and Democrats and Republicans felt more united than separate. A country where prayer is forbidden on school campuses is now proclaiming a "National Day of Prayer." On September 11, we got our priorities straight. All of this has made me more hopeful that we will not exclude God from our lives—in good times, as well as difficult times.

Elizabeth Kenney, 14: Through the tragic events of September 11, we had a chance to see "greatness." People have united in supporting each other. We saw the extraordinary and tireless efforts of firemen, policemen, everyday citizens and volunteer organizations such as the American Red Cross. They all gained my respect and admiration. There have been fundraising efforts from children to celebrities, and donations of every kind, from blood to living quarters for those in need. We're a great nation, a nation filled with "everyday heroes." After seeing all this, I think that if we can do all this for the victims of the tragedy in the attack on America, we can do it for our "brothers and sisters" in need all over the world.

Brian Nagle, 15: September 11 was a scary day for me. I was absolutely shocked that the United States was suddenly attacked. I thought about my older brother and how he could be called to war. The idea of him going off to war terrifies me, and it instantly changed my relationship with him. We used to fight a lot, but not now. I just want the time we spend together to be great. I've learned that uncertain times can cause you to be very certain about the importance of loving your family—and showing it.

Allison Little, 16: On September 11, I stood in silent horror and watched enormous buildings crumble to the ground like a child's play tower made of blocks. But, while the terrorists meant to cause splintering and chaos in our country, instead, a sense of nationalism swept the country. And, as a nation, we've turned to God in this time of tragedy. I believe that we will turn to Him in times of peace, as well.

Katelyn Abshier, 15: The events of September 11 made me think about the freedoms for which America stand. For example, Americans have the freedom to pray without fear of persecution, whereas in some countries, people risk their lives to pray. America was attacked because of the freedoms we enjoy. I think that as a result of our freedoms being attacked, at the risk of their being stripped away, we will cling to them more dearly. Maybe this will make us as bold as we profess to be. For example, I know some people who are embarrassed to pray in front of other people at a restaurant because of how they might look. Now, I don't think that will be the case.

Michelle Langowski, 17: September 11, 2001, was a sickening and tragic day for sure. But it was also a wake-up call: Because of that day, millions and millions of people are now more aware of the plight of the whole world. That can be good, because now we see the effects of all our actions collectively—and on people everywhere in the world. So each in our own way, we must all do our part. It's amazing how it all counts. I live in a fairly small town and attend a relatively small school. Still, between the efforts of parents, students and teachers, we've raised $11,000 for the families of victims. That's a lot of money for one school group to raise. Imagine if everyone, everywhere, all did something. A lot of good could be accomplished! Like every drop of water is needed to make a container full, each of us must do our part in seeing that we create a peaceful world. September 11 made that very clear to me.

Natalie Grollnek, 16: When our country was so brutally attacked, Americans everywhere, young and old, rallied, making sure everyone knew what "America" stands for—using our greatest symbol for expressing our common unity and ideals, the American flag. From the time I left school that day, to the moment I reached home, I must have seen five hundred flags. Everyone wanted and needed a flag. Within days of the tragedy, flags had sold out everywhere. As a tribute (and a way to raise money), a local radio station invited those interested to come to a huge stadium to form a "human flag." While the sponsoring radio station had anticipated 6,000 people (all pledging money for the victims' families), 72,000 people arrived—and only because they were able to get there. For miles and miles, the freeways were still backed up with people trying to get there to join in the fundraiser and show their support. It was great! Oh yes, our flag is a symbol we understand. I've posted a flag in my room, right next to some great posters of rock stars. The posters can come and go, but I intend never to take down my flag. It's permanent, like my new idea of what it really stands for.

Emily Wright, 16: I'm Canadian. When we first heard the news of these unthinkable and cowardly acts of terrorism, our initial responses were shock and disbelief; everyone was sad, and just talking about it brought tears. How amazingly fragile we found ourselves.

That night, my family and I lit candles and put them around the house in honor of those whose lives had been tragically touched by this inhumane attack. We also flew our flag at half-mast and still do. How amazingly close we felt to one another.

Personally, while I was scared for what might happen next, I knew our civilization had reached a moment of truth: Our world is more interdependent than many had imagined. I saw another truth as well: Just as it's easy to show goodwill in celebrating victories, in the wake of this horrific tragedy people from everywhere came together to comfort and care for others. We all acted like brothers and sisters to those in need. How amazingly compassionate we all found ourselves.

I'm proud that my country has united with other countries in the commitment to stop the terrorists and to bring them to justice. And so, I am hopeful. It feels to me that the whole world is beginning to stop feeling like separate entities, and while honoring our individual countries, to at least think and act like a world—one world—with the goal of protecting all humankind. In this time of tragedy, how amazingly human we have become.

Lisa Drucker: In the wake of September 11, my hope is that our leaders will be filled with wisdom and courage and compassion, and guide us all to help one another and love one another, and be instruments of divine peace and love. I hope this incomprehensible tragedy will be a springboard for us all to begin to help one another to heal, and through our support of one another, in turn heal our world. For we all are God's children, here in this lifetime to treat one another with kindness, respect and reverence.

Part 6

Voices from "Behind the Walls"

We all have two lives: the one we learn with,
and the one we live with after that.

—Elizabeth Kaye

Problems are opportunities
in work clothes.

—Henry J. Kaiser

If there were dreams to sell,
what would you buy?

—Thomas Lovell Beddoes

A Word from the Authors

In our first book in the *Taste Berries for Teens* series, *Taste Berries for Teens: Inspirational Short Stories and Encouragement on Life, Love, Friendship and Tough Issues,* we shared one story of a young man, Geremy White, who was behind bars for stealing cars. Surprisingly, Geremy was bitter and disgruntled not for his actions, but rather, because he'd been "caught." Still not ready to take responsibility for his own actions, this young man blamed his plight on his parents and teachers, believing that *if* they had "done a better job," then "I wouldn't have turned out so bad—and then I wouldn't be here" (jail). Geremy then had the audacity to ask fellow teens to send him some money "so that when I get out of here, I won't have to rely on stealing to make a living."

Geremy's story brought an avalanche of mail from our readers, nearly half of whom wanted to "set Geremy straight in his thinking." And yet, the largest percentage of teen readers commented less on Geremy and more on his circumstance, basically saying, "I know someone who is in trouble with the law," and then shared how close they personally had once come to making choices that would've had disastrous outcomes. (About 5 percent of teen readers thought that sending Geremy money would keep him from stealing again!)

Regardless of which of the three groups our readers fell into, all expressed a great deal of compassion for those who find themselves struggling with moral issues. And, they firmly believe it's only a matter of time before those with a troubled life "see the light," "right their wrongs" and "get back on the right path." Rather than judging those "behind the walls," teens offered advice—not to them, but to us: "If we would all care more about each other, people wouldn't go astray as much as they do." Then, teens told us about a particular someone ("taste berry")—or of an experience—who was key to their doing the "right thing," or "saved me from making a bad (or potentially destructive) choice." For these teens, *someone* was there for them, and it had made all the difference: It helped them set—or reset—their personal compass in the right direction. As a result, those teens were able to go forward in setting and achieving positive goals.

Just as we received hundreds and hundreds of letters from teens in junior highs and high schools around the nation, we also received hundreds of letters from those "behind the walls"—those whose address is a juvenile hall, a jail, a prison cell or some other correctional institution. These letters carried messages mostly of regrets for the choices they've made, along with the mournful message of never having had someone to encourage and guide them. Almost always, these letters were filled with sage advice along the lines of, "If I could do it again, here's what I would do differently . . . " and "Here's what you can do so as not to end up as I did. . . . " And there was hope in these letters, too, for "When I get out, I'm going to. . . . "

We also received letters from those who confirm that yes, there was a person or persons who offered guidance and direction, but "I was too stubborn" or "I thought I was clever enough on my own," and so I didn't heed the advice. Of all the letters we received from those "behind the walls," this last group wrote the longest and most impassioned letters, pleading that we share with you what they've learned from their journey thus far. Their message is straightforward: Heeding words of wisdom could have spelled the difference between being where they are now (being a ward of the court system) and where they "could" have been—living as free members within society. Then they talk freely about *why* they are stripped of their freedoms, and of their desire to once again "have a voice" and "to have my words be heard." This is most always followed by, "I want to make a difference in someone's life, starting by sharing what I've learned."

So in this unit, we bring you the words of young adults who are now paying the price for having ventured into decisions that brought on consequences and who would like to share their "voice" with you. We invite you to read their tales of "why I did what I did," and listen to their thoughts on, "If there was one thing that would have made a difference for me, it would have been. . . ." As you read these stories, keep in mind that no matter how we speak or understand the mystery of why and how our lives are as they are, we are nonetheless all on the same journey: to discover our personal truths. As we do, may we use these "creativities" as tools for self-fulfillment and to help others. Listening, supporting and encouraging others are simple gifts, but important ones. And of course, it's one way to be a taste berry—and our "brother's keeper."

❤ *Taste berries to you, Bettie and Jennifer Youngs*

The Poet in Me

My name is Andrew Philip Kegley. I am fifteen. I'm living in a group home. Before that, I was court-ordered to live in a foster home, and before that, I was on detention—which is another term for juvenile hall or juvenile jail.

Basically, group home is an alternative for jail, too. It's a place for teens who are in trouble with the law, and sometimes, it's a home for those who don't really have anyplace else to turn to for help in troubled times.

Living in a group home can be pretty tough at times. You can't leave the premises without the home's consent, and even then, you have to be with a responsible adult family member. It's very structured; you have to follow the rules and guidelines to a "T"—no exceptions, or there are consequences to pay, like having what little free time you have taken away. One of the goals is to learn, basically, that the world is about order, and how and why following rules and schedules and keeping commitments is the thing to do. It's also about "inner order," or personal rehabilitation—helping us want to be better people, and then showing us how to do that. A lot of my time is taken up with therapy sessions where a therapist helps me look at myself and understand things better. As much as I don't want to be here, it's been good for me: I've made mistakes in the past, and I want to learn from them and not repeat them.

I'm in group home because I assaulted my mother a number of times, and she realized that if she didn't get help for me, and herself, I could hurt her. I love my mother, and I don't want to hurt her. Now that I'm getting help to deal with my anger, it won't happen again. But getting my anger under control wasn't as easy as being removed from my home. I didn't hit my mother because I was mad at her; I struck out because I couldn't control me. That is an important understanding, and basically, a "light" that came on for me one day as I was reading Alana Ballen's story in the *Taste Berries for Teens* book. I identified with all she'd gone through. Like Alana, I suffered from serious depression and had terrible bouts with anger that I could not control. But now, after being diagnosed with bipolar disorder, I am on the same medications (as Alana).

Just as when Alana started on medications to control her bipolar disorder, getting the help I've needed has turned my life around. I am not a mean, angry kid who hits everyone. I suffer from an illness that makes me feel total despair. Changing my actions from an "angry kid" to instead having bipolar means that I can get the help for an illness that made me act like (and be) a mean kid. As a result, I am learning about myself and learning ways to handle myself because of my disorder.

Having been diagnosed with bipolar also means I'm treated differently: Before I was diagnosed, I was rewarded when I was "good" and punished when I acted out (angry). Being on medication means that I don't have to spend every breathing moment focused on behavior modification, managing bad versus good behavior. This whole idea has been really important. I no longer feel like a "bad apple," a "throw-away kid."

Being away from my family is really hard, but it's also good. I really did need a break from them—at least until I learn how to stop being so angry and depressed—and I'm sure they needed a break from me for a little while. Another reason being away from family has been good is that by my being in a group home, I think I may have discovered some talents I had no idea I had. The first talent is one I discovered by being in a chorus group. I find that I love to sing; it lifts my spirits and makes me feel joy. I've been in such a black hole for so long with the depression I've been in, that feeling this joy is like a miracle. Singing makes me happier. Maybe I'll be offered a scholarship to go to college to sing. You never know. Right now, it just feels so good to feel hopeful.

I've also discovered another hidden talent: I'm a poet! I've done a lot of writing and journaling, and I have written poetry. I entered a county-sponsored poetry contest and won! Since then, I've written almost thirty poems, and I'm hoping to have some published. My dream is that my work will be good enough to be "bestselling," even win awards.

Learning that I am good at these two things feels good and makes me feel that I am beginning to be someone. It also makes me realize that if I have discovered these two things about myself, maybe there are other talents, too—and so I need to keep working toward finding out who I really am. This is another reason I'm so thankful I was diagnosed and am getting the treatments I need to control my depression and anger. Now I feel more hopeful. That makes me think about my future. I'm not certain what I want to do, but I'm looking. I'm thinking that it might be interesting to go into law enforcement, or to be a paramedic. Being in a group home, I've had a chance to see both men and women doing these kinds of work. It looks like interesting work, and something that really helps people get a new start on their lives, or at least have a point to begin to change things in their lives that aren't working too well for them now—as was true for me.

So it feels really good to know that I'm beginning to look forward to my future. Even so, for now, I'm just trying to learn how to become a better person with this "time-out" from my family. I'm reevaluating myself and learning about the real me. So, in a way, having the courts order me to a group home has been good.

Here's a poem I just wrote last night. The "storm" is sort of a metaphor for my life in the last year. I hope you like it.

The Storm—My Storm

The wind is howling through the trees
And it ain't no gentle breeze
The rain is splashing
The thunder crashing
Lord knows, a storm's a'comin'!

Now lightning cracks across the sky
And the peaceful day has died
The limbs are landing on the roofs
Sounds of thunder, like a million horses' hoofs
Lord knows, it's going to be one mighty storm!

No more sound of birds a'chirpin'
No distant church bells a'ringin'
All have been drowned asunder
Deafened by rolling thunder
Lord knows, I'm in the center of one horrific storm!

But ah, a new dawn is shining:
The sky is clear, a silver lining
Clouds no longer block the sun
Happier days on a blue horizon
Lord knows, this storm—*my* storm—is over!

Andrew Philip Kegley, 15

"That 'New' Geek"

I had, once again, started a new school in a new town. My family moved a lot, so being the "new kid" seemed to be the story of my life. It's really tough being a new kid in a new school—especially those first few weeks where you have to prove yourself to everyone. I'm here in a state school because I tried to prove myself in a way that got me in a lot of trouble.

What happened was that I found myself, once again, a new face at school that was five months into the school year. Sure enough, as usual, the first day was about everyone checking me out, just sort of looking at me from a distance. The second day, I got a few basic questions: "What's your name?" "Where you from?" Stuff like that.

Then, as usual, once a little familiarity set in, the name-calling began. First, there was being called by my last name only (never a good sign). Either that or "That *new* geek." Kids deemed good enough to be considered one of the "in" crowd are always respectfully called by their first names. The really popular kids, and the ones who are really liked by everybody, are called by nicknames, like Bennett O'Brien at the school was called "Bennie-o" or Kate Belleview was called Katie-Bell. Things like that. I, on the other hand, was called by my last name, or worse, names like "fatso," or "four-eyes." I do wear thick glasses because my eyesight is pretty bad. I mean, in the morning, I have to feel around for my glasses because I can't see without them. And I am about twenty-five pounds heavier than I'd like to be, but still, that doesn't give others the right to have a name-calling free-for-all at my expense.

Still, the name-calling is not the worst of it. The taunting is what drives me absolutely livid! And what happened on the day that got me here where I am today was something that made me really furious, and I mean "I can't and won't take it anymore" serious. I was putting books in my locker when a big bully-like guy came running by, intentionally ramming himself into my locker. I was getting books down from the upper shelf, and because the locker door slammed into me, I fell into my locker— which caused me to drop the books I was holding—and my glasses fell off. When this guy saw my glasses go flying (several feet from my locker) he laughed, and then gave my glasses a good swift kick. This sent them sliding down the hallway to a kid who kicked my glasses to yet another guy. Of course everyone thought it was really funny.

Really upset—and now as blind as a bat—I couldn't see well enough to get my glasses so I just sort of ran after the guy about to take the next kick. Realizing that by my entering into their game, it became a contest, I stopped doing that, and that did stop them from kicking my glasses around, but not me.

Knowing my glasses lay somewhere on the floor, I got down on my knees, crawling around feeling for the glasses, then some guy kicked me in the butt. It hurt and made me slam belly first onto the floor. It seemed to me that practically everyone in the hall laughed. Luckily, in the same moment, the bell rang and everyone just went on his or her way to class. I was embarrassed, but really mad, too. I found my glasses, got my books, and instead of going to class, left the school building and headed for home.

The next day, at the very same time, this same boy once again slammed into my locker when I was getting books. This time, I let my books go flying, but clung to my glasses. But the guy wasn't satisfied that I should only have my body rammed into the locker (and my arm bruised from shielding the locker door from knocking me over). Seeing my glasses still on my face, he came up and flicked them from my face. I grabbed for them, but once again they ended up on the floor where a similar "game" of hockey— with my glasses being the puck—started.

The next day, I brought a gun to school.

I did not bring bullets; I did not intend to hurt anyone. Only to frighten the bullyboys. My plan was to get to my locker about the time they'd be coming to their lockers, and then, instead of my retrieving books from the locker, I'd have the gun in my hand, casually looking it over. I figured this would let them know they'd better stop messing me over—because maybe I wasn't such easy prey as they thought (I felt they thought I wouldn't get in their face, or defend myself). So by seeing me with a gun, they would think that I just might not be as wimpy as they thought.

Things played out as I knew they would, and then, when I took out the gun and coolly looked it over, the other kids looked on in disbelief—and no one rammed my locker or bothered to knock my glasses from my face. The plan had worked. I had scared respect into them. Surely they would leave me alone from then on.

What didn't happen according to my plan was that fifteen minutes later, two policemen came into the classroom, handcuffed me and took me to the police station. I was sentenced to seven years. With "good behavior" maybe I can get out earlier, maybe even in a year.

I know that what I did wasn't the best way to go about things. And I wish I could have a chance to do things differently. But that's not the way things are for me now. And I'm paying the price for the way I handled things.

Still, I want you all to know that it's a terrible thing to tease and taunt others—especially when you know it takes them to the edge. What I did was a drastic attempt to stop others from the insults, the harassment, but you know, at the time, I thought it would make the misery of being bullied stop.

So from this position, now in state school, all I can do is ask you to please consider the person on the other end of being "that new geek" or being tortured or bullied and cut that person a little slack. I always felt like "that new geek." That others felt so free to go out of their way to make me feel that way just isn't right. So, please, don't do it. Forcing others to defend themselves from the rude and inconsiderate behaviors of others is more than contemptible. Quite possibly, you could be helping someone get angry to the point of committing a crime.

Craig North, 16

I'm What They Call a "Troubled Teen"

I've just turned fifteen. I'm what society calls a "troubled teen." I've been in and out of county juvenile hall eleven times since May 1998. I've been in five different group homes.

When did my life fall apart? Well, maybe it was doomed from the beginning, but for me it seemed that life changed the day my mother died—which was October 2, 1995. Everything went downhill for me from that day on. For one, I was so sad I couldn't even function. I didn't want to get out of bed, let alone get up and go to school. So, mostly I didn't. Because of that, I was labeled "truant" (which, of course, I was).

I never knew my dad; in fact, I'd never even met him. So when my mother died, I went to live with my sister. She was twenty-five, and with a life of her own she really didn't want or need a kid around. Realizing that I was just in the way, and that she was trying to make a life for me when she really just wanted to be with her own friends and come and go as she pleased, I knew it would be better if I left. So one day I did. She got worried and called the police—who found me and took me to a detention facility. There I was labeled "homeless."

Then the courts sent me to a group home. It just didn't seem to me like I belonged there, because the kids placed in the group home had done some pretty bad things, like stealing, using drugs and even beating up on others. I hadn't done any of that. I'd never stolen or used drugs. I had committed no crimes what-soever. The only thing I'd done was "leave" when I didn't feel I belonged. I don't consider myself a bad guy, and I am fairly bright. In school, I even got pretty good grades. So while the court system sees me as a "troubled teen," I really don't see myself that way at all. More than anything else, I see myself as a boy without parents—and that's a problem. You've got to live somewhere, and it's just logical to live with your parents, even if your relationship is rocky. At least you have a home. Not having a home—at least one where I felt like I belonged—has been a real problem for me.

So feeling the group home was not for me, one day I just slipped out. Once again, the police found me and brought me back. Then I was labeled a "runaway."

I was returned to the group home, and I decided to stop running, because I didn't want any new labels—each one seemed to carry a really terrible penalty. But now I get released in thirteen days. The even better news is that I've met my dad, and he has agreed to have me come live with him.

I'm hopeful that my life is going to have a "storybook" ending. I really hope that my dad and I become a real family and everything is just great between us. I know it won't be easy, but I'm going to try to make it work. I'm going to be living with a person who, while he is my "father," I don't know. I am hoping my father (I keep saying that word because it is so new to me, and seeing it in writing is both frightening and awesome) will be someone who is going to let me have my feelings, and not tell me to "buck up and be a man" as I was told by one man at the group home. I am still very sad about my mother's death, and I hope that it's okay with him if I talk about her. And, I hope, too, that it'll be okay with him if I cry over her. I hope he's a nice guy and ready to be a father. I'm hoping he wants me in his life and that he doesn't feel that he's getting stuck with me, as did my sister. I hope he likes me and feels okay about taking care of me. And most especially, I hope he won't think badly of me because of all those labels. I really don't want him to think of me as a "troubled kid."

I'm hoping for other things, too. Like I'm looking forward to going back to school and having friends. I'm hoping the labels I've picked up and the places I've been—group home and all— won't keep me from having nice friends. So if you meet me, or someone like me, please be open-minded and give me a chance to just be a good friend. I'd like you to keep in mind that not everyone with a past is a bad person, just a person who's been down on his or her luck.

Clark Brown, 15

Have You Ever Been to Juvenile Hall —Even to Visit Someone?

When I was twelve, I lived with my mother and my sister, Susan, in Phoenix, Arizona. I liked my school and friends, and I especially liked Sean Andrews.

Then, my sister Susan and I had to go live with my father in Florida. I had to leave my mom and all my friends behind. Sean, too.

Once in Florida, I didn't think I'd ever see him again. So I tried to just get on with my life. The new school was okay and all, and I made some really nice friends, but I missed Sean *so* much. I thought about him all the time, daydreaming about him while sitting in my classes, and especially missing him when I'd be laying in bed thinking about my life in Phoenix—my mom, my room at Mom's house and my friends. Sometimes I'd be so homesick for all of them that I'd just lie in bed and sob.

With every passing week, I became more homesick. My father must have noticed, because after just that one semester with our father, my parents agreed that my sister and I would return the next year to Arizona to live with our mother again—which, of course, meant we'd be going to school there again. The moment I learned this, my heart felt such a huge relief. I was happy just knowing the days were ticking off, and soon I wouldn't be a zillion miles away from all the things I loved in Phoenix any longer. I just hoped Sean hadn't moved away—and didn't have a girlfriend like so many of the boys in my school had.

Though the semester couldn't end soon enough for me, it did end and I was on my way back to Phoenix.

The second I arrived at my mother's house and settled back into my room, I called around to my friends, casually asking them about Sean. Was he still around? Did he have a girlfriend (or even like anyone)? Had he ever mentioned me? Stuff like that. I found out that yes, Sean was still around, and no, there was no girlfriend, and no, my name had never come up in his conversations—at least any that anyone knew about or was letting on to.

Excited that there was still a chance he was "available," my dreams were no longer of missing Sean, but of how I could meet up with him—and of how I could let him know I liked him. Of course, all this was in the middle of stressing out about the possibility that he might be mad that I did like him. Some boys are like that, and I really didn't know how Sean was about these things.

The answers to all my "how" questions plopped in my lap one week later, when I was sitting at home watching TV. My sister, who had been visiting her girlfriend (who lived in the neighborhood), came dashing into the TV room. Grabbing my hand and practically pulling me off the couch, she exclaimed, "I was just over at my friend's house, and guess who is there playing basketball? Sean! So get up and go get dressed up!" Out of breath and obviously excited, she added, "I'll take you over there. You can see Sean! Hurry up, or you'll miss him."

My sister and I practically ran to her friend's house. I was excited, and nervous, too. We got there just as Sean and his friends were taking a break from their game. "Hey, look who's back!" Sean said the moment he saw me. It felt so good to have him start things off like that; it really took the pressure off. Then came his words, "Want to go for a walk?"

"Sure," I said, thinking the best and feeling all giddy inside. So we left our friends and started walking down the sidewalk. And that's when Sean told me something I could hardly believe. "Look," he said, "I've liked you for almost three years, so when you left to go to Florida, I was really upset about it. And I missed you."

So that's how our "real" relationship, our "true love" relationship, began.

For the next two months, Sean was my boyfriend, and I was his girlfriend. It was a really happy time.

I don't know why I started doing drugs, but I did. Maybe it was because some of my friends were using, but it's gotten me in a whole lot of trouble, and I've ended up in a detention center as a result. I've ruined my life! Now, I'm living thirty-five miles away from home because I have to spend the next ten months here in the center. Not only is my life terrible being here, but I also don't get to see Sean. And it's my entire fault—again. Sean knew when I started doing drugs because I asked him if he wanted to try some, too, but he refused. He also told me that I shouldn't use either. He even told me that if I continued to do drugs, he wouldn't be my boyfriend. But even with that warning, I still used.

I can't believe I screwed up my life so bad.

Being in a detention center is just totally awful. Your whole life is "detained." You're cut off from everything that is fun and carefree. Your life isn't even your own; there are meetings, rules and kitchen chores, duties with schedules that are far worse than your parents would ever assign. There are even very strict curfews—and not just for going to bed, but even on the weekends. Plus, you're told what you can wear, when you can eat, when you have reading time, when you can shower and what time you must have all the lights in your room off. You can't even listen to music. During the day, you have to get permission to use the bathroom. It's just awful. I miss my mom, my sister, my friends, and worse than when I was in Florida, I'm without Sean again. I miss him so much. Who knows if I'll ever have a chance to be his girlfriend again? Maybe he won't even want to speak to me again.

I'm so stressed out. I think knowing that I did this all to myself makes it even worse. I feel so awful about what I've done to my life—in every way. I'm definitely overwhelmed. Nothing could be worse than my life right now. So, think twice about using drugs, because it's not worth it. It is not worth it!

Victoria Moore, 15
(adapted from A Taste-Berry Teen's Guide
to Managing the Stress and Pressures of Life*)*

A Room . . . That's Mine

A glaring bulb above my head,
A broken promise for every tear I've shed.
Stone cold walls, dead cold eyes,
Why? 'Cause I started early, learned all the lies.

Lost souls abound, mine sinks within,
When I think of all I might have been.
This is all that I am, a troubled teen,
All that is left of wild, hopeless dreams.

A flicker of heart, glimmer of hope.
This isn't how I'd planned to cope.
A small ray of light a ways off ahead,
And so hard to see from this cold, hard bed.

"Time's up—lights out" someone yells,
Each night these words echo off my cell.
Another day over—lost, out of sight,
No one but myself to wish a good-night.

I need a song to sing in troubled times,
A thought to soothe my raging mind.
And peace when I grow afraid,
. . . Small comforts when I'm dismayed.

I want to play and be heard once more,
To fly high again, to be free, to soar.
To live again, and leave pain behind,
To feel love's touch, gentle and kind.

I need a new life, a chance, and a plan,
Somewhere to build on rock, not sand.
Need to find new friends, have some good times,
And live in a house with a room . . . that's mine.

Delilah Burton, 17

Rhythm—and Blues

My mother, Mary Butler, was sixteen years old when she had me. My father was eighteen at the time, so the relationship broke apart before I was even born. Heartbroken, and all alone with an infant, my mother set out for California to live with her sister.

Within a couple of years, my mother met and married, and gave birth to twin girls. It was a pretty good time for us, with the exception that, because my stepfather was in the Navy, we moved around a lot. Times were not so good for my mother. My stepfather was physically abusive to my mother, so she divorced him.

The next few years were relatively good ones for my mother and for us three kids. My mother returned to California, got a job and set about raising her children. During this time I was doing okay in school, but discovered music and learned that I had a real talent for it. It wasn't long before I was playing several instruments, as well as writing and singing my own music.

Because of my music, I made a lot of friends, especially those who were also musically inclined. I met a guy named Dwayne Marston—a whiz on the guitar—and we became really good buddies. Dwayne and I were as close as brothers. In fact, a lot of people thought we were blood brothers, since we look a lot alike. By the time high school rolled around, the two of us had formed a band. Our sound was rhythm-and-blues, sort of a combo of Earth, Wind, and Fire, and Michael Styles with a touch of Sting. We were cool!

We had big plans. Dwayne and I, along with his younger brother, were going to be the best and hottest band in the world. We certainly wanted to be. We worked hard at putting together a look and sound that we thought were unique. But then things began to get dicey: Jealousy among the members of the band set in.

I don't know how it happened, or why, but out of the blue, the other members decided to "vote" me out of the group, saying I was "conceited and big-headed." This was such a huge blow to me, and worse, it came right at the same time that our group began contract negotiations with a large and well-known record company in California. As I see it now, I think the group was determined to get me out of the group before the contract was signed because shortly after this happened, they signed the contract. Soon thereafter, they released their first album. Within what seemed like a matter of months, they released three singles, all of which went "gold."

I'd like to say I was happy for them, but all I can say is that I was devastated. Here was a group with whom I'd been an original member and had been in on the ground floor since day one. Now, here they were, with fame and fortune, and I with nothing. Zip. And I'd worked so hard and dreamed of the very things they were now realizing. The success I was missing out on wasn't just small potatoes. I mean, the group was on TV, radio and in concert. For me, a sadness and bitterness set in followed by anger. And then a deep depression.

I panicked. How could I come up with a "get-rich-quick scheme"—and quick?

I'm ashamed to tell you, but I began using and selling drugs to pay for my livelihood and the equipment and things I needed to put together a new musical career. As you would expect, it was too difficult to escape the power of drugs, and soon I became more and more involved in using and selling. Drugs just took over my entire life. I fell into an even deeper depression, and it wasn't long before I lost faith in myself as a musician. I was giving up on music. And on myself.

Then I was arrested for trafficking. So now, here I sit in the penitentiary with five years to do.

Along with my regrets of having shortchanged myself (and many others along the way) of having a music career, I've had to face the incredible heartbreak of lost years with the people I love. Even worse, while in here, my mother died from complications during surgery (she was only forty-three years old). That she died without me at her side—not to mention all the time she didn't get to be proud of her son—made me feel like a complete failure. She'd worked so hard to raise us kids, and she was so good to us. Ever since I was young, it was my dream that one day I'd have enough money to build her a home of her very own. It's pretty hard to do that when you're in prison. I've lost other people important to my life, too. My girlfriend of five years waited for as long as she could, then said she had to "move on"—without me.

I just have so many regrets. But that makes it all the more reason I've got to get a grip—to take hold of my life and make something out of it. I've started doing that. Luckily, I am still a young man. Thankfully, I am very talented. Hopefully, I've learned some things, such as to stay far away from drugs, and that there are no shortcuts to success, so working towards goals—and I do have some again—is about taking it one step at a time. I plan to get back into music, to write and play it. One day, I intend to launch my own music production company.

I'm not blowing smoke: I really am being serious about my (delayed—but no more) goals. I write every day—songs, poetry and a journal of my thoughts (which I want to turn into verse and lyrics). And, I read, read and read.

Even though I am a few years older than most of your teen readers, I have read all the *Taste Berries for Teens* books. It's a great series. In so many of the stories, I saw myself as a young guy again, a teen again, and remembered when I was filled with dreams and ideals and never for a moment believed I'd "shoot myself in the foot" as I've done. Reading the stories makes me remember exactly the moment when, as a teen, I lost hope. And that's why I'm writing this now. I want to tell teens that *hope is hope,* anywhere you can find it. I guess the point is to have hope, and hang on to it and not allow life's disappointments to take it away from you.

When you mess up, do whatever you can to stay in touch with believing that you can "re-do" your life. It's the biggest thing I face now. I'm over the hurdle of feeling lost or defeated. I've reclaimed my desire to get going and to have a worthwhile and productive life, one in which I use my talents to express myself, and to make a good living for myself and those I love. Now, my goal is to accomplish my dreams. Along the way, I'm sure I'll have to overcome those who reject me because I "served time." I believe I can. I want to.

I want to do it for me, the new me. And because I want to honor my mother, and to be worthy of all she invested in me. I owe her so much. I can tell you firsthand that if living behind the walls won't scare you from bad dealings, thinking about letting your parents down should. I'm more ashamed of the sadness and heartache I've put my mother through than almost anything I can think of. The pain in my heart over the lost years with her is a searing one. But I'm moving forward now. For her. For me. And, for your belief in me as a fellow human walking the earth together. You can trust me.

I hope that one day soon, you will be hearing my new tunes, and that when you do, you will enjoy them. I'd also like you to remember my journey in bringing them to you.

I hope you'll respect me and others who have paid a price and learned a lesson, and who got up and continued their journey. I am. And if I can, you can. Just remember, keep the faith. And never, never lose hope that you can. And always know that I'll be your taste berry any day—and every day. Although I owe this to my mother, I want to do it for you, too. I'm ready to give back. Starting today. Starting with you.

Terrance Butler

You Promised

You promised me your love
You promised me understanding
You promised, "I'll make you happy!"
You promised my "best interests at heart"
You promised you'd never turn your back
You promised you'd never leave
You promised to stick by me "no matter what"
You promised. You promised. You promised.

You broke every single promise.

You walked away
And when they asked, you said, "Don't know her!"
How does it feel to have betrayed me?
To let me pay the sole price
Of a crime planned by two?
So now I'm locked away . . . for ten months
Because of you—
And what you asked me to do.
So here I am, behind walls,
While you're out there, free.
They say you've found someone new,
So tell me, are you sweet-talking her,
And asking her to do your dirty work?
Does she know the price?
Oh, please do have her write to me
I'll let her know that your promises
Are like your love—all lies, total deceit
And come at a huge cost
Or maybe I'll tell her myself when she finds herself in the cell
    next to me!

Linda Jeanette Belmontes, 18

#784104

My name is Christopher Lee Byrd, better known as #784104. For the past eleven years, I've been living in the Texas Department of Criminal Justice System. In short, my home is a prison cell.

I was introduced to drugs at a very young age. Because drugs are so insidiously addictive, I got hooked. It wasn't long before I was living on the streets, and then became a part of its corruption. Even though I was smart enough to see that my using was turning me into a criminal, I prided myself on having survived the day. It's no way to live—or die.

It's amazing that even when you only know an ugly lifestyle—and for me the streets were just that—you need to drown out the cries from your heart and soul that keep hoping you'll be a "decent person." A good part of the reason I used was to numb myself from the reality of the life I was living—and not face the truth of what I had become. It didn't work.

But while using and selling drugs seemed like the only way I could survive, the truth is, drugs led to my destruction (I became a criminal) and physical and mental deterioration. I nearly lost my life a thousand times. It could have been from overdosing or being killed because of a drug deal I was involved in. I've had stretches where I had a lot of money in my pockets, and times when I didn't have a place to take a shower. I've been without basic necessities, and had times when I was tired, wet, cold and hungry, slept in ditches, under bridges, in parks, trains, restaurant bathrooms, and alleyways. Not cool. Not good.

Living on the streets is a hard and terrible life. I'm one out of tens of thousands who know. The thing is, I *was* smart enough and had what it takes to succeed in the world outside of the life I was living. I knew this. I convinced myself that I didn't know how to break out of the life I'd come to know. But all that was an excuse, too.

By the time I was ready to give up this excuse, the consequences of my crimes caught up with me—for which, as odd as
it may seem, I am thankful. It's put an end to the bizarre and
crazy and criminal life I was leading. Not that prison is a lovely
place to be—because it's not. It's just that the streets can only
lead to pain, crime and eventually death. After you've committed a crime and ripped someone off, things can only get worse
because you have to grow eyes in the back of your head to stay
alert for all the danger coming. The law—as well as a bullet—
will always be looking for you. Doing this will take your mind
and play a million games with it—which are not fun to play on
any level.

My life being what it is—a prison inmate—here's what I'd
like to say to you (if you will be so kind and patient to hear my
words). If you are in trouble—or know you're heading there—I
think there are two things you can do that will make all the difference in your life. (I know they would have changed my life
for the better, and I've talked to hundreds of others like me, and
they agree.) *First, examine your thinking: Are you developing a devi-
ous mind?* For example, do you believe it's okay to take things
that belong to someone else (whether or not they find out about
it)? Do you feel that you need to "get yours," that you are
entitled? Do you believe in shortcuts to having what you want—
that you can have something without working for it? These are
all a part of developing what behind the walls we call a "criminal mentality." So if these describe you, change this mind-set
instantly.

After spending some time here behind walls, it dawned on me
that I think like a criminal: I thought more about how to "get
away" with something, than going about being an honest,
decent, straightforward person. So then I had to think about if I
was willing to change my life, to set and get on a new course. I'd
already lost years of my life being jailed. I had to ask myself if I
was willing to lose more.

It's impossible to change your thinking overnight, but you can do it little by little. Start spending more time with a more positive crowd. This will give you a little more incentive to want to change. I wish I would have. It might have changed my life a lot sooner. You have to be very dedicated to want to change. Believe me, I know! It took me about eight years being in before I really got serious about it (yes, obviously I'm a slow learner!). But changing your way of thinking is the only way you will keep from finding yourself living behind walls.

The second piece of advice I have for you is to *find someone you believe in, and please let them guide you.* It can be your mom or dad, a teacher, or someone you admire—someone you know who will keep you on the straight and narrow. Don't wait for that person to come to you, because maybe that won't happen. Just know that it can be a really good thing to have someone looking objectively at you and your life—and believing in you enough so they'll tell it to you straight.

Do it now. Start today. Yes, you're young, and it seems like you have forever, but you can't believe how fast even slow days tick away. I waited for someone to walk up and hand me a life for so long and you know, it never happened. Decide today that you're in charge of your life. Doing that can make the difference between wasting your life and having a decent one.

As a child, my life was a mess (and I messed it up more, bigtime). Even so, I did have people who actually cared about me; people who tried to get me to "wake up and see where my life was headed if I didn't straighten up." Had I listened, had I followed their suggestions and advice (and let them help me), everything could have been different for me. But I felt, "You can't tell me; I already know all I need to know," so I never listened to the words of wisdom from others. And I felt, "If only everyone would just let me live my life and quit bugging me." Don't turn down the offer to have someone give you a hand in making a decent life for yourself. If you are fortunate enough to have people in your life who are trying to get you to see a different and better way of doing something, please think about what they are saying. Consider that I am in prison because I didn't take the time to listen.

If you need further prodding, think about the price I'm paying: forfeiting the chance to do what I want, when I want, where I want, and to lay my head on a pillow each night without regrets and guilt. If you do not have anyone you feel is interested in helping you go forward (or to turn your life around before it is too late), seek out a person. I had teachers, coaches, counselors, neighbors and others interested in my well-being, and probably you have, too.

I have a hundred other things to say, but I'll settle for those important points. I really hope you won't make the mistakes I did. Even if your life seemed doomed from the beginning (as mine did to me), I hope you will have the willpower and heart to get yourself some help.

So I'm praying for you—just as I pray for me—to find those (taste berries) who can help you prevent yourself from being in my shoes. Prison is a violent way of life. But it doesn't compare to the mental anguish of knowing you've wasted years of your life, and missed out on being loved and loving others.

We all need someone who cares and believes in us. I believe in you. So you believe in you. Even in your most hopeless moments, don't give up on yourself. Ever.

Christopher Lee Byrd, #784104

"Residential Burglar"

I'm ashamed to say that I have been in and out of prison since I was seventeen. But I have been. It's with a good deal of remorse that I say these words, but it is with a great deal of soul-searching that I'm also able to say that I've changed more (for the better) in the last year and a half than in the first seventeen years of my life. One of the biggest changes is in my thinking. I'd say that before two years ago, I really never imagined that "how" I thought was the key to my actions. But now I can see it has a lot to do with everything.

Just as "how" I thought landed me in prison in the first place, changing the way I think is literally turning my life around. Doing that has changed the way I see myself. For example, until recently, I would have told you with a straight face that I considered myself an expert on being a failure, but now I see the importance of not thinking of myself as a failure, but rather, thinking of myself as someone who needs to work hard at putting in place what I call the "building blocks" of being a decent person: self-honesty; keeping my word; being disciplined; having goals; and reading about others and how they overcame the obstacles in their lives.

I'm really happy to have a chance to be writing this. When I first read one of the *Taste Berries for Teens* books, I knew I wanted to share what I learned with you. Let me begin.

Why I'm incarcerated: After a great deal of thinking about it, I've decided not to go into detail about my "story," other than that I am serving six years for residential burglary. I was a thief; I stole from someone. To me, it doesn't serve much purpose to embellish the crime, and takes away from what's important—which is that I am paying a price because I did a crime. The crime, the act itself, was stupid and senseless. More importantly, there are 101 reasons why I could have prevented myself from going down that path (of crime), and as a result, having gone to prison.

My biggest loss: As a result of my actions, there are some things I can never get back. For example, I can't vote, and the police can even search my house—for the rest of my entire life— at any time (without a warrant). But there are even bigger losses. A sobering realization came one day when I realized that one of the biggest personal losses of being incarcerated was the loss of my "voice"—my opinions and words didn't matter much to *anyone*. Only my actions matter now—because I've blown my chance to have my words trusted. This idea became crystal clear one day as I watched other inmates around me on visitation days—which are so important to us. When those we care about come to visit us, we hang on to their every word. And yet, when we would utter words like I did once, when I told someone "I love you," that person looked at me and said, "Then show it in your actions. Sort yourself out and straighten up so we can trust you and have you in our lives—our real lives."

I'll bet that for many of you reading this, those around you, friends, teachers and parents hang on to your every word. And they believe and trust what you say. That doesn't happen for me. Others pretty much believe that what I have to say has little value, even that I may be telling them what they want me to say, not the truth. In the past, most of the time they'd be right. But now I can trust the words I say and write. I hope you will, too.

Serious errors I've made: There have been lots of them, of course, but what troubles me most—when I'm down on myself the most—aside from the laws I've broken, here's where I really screwed up: As a teen, I never gave any serious thought to my future. I had no long-range goals. My future consisted of the weekend coming up. Since I really hadn't thought about working toward a specific thing, I had no direction. So then, feeling so far behind the achievements of others, like having a job and decent lifestyle, the second serious error I made was to look for a shortcut: stealing. I've since learned there are few shortcuts in life. I've got a lot to catch up on; it's going to take a plan and effort to rebuild a life and lifestyle I can respect.

My goals and plans for the future: Having gotten so far behind in life, you'd think I would have given up on any chance of living a normal life. While I did for a long time, now I want to design a new life. I know it starts with having to change many things—most having to do with me. Being dissatisfied with my life—and seeing the sad acceptance of prison life by those around me—has given me a reason to want to change my life. Fortunately for the majority of you who may be reading this, your lives and hopes for the future are still in the making. You have a chance, take it. Don't screw it up. It is not worth it.

I'm going to be released in a short while, and for the first time, I know that I will commit myself to a serious path of doing a few simple things: I want to get and hold down a job. I want to slowly build relationships with others who care about me, who will be able to trust me and believe in me. And I want to work on having people know that no matter what circumstances come about, they can trust me and trust in me. I want them to believe I'll come to their defense when the chips are down. I'd like them to do that for me.

I'd like to earn the love of others, to have love in my life that brings me joy and contentment. I know that this, too, will require dedicated work and effort, but I welcome that. And, I'd like to further my education. I really do believe that education is power. I'd like to have others think of me as intelligent, and not just "clever." I'm spending a lot of time reading and going to classes. Learning is important to me—maybe for the first time ever. Don't wait as long as I did to value the satisfaction of learning good and positive things.

Advice from a person behind the walls: Probably, it will take a long time to have in my life what many of you teens have in your lives right now. So my hope is that you won't allow yourself to get off course and have those things taken from you. I can't stress enough just how important it is to set goals for yourself because this gives meaning to your life. Plus, it gives you direction as you go about your days. And another truth about having goals is that others will look up to you and respect you. Nobody really tells you this, but it's true. Having goals is also good for your self-esteem and to your feeling as though you're not as worthless as you can sometimes feel.

What I'd like to ask of you: I'm getting a late start on what my life should have been. Still, I ask that you don't discount me; what I have to say has merit, if for no other reason than the fact I'm here for a reason. And I ask that you don't pity me and don't reject me because I didn't see the light when I should have. Instead, I hope you'll understand that the price I've paid for the mistakes I've made could have been avoided, if only I would've done some things differently. And it is a big, big price. When you're behind the walls, you lose your freedoms—the ones in the outside world, of course, but also those freedoms on the inside of your guts that allow you to respect yourself and think of yourself as an honorable person. The loss of self-respect is one of the greatest losses imaginable. I know.

In closing, I'd tell you that life is short and precious, so don't waste it. Do all that you can to live your life so that you *own* yourself. And, so that when you put your head on the pillow at night, you are right with the world, and right with the most important person you spend it with—yourself. And one last thing, thank you for reading my words—and for allowing me my voice. It means more to me than you can ever know.

Stephen Russell

Part 7

Coping with Private Pain

In the depth of winter, I finally learned that within me there lay an invincible summer.

—Albert Camus

Inside each of us resides the memories that comfort, recollections that soothe, remembrances we treasure. These can heal and mend—now and forevermore.

—Source Unknown

Pain is part of being alive, and we need to learn that. Pain does not last forever, nor is it necessarily unbearable, and we need to be taught that.

—Rabbi Harold Kushner

A Word from the Authors

Are you sad or hurting? Are you feeling lonely or alone? Do you feel as though no one understands you, or cares about you as much as you would like? Do you feel overwhelmed with the stress of meeting the expectations placed upon you? Are you feeling depressed, or just "blah"—wishing that your life was more exciting, or bigger, brighter and better than you feel it is? In working on this unit, we found that *many* teens face sad and painful times—be it a breakup with a special someone; the death of a loved one; or, the loss of an ideal (such as admiring or trusting someone, only to discover that person is not all you had believed him or her to be). Pain hurts. It's doubtful that the words in this unit can make your hurt go away, but they can help you feel more hopeful and leave you with a new appreciation not only for your resilience, but your personal courage.

"You know, Mom, because I've personally had such a painful year, I can really relate to what so many teens referred to as 'private pain.' What makes it 'private' is that while you turn to others for comfort and support, you know they can only do so much. The pain rumbling around inside of your heart is largely your *own* to get through. It's like when the love of your life wants to break up with you. Your parents and friends can be extra kind and caring toward you, and while that is so very appreciated—

still your heart knows it would prefer to find a corner of its very own to go cry in, rather than be at a crowded party with all your friends. (Then, when you've moved through the worst of the pain, you definitely want the crowded party with all your friends!) It's just that initially, when pain sets in, it holds you captive, and it puts the *enjoyment* of all the other things in your life on hold.

"Many adults have experienced this sort of thing—either from facing a family crisis, such as divorce, or job loss, a personal humiliation or a health crisis. But seldom do we ask teens how they're feeling—and faring—with the circumstance and experiences within their lives. And that is what's so poignant about this unit—it highlights how teens themselves have to face some pretty deep experiences—like the death of friends through car crashes or overdosing from drugs; the illness (or death) of friends from AIDS or anorexia; the aftermath of an abortion (self or friend); drug or alcohol addictions; or mental-health concerns (self or peers). In short, teen life today is not as placid as many believe it to be."

"It's an enormous realization, to be sure, Jennifer. You have had a year filled with heartbreak. Given what you've been through, what's been the heart of the process—the getting through your painful times?"

"Well, I'd say I'm not *completely* through it yet, but I am committed to finding healthy ways to cope with things as I go along—which is new, because at first, I just froze up. But I have made some amazing discoveries—like how often we sort of 'stuff' our pains away and not deal with them at the time. But sooner or later, these are going to come barreling back, and probably at a time when we're feeling our most vulnerable. That was true for me this past year when my grandmother suddenly became ill and died. It was a pain of its own, of course, but unearthed some 'stuffed' pain, too.

"I loved my grandmother so much, and we had such an

enormous bond, that losing her left this huge gash in my heart. When I had something on my mind, talking it over with her was especially gratifying because she saw life through divine eyes, and so the 'answer'—as she saw it—was always a simple and non-complicated one. It was just so perfect for me. *She* was just so perfect for me. My grandmother soothed, mended and expanded parts of me in the ways only she could. The loneliness I feel for her is so extreme, still, that on some days, I just can't get it together. Worse, on some days I go into this 'funk,' this depression.

"My sadness over her death was the beginning of not only grieving for her, but grieving for me as well. In mourning her, it was like the floodgates had opened and a dam of hurts, pains and minor transgressions (which suddenly felt like huge injustices) came cascading down. Traumas, dramas and ills from seemingly every corner of my life (from early childhood to present) came gushing out. I grieved for every imaginable loss there was, from the death of my favorite pet to my favorite uncle who had died the year before. I longed for those times you took me to school each morning. For me, these were cherished times because you were always so loving and positive. When I was dropped off for school, I felt upbeat and at my personal best. That these times were a thing of the past suddenly seemed unfair—even though at that time, I couldn't wait to have a car so I could drive to school on my own.

"I mourned for the carefree times of being a child—even though they seemed anything but simple then. It was as though there had been a million and one losses from childhood and my teen years. Worse, apparently I'd swept them under a rug and not dealt with them—either because my world was too busy to be bothered by grieving for them at the time or because I didn't want to deal with them then. Who does? When a good friend betrays you, it's not like you dwell on it for long, or at least not for as long as your heart is hurting. You're a teen; you're cool. You have to act like it's no big deal because you have other friends—and it's not like you want others to see you 'weak.'

"But when Grandma died, suddenly my heart refused to delay grieving for any pain, past or present. I just wept—for the longest time. This, too, produced a surprise for me. I wondered how sadness could be so intense and last for such a long time. My tears—a reservoir of tears—were endless. There were tears over missing Grandma, and tears for the kitty I had to give away because we couldn't keep her where we lived. There were tears for having to sell my beloved horse (even when it was my deci- sion); tears for the beautiful and sunlit bedroom I'd decorated and then had to leave behind because we sold that house and bought another.

"There were tears for the days of being a high-school athlete when I was a valued member of several sport teams, and for my many like-minded friends who'd even given me a nickname (a real sign of belonging); and tears for that friend who betrayed me. There were tears for a friendship that ended badly; for the boyfriend's heart I broke because I went out with someone new *before* I officially broke off with him. There were tears for the heartthrob who left for college and found a new sweetheart. There were tears for bygone days of living with my parents where a hug and a bowl of my favorite sugar cereal was just an arm's length away. It was an endless list.

"In the months following Grandma's death, I felt as though I were going to drown in all the despair I felt at remembering and mourning all these things—which, of course, made me miss her even more! I knew I needed comforting. Then came the crush- ing realization: My grandmother, always the first person I turned to when I needed as much comforting as I needed now, was gone.

"It was a seriously low point in my life, one that seemed to take me deeper into my sadness—a paralyzing one. I felt guilty that I couldn't comfort you more than I did. You'd lost your very own mother—your twin soul in the world. I believed your loss to be even greater than my own. I wanted to soothe you, but I couldn't. I was too depleted—which made me feel even more helpless, and in a way, useless—which added to my own feeling of inadequacy. This produced even more pain.

"I needed a lifeline, but was too fragile to call out or communicate clearly to get the help I desperately needed. It was a harrowing time. My pain reached a point where I seriously worried about myself!"

"Jennifer, my heart feels your pain, now and then, too. My mother, your grandmother, was such an exquisite and loving woman in our lives. We will always miss her presence, even though you and I both feel that she is with us in spirit, still. It's good that we sought counseling to help us grieve for our loss and, to help us draw strength from the ways she loved us. It was also important to apply the consoling words from our family and friends."

"Mom, I've come to understand private pain as a way to love and honor our own inner God-Nature. Believing this has helped me accept—as opposed to reject—that part of me that is 'the griever' and that can be really important. But that doesn't mean we need to walk through our pain alone. Luckily for me, you've always had big antennae when it comes to my feelings, so you always know what's up. That we can tell when others are hurting is good news.

"Luckily, the more we try to hide our pain, the larger it gets, and the more tender we get, so it's as though we shine a spotlight on our pains—which is probably the intention of hurting in the first place. Hurting helps remind us how fragile we really are, and shows us how much we need each other. In reaching out, we draw closer and are strengthened by this unity. In turn, sharing our burdens lightens our load. It's in this way that we are each a *taste berry* to each other."

The pain we feel may be nature's way of telling us it's time to take notice of our inner-selves—and to take extra good care of ourselves. Should you be facing painful times, rather than suffer alone or resort to doing things that are self-destructive (such as using alcohol or drugs), we urge you to reach out to get the help and support you need. Maybe you believe that no one will empathize with you—because it can be difficult to see another's worry, concern and pain as being as significant as you see it. Maybe you feel you shouldn't expose your pain—since you're supposed to be cool and act like you can handle things. Maybe you feel the price for revealing your pain is too big to pay, that you may get more scrutiny and even lose some privileges for fear you aren't as capable or "strong" as others—parents, teachers, friends—thought you to be.

Even though you may feel that no one can help you get *over* your pain, the important thing is to reach out. Here are seven positive ways to cope with private pain.

Positive Ways to Cope with Private Pain

1. **Don't trivialize your pain; *hurting* is a symptom.** Whether you're deeply saddened over a breakup with a special someone, or grieving over the death of a loved one, what's most important is that you recognize "hurting" for what it is: a symptom, a siren or bell that sounds when your heart and soul are in need of your personal attention. It's time to "tune in," not "tune out."

2. **Don't keep it all inside; talk about what hurts.** Talking about what hurts is an important first step in coping. Even if you feel that no one can do anything to make the hurt go away, talking to someone can ease the weight of painful feelings. Confide in someone you trust with your feelings. Tell your parents. If you feel you can't talk with them, talk with a favorite aunt or uncle, a grandma or grandpa, a special teacher, the school nurse, counselor or principal, the pastor or bishop of your church. The important thing is to not harbor your pain, or to think that others will think less

of you for needing their help and support in changing or getting through the situation you're facing.

3. **Join a support group (or start one).** Support groups, whether teens helping teens or adults helping teens, are an excellent way of working through the pains of life. Check to see if your school offers "Peer Counseling"—a certified program where teens are trained to help teens. Also check to see if your church has a similar program (many do), and be sure to ask your mom or dad if their place of employment offers a program to assist teens (again, many do).

4. **See a professional counselor.** A trained professional is an excellent way to work through painful times. Ask your parents or school nurse or counselor to help you find one. If you're looking for a counselor without their help, begin by looking in the social services section of the yellow pages for the various agencies that assist teens. Once you find a professional who specializes in working with teens, ask what he or she charges. Also check to see if your family's health insurance covers all or a portion of the assistance you are seeking. (In special circumstances, counseling may be without a cost. Ask so you know for sure.)

5. **Allow your faith to comfort and guide you through painful times.** Drawing on the strength and power of a loving and caring power is the essence of faith. You may do this privately or with the guidance of a clergyperson.

6. **Be extra good to you.** Especially when life hurts, it's time to take extra good care of you. In addition to talking things over with others, get adequate rest, eat properly, and get the exercise your body needs to burn off tension. Be patient with yourself, take time to relax and listen to soothing music, and don't forget those extra hugs for your pet. You know what a source of comfort you are to others; be sure to be that for yourself, as well.

7. **Journal.** Keeping a journal is a good way to "talk" about

what's on your mind. Because it's private, it allows you to say those things you may not yet be ready to say to someone else. And it's a good way to measure your progress of working through and "getting to the other side" of things. Be sure to date each entry; that way when you read how you felt about something a week or a month ago, and then read how you feel about it today or yesterday, you'll see how you are coping. Should you feel things aren't getting better, that is good information, too. It means you may need more outside comfort and support than you're getting.

In this unit, teens share their stories of hurt-filled times and how they are working toward (or have reached) the other side. As we learn from the teens in this unit, as painful as their stories are, such times can help us be more resilient, more accepting and thrive in a difficult world. If your life is pain-free, we hope that reading these stories helps you develop compassion and empathy for those who are going through such a hard time and be inspired by their courage.

May we all take to heart the sage advice of philosopher Rumi in the beautifully touching quote: "Be a lamp, or a lifeboat, or a ladder. Help someone's soul heal. Walk out of your house like a shepherd." So if you see someone hurting, be gentle, kind and loving. It's what a taste berry is all about.

❤ *Taste berries to you, Bettie and Jennifer Youngs*

Adopted at Age Thirteen

When I was two, my parents divorced. Even though my parents weren't married, my father and I were always together—on weekends, holidays and for six weeks each summer. I was his "spoiled princess." Even being so young, I knew I was the "apple of his eye." It was great!

Then one summer (when I was six) my father tried to convince me that my mother was an evil person and hated me. He also said that I should tell the judge at the courthouse that she was mean to me and tried to hurt me—and that I loved my daddy more than I did my mother and wanted to live with him full time. That confused me, because I knew my mother loved me, and she was never mean to me.

The next thing I knew, I wasn't allowed to be with my father again without a social worker present. When I asked the social worker why she had to be along, she said it was for my protection so that my father wouldn't hurt me. That seemed strange to me, because my father never hurt me—and having someone tag along with us was really an intrusion of the happy times spent with my father.

Then, for my seventh birthday, my dad promised to take me to Disney World. On the day he was to pick me up, I waited and waited for him. He never came.

I didn't hear from him again until my twelfth birthday—when he sent me a birthday card congratulating me on turning eleven!

My mother has remarried. Her new husband is a nice person, and I do appreciate all the things he does for me and all the ways he tries to fill in as my father. Still, having someone "fill in" is not the same as your own father. I miss my dad—even though I'm angry with him, too.

When my friends talk about their dads, especially about all the cool things they're doing or the vacations they take together,

I miss my father even more. When they tell me about all the time they spend with their dads or the things they get—like cleats for soccer or gloves for baseball or clothes for school—I resent my own father for no longer buying me things. He once did. And when their dads spend time with them, like attend their school athletic competitions—and sometimes come and sit in the stands just to watch them practice—I'm sad that my own father isn't there. Obviously, he doesn't want to be there. I miss him and feel as though I've literally lost my father.

Now, my new stepdad is in the process of adopting me. I have very mixed emotions about this. One day, I want it to happen, the next I don't. But, regardless of what I want, it's going to happen. Maybe it will be good in that we will all be a family with the same last name and all. And maybe this will help my stepfather feel that I'm worth all the time he spends with me, because after all, I'll have his last name, too. Maybe then I'll be as spoiled by my stepfather as I was by my father. I watch him with my three-year-old half-brother—his son with my mother—and it's easy to tell he adores his "real" son. My stepfather has a daughter from a previous marriage. He sees her every weekend, and he's never late picking her up. Plus, he always calls her and he's always making sure everything is okay in her life.

So I'm hoping that my being adopted will make my life better, and that I'll feel like I have a real father again. Going through the adoption isn't easy, but I am looking forward to all of us kids having the same last name. I wish we all had the same blood, but that's never going to be. But at least with the adoption, I'll be able to tell my friends, "My dad . . ." But like I said, I'm hesitant, too. I wonder if next year I will feel okay about having been adopted, or ten years from now when I hope to be married and have kids of my own. And I worry what my real father will say when he learns of the adoption. Right now, the adoption is top secret, because my mother doesn't want any more legal hassles than necessary from my father or his relatives—especially from his parents, my grandparents.

Sometimes I think that if parents could see how much they hurt their children, hopefully, they'd try not to. It's really hard to watch your parents be so mad and mean to each other and even harder when you're in the middle—especially when you're young, and there's not a lot you can do about it.

When I get married and have kids, I'm going to make very sure that my husband is "Mr. Right." I can tell you right now that if he's not, I will not have kids with him. I will not let my children go through an experience like this.

Cara James, 13

February 12, 2000, 3:56 A.M.

The fair comes to our town once a year. For days before it arrives, it's the most talked-about event—and most definitely a topic of discussion for a long time after it's gone on to the next town. *Everyone* goes. "Being there" is very cool for the obvious reasons: It's a fun way to let loose with your friends and a great place for people-watching—especially to see some *new faces* from other schools around town!

It was Friday, the opening night of the fair, and everyone I knew was "amped" to go! It's very cool to go opening night, so of course my two best friends (Ashley and Stacy) and I decided we'd go. But the "best" time to be at the fair is between midnight and closing time (which is 3:00 A.M.)—called "Midnight Madness." So the three of us got permission from our parents to go to Midnight Madness—and off we went. We had *so* much fun and hoped to return again the next night.

I asked my parents, but they said we had "family plans" and I needed to be well-rested, so I couldn't go the second evening "but maybe the following evening." So I called Stacy, who said she couldn't go the second evening either. She'd gotten a baby-sitting job, but hoped to go the third evening. Stacy said she'd call Ashley with the news that the two of us couldn't go on the second night, and to see if we could cook up plans to go on the third night.

As it turned out, Ashley already had permission from her parents to attend the second night, and so she made plans with another friend of ours, Angelique. She said she'd also go with us on the third night.

We never got that opportunity.

Ashley and Angelique had gone to Midnight Madness as planned on the second night. At closing time, they'd planned to take a cab back to Angelique's house. But as they were waiting to catch the cab, two guys from their school saw them and asked if they'd like to go get something to eat and then catch a ride home. Who wouldn't take that offer? Both Angelique and Ashley did.

Maybe it was because it was a very foggy night. Maybe it was because of an unexpected turn coming all too quickly. Or maybe it was because the car—traveling at seventy miles an hour—hit the curb, bounced off and went airborne, sailing approximately fifteen feet before it hit a tree. Maybe it was because the five people in the car weren't wearing seatbelts. Maybe it was because the driver was more preoccupied with what was going on inside the car than out, or was fooling with the car stereo. Or maybe something fell onto the floorboard and he reached to get it; or maybe he was dodging an animal in the road. *Who knows?* That fateful night, my friend—and one other person in the car— lost their lives. At exactly 3:56 in the morning, February 12, 2000, Ashley died. They said she was killed instantly on impact.

My friend, Ashley, is dead.

Ashley dead? When I got the news, it was like I couldn't take another breath. Dead! Even now, I can't really believe it—for sure I don't want to. How terribly much I miss her. It feels like a piece of my life has been taken. I have lost the person who knew me so well, maybe even better than anyone else. The friend I exchanged clothes with and tried new things with, shopped at the mall with, talked about boys with, traded lipstick and dreams with. We had talked on the phone . . . literally hours before she died!

Every night in my dreams I try to put the pieces together of what happened that fateful night. And always there is this haunting about how I could have been in that car that night. It's a terrible reality and one I never discuss with anyone else.

I am saddened. On some days I walk around in a complete daze. Who would have ever imagined that when the fair came to town it would leave among its memories a tragedy such as this? I don't think I will ever be able to go to the fair again. For sure, I will never see my best friend again. I've come away from all this with a new respect for safety. The moment I get in anyone's car, I put on my seat belt, and when I'm in a car with my friends, while it's easy to get distracted, I'm always aware of what's going on and how it affects the driver and his or her attention to the road. And I have a very real respect for life, and how precious—and fleeting—it is.

Megan Demonbreun, 16

I'm in Love—A "Goner," as They Say

We met at a very crowded party—and were instantly drawn to each other. Unfortunately, he and his friends had plans to leave early, so we didn't have much time together. When his two friends announced they were leaving, he said good-bye and turned to leave. I missed him instantly and felt pangs of panic, too. He must have been feeling the same way because just as he reached the door, he turned back, searching the room. I hoped—but knew, too—he was looking for me.

I was right. Spotting me, his eyes lit up and he edged his way back through the crowd and asked me for my phone number. I'd already written it down on the corner of a napkin. He took it, repeated the number twice, and then handed it back to me. Obviously, he wanted to show me that he'd logged my number in his head, thoroughly memorized. I was thoroughly impressed—and took it as yet another sign of our powerful and unmistakable connection.

I was also totally and completely in love—"a goner," as my friends say.

He called the very next day. I'd been planning a little Fourth of July get-together for a handful of friends. "I'm there," he said when I asked him to come. And then, while the fireworks were filling the sky with splendor and magic, he pulled me close and said, "I've got feelings for you. Be mine." Just like that. It was a perfect moment, a perfect party and now, I had a perfect life. I knew beyond a shadow of a doubt, this was the man I'd marry; this was the person with whom I'd share my life. He'd be the father of my children and the person with whom I'd grow old. This was my partner—for life. It had been so simple. A chance meeting, and suddenly my life was bursting with magic. I knew we were meant to be. Soul mate was a term that now applied to me. To us.

We attended different schools, but saw each other as much as we could. We dated every Saturday night, and sometimes he would drive over to my house during the week. We called each other every day—and dearly missed each other when we were apart. I loved being with him. And I loved that feeling of feeling so lovesick when we weren't together. I was so sure of him, so sure of us, that I gave myself completely to him.

Maybe that's what went wrong—the giving of myself to him. For two months we were hot and heavy, and then, things changed. At first I couldn't quite put my finger on just exactly what had gone wrong; I only knew that our togetherness had lost its sweetness—and our relationship had become mostly a physical one.

"What's wrong?" I asked.

"What do you mean?" came the reply.

"I miss the way we were," I said. "Things seem so different."

He offered excuses about why we couldn't be together more often: homework, the part-time job, time with friends, things like that. Standing alone, the excuses made sense until he said, "Get off my back, will you?" It was an expression said in a tone I would never have imagined from him.

Two days later, his "we need to talk" call came. He said that he'd been friends with a girl he'd known for a long time and had "feelings for her."

So how does that work? How could he have feelings for me and suddenly turn them off and have "feelings" for someone else? I am completely confused how love can come barreling in your life and be such a sure thing, and then with the speed of a bullet train, leave you standing in the dust—alone.

I am devastated.

He's gone, off to the new girl for whom he has "feelings."

I am so brokenhearted.

I think back on every moment, from the time we met to our last phone call. I examine everything a hundred times. I'm still trying to figure out what went wrong. If we'd taken things more slowly, would things have been different between us—is that the reason? I don't know. I only know that it hurts just to see his cards and love letters—and there were many.

I can't stop seeing the two of them together. It's indescribably painful to know that it is someone else—and not me—who receives his love letters and his phone calls now; and that it is someone other than me who gets to feel the touch of his kiss and the warmth of his hand holding on so tightly.

This isn't the first time I've been in love or had love fall apart. But it's the first time I know for sure that every breakup does *not* feel the same. This is an around-the-clock heartache. I'd wanted him forever. But all I have right now is a heartache that feels as though it will last forever. I do know it won't, of course.

I'm coping as best as I can. I'm staying close to my parents and good friends; they all know what's going on, and they're all being so kind to me—which feels really good. My best girlfriend says I should start dating right away. I'm not ready just yet, though I do go with my friends to our crowd's hangout. It feels good just to be around friends—but not "with" anyone right now. But I know in time, I will. Just as I know that in time, there will be another soul mate out there for me.

Katerina Marie Kothen, 18

Crohn's: Feeling Freaky

I love sports. When I was eleven, I was named most valuable player on the West Denison softball team. When I turned twelve, I became too ill to play sports of any kind.

It started off as stomach pains. But then the pains got so bad I couldn't eat. Sometimes it hurt to breathe. My stepmom took me to the Cleveland Clinic for tests. The test showed I had ulcers! I was put on a special diet—no spicy foods—and I had to take three different kinds of pills every day. It was inconvenient, but I could live with it.

But the next year, my problems got worse. My intestines started bleeding inside, and they cracked open. I was rushed to the clinic, and I received my first blood transfusion. For two weeks, they ran painful tests. They said my ulcers had turned into Crohn's disease. That year, I spent a lot of time at the Cleveland Clinic. My life had changed so much. I missed being on the baseball team the most—but I wasn't even able to walk that well, let alone tear around the bases.

By the time I turned fourteen, I was taking seven different pills and was sick more than I was well. I had to be home-schooled. I missed school and being with all my friends all day long. When you don't spend time with your friends on a regular basis, they soon forget about you. Even the ones who in the beginning came over quite a bit, soon stopped coming around. I was so lonely without them. Then depression set in, as did other health problems. I became diabetic and needed to control it by injecting myself with insulin (three shots a day!). I was a mess. I couldn't eat the food I needed for Crohn's because I was a diabetic. And vice versa. It felt like a bread and water diet. By this time, I felt my life sucked! It was not very much fun being me.

By the time I turned fifteen, I was positively sure that things couldn't get worse: Wrong again! Now I'd also become anemic. One night I laid on my bed staring at the ceiling, listening to music and just praying that there would be a time—and real soon—that I would be free of these terrible and crazy diseases. Well, it's finally beginning to happen. My life is starting to improve. I'm finally off my shots, and I'm no longer a diabetic. I am not anemic either. And I can walk, so I can do a lot more. I still can't play ball, but I've got my fingers crossed. I'm back attending school—and recently I made the honor roll! The only disease I have is Crohn's, and it's in remission—so I'm feeling hopeful. I have friends now, and a boyfriend, too. He is very special.

Although my life is getting better, I will never really have the same life as my friends because my health is "fragile." I have to "take it easy," when instead I'd like to return to my life as I once knew it. And boy does that seem like a long time ago! So be good to those you meet. Have a good heart and a generous spirit to wish them well. Just normal life is pretty tough for a teen; battling things such as I went through is incredibly tough—which can make one's life feel unbearable. So, just be really nice to everyone you meet.

Jessica Mossage, 17

A Letter to My Darling

Six days ago, my dog had puppies, seven of them—four "boys" and three "girls." She's a wonderful mother, constantly feeding them, licking them and looking out for them—watching their every move. It's just amazing to see how fiercely she protects them.

As I watch the mother dog guarding and protecting her puppies, my stomach sickens, and I am saddened beyond words. Oh my little darling, I'd like to think that I would have protected you with all my being as does the mother dog her puppies.

But I didn't.

Oh, Honey, I don't know how to begin writing this letter to you. I only know I must. How do I explain things? I suppose it doesn't make any difference if I tell you that I was *advised* to have the abortion—because in the end I did. Still, it's incredibly important to me to let you know that what happened had nothing to do with you—you did nothing wrong; there was nothing *wrong* with *YOU*. You were an innocent little person who wanted to be born.

I couldn't believe I had a baby growing inside me. I was so terribly afraid. I don't even know how to do algebra yet. But that doesn't change the facts. What I've done will haunt my body and mind forever. I wish I could go back in time and never get pregnant in the first place. An *abortion*. It sounded harsh to my ears even then. Now I can hardly say the word because it is so cruel. It was also a terrible and harsh insult on my body. And on my heart, as well.

I'd like to think that you were a little girl; at least my heart tells me so. In my mind, I picture you as a tiny little thing with pink soft skin and large brown eyes—like mine. My secret name for you little girl is *Hope*. It's a pretty name, isn't it? I've named you this because I have a lot of hopes for you—even if it will take some time before any of them can come true. My little Hope, I can tell you that I am really scared about all the things that have happened. I don't know how to tell you that I'm sorry, but I am. I'm sorry for me, too, and for the "us" that could have been. This whole thing has made me begin to think seriously about heaven. I'd like to think that even though I've made this big mistake, you and I will still meet again—in heaven. I've seen it a hundred thousand times in my mind—we see each other and run to be in each other's arms.

When I pray, I pray for you and me. I hope that you're looking down on me because then you can see that every day I think of you. And you'll know that I love you more than anything else in the whole world.

Please forgive me for hurting you in the ways I have. I love you little darling. When I am older, will you come to me again? Please give me another chance to care for you, to guard you and protect you. Know that I will. I promise you this with all my heart.

Love, your mommy—still.

Samil Ousley, 15

Child of the Lost

Sometimes I feel like a child of the lost
With nowhere to go
No one to run to
A dark little angel with a very dark past.

Everywhere I turn
It seems like a stranger in the dark shadows
Engulfs me
Follows me
Haunts me.
No relief
No end in sight
From this painful stress-filled life.

Memory haunting memory
Of that troubled child inside
Wishing for:
A shoulder to lean on
A safe sure hand to hold
A loving heart to talk with
A trusting soul in whom to confide
A someone to lead me
Out of the darkness
And into the sunshine.

Where is that someone?
I'm searching
And I know you are there
My heart tells me so
Everyone cares
About everyone

Most especially,
Those who feel
Like a child of the lost.

Sahah Botzek, 14

Why Do You Talk to Me That Way?

I love my mom; I really do. But I'm so hurt over the way she treats me. Sometimes I feel as though she doesn't like me, but I really try not to believe that. The problem is, she's so negative. She often yells and swears at me—which really hurts my feelings. And she has a way of putting me down that makes me feel bad about myself.

She doesn't get home from work until around 6:30. The moment she's home she starts in, making comments like, "I suppose you haven't done your homework, yet. Right?" or, "So tell me, how late were you in getting home from school today?" Should she be checking to see how I did on an assignment or test at school, instead of just asking, she'll say, "Tell me you didn't fail your test! Did you?" I think it's a really terrible way of talking to someone you're supposed to love. It's always about looking at the negative side of things, thinking I haven't done what I'm supposed to do. I'm wrong even before I begin.

It makes me sad. The other day I was in my room, and she was yelling, and I thought, *Why doesn't she just remember all the nice things I've done for her, like the extra special thought and time I put into getting her things like Christmas and Mother's Day presents? Even flowers when there isn't a special occasion.* I believe that if my mother would stop and think about how considerate I am of her feelings, she would think of me as more special than she obviously does.

I know things aren't this way for every teen. When I go to the house of other friends, their mothers talk nicely, even sweetly to them. They say things like, "Have you done your homework, Sweetie?" That's a far cry from my mother. It's disappointing.

I wish my mother could understand how she makes me feel. Every insult feels like a blow. It hurts, and I can't talk back or scream back and tell her how it feels, because that will only make things worse. I'll lose phone privileges and then suffer the consequences of not being able to talk with my friends.

I need her to love me—and want her to love me. I've talked this over with my friends, and they suggest that I just tell her how she makes me feel bad. I don't think that will make us feel closer. I've also talked to my school counselor, who has been very helpful suggesting ways I can tell my mother about my feelings and get more positive results. So far I've tried several things the counselor suggested—like when my mother does say something loving and supportive, I give her feedback right away on how great that makes me feel. I can see this approach is paying off, because when I tell my mom how good that makes me feel, both of us feel close, and then for the next couple of hours, there is a good mood around the house. So, I'm hoping things get better. I'm doing my part and hoping my mom will do hers.

Ashley Lin, 12

A Football State of Mind

In the fall, Friday is *always* the best day of the whole week, first, because the school week is over, and also because Friday is the day of our high school's football games! At our school, these games are always a big deal. Practically everyone in town attends! Everyone! Maybe it's because we live in Texas (the football state), or maybe it's that in Katy, Texas, football isn't just a sport, it's a way of life! For sure it's how my brother Kyle, and his best friend, Trey, felt. Both were good players with serious intentions to one day play pro football. Everyone knew they would: "Nothing but pigskins in their futures!" everyone said.

My dad was a big fan and supporter of our school, and in particular, his son and Trey (who my dad called his "second son"). My dad had wanted to be a professional football player himself, but a knee injury his senior year in college derailed his plans. So my father was really excited to have his son "go all the way" in a football career. When my father and "sons" were together, you could be sure they'd be talking "football."

If regular Friday night football was "huge," homecoming was larger than life! It wasn't just our school and the parents of students at our school who attended. People came from miles around to watch homecoming games—die-hard fans who came wearing T-shirts, sweatshirts, hats and other garb—all in school colors. Maybe it was the energy and expectations of the crowd, or maybe our players were just always great, or maybe it was just something in the air—whatever it was, in the history of our school, our school NEVER, ever, lost a homecoming game.

Homecoming was fast approaching. Everyone was buzzing around in preparation. Floats were being designed; the school was bathed in rah-rah signs; teams of kids were selling advertising slots throughout the town for the game day's program of activities. And of course, the football team was hard at work—or harder at work than for regular games. The school had a new coach, and with a record of solid wins to follow, he knew he needed to make darn sure "his" team won this game.

I know I was looking forward to it—and hoping my date for the big game was a certain football guy—Trey! Though we weren't "an item," he and I had eyes for each other, and I was hoping that the big dance following the homecoming game would be the time when we hooked up. It was intuition on my part, because he hadn't asked me formally to the dance, though he had asked if I'd come to his practices the week prior to homecoming—which of course, I did! Every opportunity he got, Trey would look up at the bleachers to see if I was there, and when he saw me, he'd wave. And when he'd just made an especially cool play, he'd look to see if I'd been watching. I had!

Two days before homecoming, as soon I got home from school, my mother told me we had to leave immediately for the hospital. Trey had landed on his head in football practice and had a concussion. The doctors told him that he'd be "fine," but even so, he shouldn't get his hopes up about playing in the homecoming game. I knew that had to disappoint him. But even though he wasn't going to play, the next day, he still went to practice. The coach said it was too soon for him to play (for fear of getting hurt again). But Trey wanted to practice and play Friday night, and said he was up for it. Still the coach wouldn't put him in. So that night Trey came over to speak to my dad, telling him he wanted in and could my dad please convince the coach how important it was he play in the homecoming game.

My dad told him, "No way," that it was too dangerous. So though I knew Trey would probably sit with his team, I was hopeful that he just might sit with me in the bleachers. The next day was homecoming, and everyone was anticipating a spectacular night! Kyle told my parents that he was going to meet up with Trey for a quick pregame dinner at a favorite teen hangout and then head over to the school. He asked me if I wanted to come, and I absolutely did. We waited at the restaurant, but Trey never came. We thought that was odd, since he and my brother were the best of friends, and Trey just wouldn't stand my brother up like that. So my brother called home to see if Trey had called and changed where to meet up. My dad informed us that Trey had called, saying he had a headache and was going to skip meeting us at the restaurant, and instead, rest up and then meet Kyle at the game.

When my brother and I arrived at the playing field, Trey still had not arrived. And, he still hadn't arrived by the time our school band played the opening pregame ceremonies. Nor had he arrived for the game kickoff. Trey never played in the homecoming game that night. On the way to the game, Trey had blacked out, and as a result, his car had careened into a light pole.

He died on impact.

When I heard the news, I closed my eyes and just cried. My brother sank to his knees and beat the ground with his fists, calling out, "No! No!" It was so heartbreaking to watch. It was the last football game at our school that I attended. Nor has my brother taken the field again. He said he was too scared that something like that might happen to him.

We don't talk too much about football in our family any more, but we do talk about Trey. At first no one wanted to mention his name, but for the past month, we've had a family counselor who comes to the house, and we all sit on the couch and talk about things. Sometimes we talk about our feelings about missing Trey, but mostly we talk about listening to and supporting each other. I've noticed that the more we do this, the more we are starting to talk about Trey again. My brother has even mentioned that he may try out for spring training next year at college.

So, we're all getting on with our lives now, but the death of our friend is something we will never forget. For me, there is a sadness I carry—for the friendship I will never have with Trey, and for the ways he was a friend to my family. Trey definitely left a piece of his heart with all who knew him.

Amber Mendoza, 16

In Person

I wish I could see you today,
In person,
Talk with you,
Tell you about what's going on
Ask you how I should handle things
Pray together as we used to do.

I know you're in a "better place," still,
I miss our bond, our soul connection,
Knowing that for the rest of my life,
No one will ever love me as deeply as you did.
I miss the heart-to-heart talks—
Discussing the plight of the world, the nature of bees.

I miss our laughter, and the knowing smiles we exchanged,
I miss loving someone as much as we loved each other—and all
    the ways we knew it.
I miss the things we used to do
    to honor, support and encourage each other.
You knew me inside and out—my highs, my lows
You helped me work through the tough stuff,
Showed me why and how to choose the best road, the "high
    road,"
You had the right words to soothe, comfort and reassure
You were so wise and good
I feel so alone without you—and sometimes, even lost.
Some days are longer than others
It's those times when I'd most like to see your shining eyes, your
    smiling face
To hug each other the way we did, as you slowly stroked my hair.
I keep hearing these voices in my head,

I wrestle with them a lot these days
They keep telling me to go to church.
I do, of course,
But so far, Mom, it hasn't stopped the pain of not having you here
In person,
To talk with,
To share what's going on
To ask you about how I should handle things,
And to pray together as we used to do.

Bettie B. Youngs

Acting Lessons

I'm so surprised to be here,
It was such an awesome start.
What began a playful liking
Ended up a broken heart.

I didn't see it coming,
But now it all makes sense,
And sad as it may seem
I guess I'm pretty dense.

You seemed embarrassed to be seen with me,
Yet in private, called me "cute" and "sweet,"
When alone you teased and flirted,
But with friends mocked, "What a geek!"

I tried to justify it all as just a "stage,"
And, "Hang in there; it will end."
But what about those two faces,
One for me—and one for your friends?

So it's time to gather up the pieces,
To put me back together once again,
To find someone more evolved
One face, one act, one friend.

Brooke Drake, 15

Part 8

Dear Dr. Youngs: What Should I Do?

*At some point in your life,
you have to be willing to take the
circumstance that's been handed to you
and make something out of it.*

—Gloria Wilder-Brathwaite, M.D.

*What is the meaning of life?
The great revelation never did come.
Instead there were little daily miracles,
illuminations, matches struck
unexpectedly in the dark.*

—Virginia Woolf

A Word from the Authors

We work with hundreds and hundreds of teens across the nation, either in workshops within their schools, or after having read one or more of our books in the *Taste Berries for Teens* series, a teen submits a story of his or her own for one of our upcoming books (in which case we work with teens via mail, phone or e-mail). As you can imagine, along the way we make many friends and get a chance to talk about many of the things going on in the busy lives of today's teens.

As always, we are most interested in learning all the positive things teens are doing, and all the ways they are making a difference within their families, schools and communities. In other words, being a taste berry. As authors, and in keeping with our taste-berry theme (a definition explained in the introduction of this book), we primarily publish those stories (by teens for teens) showing how real teens are personally working through real-life issues and doing so in "taste-berry" style—giving it their personal best.

But many times, teens aren't writing, calling or e-mailing to offer advice to other teens, but rather, because they're looking for an "answer" to a particular problem they're facing. Among the most "popular" questions are those centering on these themes:

Self-improvement:

- I want to be more popular (or "cool"). What can I do?
- I get teased about the way I look (hair, weight, complexion, clothing style). What can I do?
- Other kids in my school have more friends than I do; how can I have more friends?
- A lot of the kids in my school are diagnosed with things such as bipolar disorder, anorexia, bulimia, dyslexia, ADHD or a learning disorder of one type or another. I feel depressed all the time, and sometimes have really weird thoughts. How do I find out if anything is wrong with me—if one of those "labels" applies to me? If so, what then?

Friendships:

- A certain someone and I have been best friends for a couple of years. But I can sense that now he/she is pulling away. He/she doesn't want to talk about it, so now what do I do to find out what is wrong? I want to stay friends.
- My best friend and I used to confide in each other only. But now she/he wants to be friends with a lot of other students in our school. What can I do to convince my friend to be just *my* friend?
- My good friend is using drugs (or drinking). It's really messing up my friend—he's/she's starting to skip school and be in trouble all the time. What can I do?
- Someone I thought was a true friend has started "back-stabbing" me (saying or doing things that are not support-ive) to the other kids at school. How can I get my friend to stop? (I've tried telling her to stop, but she only laughs it off and says, "Oh, you know I was only kidding!")

Love (and sex):

- My good friend has started flirting with my boy/girlfriend. How do I find out if anything is going on between them?
- I'm being pressured to have sex. What is the best "line" to use—because I don't want to break up? I just do not want to have sex yet.
- I think I (or a good friend) might be pregnant. I'm scared. How can I find out for sure, and if I am, what should I do then?
- My boy/girlfriend is always giving me ultimatums. How do I get him/her to back off—without breaking up?
- I really would like to have a boy/girlfriend. Nothing I've done so far seems to be working. Is there something I'm doing wrong?

Coping with bereavement/grieving/inner sadness:

- Several months ago, my grandma (grandpa/friend/class-mate/pet) died. I can't stop thinking about it. I'm so sad, and I cry all the time. What can I do to make some of the pain I feel go away?
- My friend's little brother (sister/cousin) died from leukemia (cancer/car crash/accident). What can I say (or do) to make her/him feel less sad?
- I feel "down" all the time. Is this normal?

The rumor mill:

- There is a rumor going around at school about me (or a friend). It feels creepy to walk down the halls having every-one stare in my direction, and I know they're saying things about me (or my friend). What can I do?
- I started a rumor around school, and everyone knows I did it. The thing is, everyone seems to be upset with me. What can I do now?

- A nasty rumor is circulating around about me. Unfortunately, it's true. What can I do to clean up my reputation?

Threats/harassment:

- A kid at school has threatened to "kick my butt" if I don't turn over my lunch money (allow him/her to copy my homework; be his/her "gopher"/"stooge"). I know he's/she's serious about it. What can I do?
- There are a couple of kids at our school who yell, swear and/or threaten some of the others. We try to ignore them or deal with their taunts as best we can, but with all the school shootings, there are some of us who are afraid that maybe the bullies will eventually do something really bad. What is the best thing to do so that no one gets hurt—and so that those who "tell" won't get found out?

Parent issues:

- I want a longer curfew. How do I convince my parents to let me stay out later?
- My mother/father always pries into what's going on between my friends and me. They even call my friends' parents to check on things. I get embarrassed and my friends don't like it. What can I do to make them stop—and to trust me more than they do?
- My mother/father yells at me all the time. How can I get her/him to talk to me like a normal person?
- I think I'm going to be getting a lower grade than expected in a class at school. My parents are going to be really upset. How can I prepare them ahead of time so I don't get put on restriction?

Whether wanting to know how to help your friend through a problem they're facing, or wanting to know the best way to get through one of your own, teens everywhere are looking for answers. While we answer as many of these letters as we can, we can't get around to all of them. So in this book, we've decided to share with you some of the "Dear Dr. Youngs, can you help me . . ." letters we receive—along with our responses to them. By doing so, we hope that you will be encouraged and supported in working through the problems and concerns you may be facing.

We've noticed that for the teens seeking advice, many explain their problem and then inform us that the problem they're "wading through" has been going on for some time. Sometimes a problem lingers because we're afraid to *implement* the best or most logical "answer"—either because we lack courage or fear the consequence of doing so. For example, sometimes, no matter how difficult it is to disclose to your parents a secret you've been harboring, you should—because you need them on board to help you. This was true for a teen you'll read about in this unit, who made friends with a girl who, as it turned out, was involved in illegal activities. The point is, the sooner her mother was aware of the problem, the quicker she was relieved of feeling it was hers and hers alone to work through.

Another reason a problem can linger (causing you stress and anguish in the meanwhile) is because, even though you may know how best to resolve it, you may be reluctant to take action. Sometimes the solution to a particular problem calls for a hard, swift and certain action—*now*. Sometimes there is no better way to handle things than to "draw a line in the sand" and move forward. For example, maybe you know that a relationship with a special someone is not a healthy one, and that you really must break up with that person—even if your heart is hoping you'll stay "just a little longer"—as is the case for a teen in this unit. And sometimes, it's not so much about finding a "solution" to a problem, as much as it is a matter of working through a feeling or emotion—such as when someone you care about moves away, becomes very ill or even dies. While others can offer comfort and soothing, only time and devotion to your feelings can lessen the pain you're feeling.

As always, we remind you that you mustn't feel that you have to solve all problems on your own—nor should you. Some problems are far too complex—even dangerous—to work through alone. This is particularly true should you be feeling despondent, suspect you are pregnant, are using drugs or alcohol, or facing emotional or physical abuse. As always, we encourage you to confide in a trusted adult friend. That person may not have the "answer" either—or the one you're hoping to hear—but discussing it can help the two of you decide who is best qualified to help you work it through. And, of course, you are welcome to write to us. In the true spirit of a taste berry, we will help you as best as we can, or refer you to those we believe can be of help.

❤ *Taste berries to you, Bettie and Jennifer Youngs*

I'm Afraid to Ask . . .
a Special Someone . . .

Dear Dr. Youngs,

My problem is not as serious as making world hunger go away, but it's pretty serious to me. I'd like Tara Blane to go with me to the homecoming dance—which is only a couple of weeks away—but I'm too afraid to ask her. Tara doesn't have a boyfriend yet, but there are 103 guys in our school, and I'm sure that with the exception of about ten who already have girlfriends, every last one of them would like to ask her to the dance.

Tara is positively the best and nicest girl in our class. She is also the epitome of cool—unlike me! Every time I see her, I drop things and trip over my own feet. When she's standing nearby or talks to me, I turn beet red and get so tongue-tied that I can hardly speak. And when I do, honestly, sometimes the dumbest things come out of my mouth. I mean, I'm a total mess—which is one reason I'm afraid of just walking up to her and asking her to the dance.

I'm amazed that she doesn't think I'm an idiot—but I don't think she does, because whenever she sees me she says "Hi!" She even waves at me when she sees me from a distance, and just last week, she was sitting with a group of girls after school in the bleachers watching our soccer team practice. When I noticed her, she waved—so that's got to mean something.

Even so, I'd be totally devastated if I asked her to the dance and she said "No." I don't think I could handle the rejection. I mean, it would almost be better to not ask and at least think she hasn't shut me out. So, I don't know what to do. Do you think I should just wait for the night of the dance and then go up to her and ask her to dance (though if another boy asks her to the dance, she will probably feel obligated to dance with only him—because in our school, that's sort of one of the rules for "proper behavior")? Or, do you think it would be best just to write her a note and get it to her somehow? What do you think is the best way to ask a girl like Tara to the homecoming dance?

Brian Burres, 16

Dear Brian,

Every day we get letters asking pretty much the same thing about the opposite sex: "I'm wanting to be with so-and-so but afraid to take the first step to doing that, or afraid that whatever it is I do, I'll be turned down." First, I'd like to answer your question, "What do you think is the best way to ask a girl like Tara to the school dance?" The best way is to go up to her and simply say, "Would you like to go with me to the homecoming dance?"

Since that probably sounds too intimidating for you to do right now, here is a simple but effective exercise that can help you rally the courage to ask out a special someone. Go to your bathroom, close the door, and then, standing in front of the mirror, have a talk with yourself. It should follow these steps:

1. *Reassure yourself.* "Brian, you are a nice guy, and Tara deserves the chance to be asked to the dance by you. But she can't say 'Yes' (or 'No') unless you ask."

2. *Motivate yourself to take action.* "Brian, you know that if you don't ask Tara soon, she may get asked to the dance by one of those 103 other guys at school, and then you won't even get to have one dance with her. So, you'd better hop to it; ask ASAP!"

3. *Rehearse all the possible things likely to come out of your mouth, and then decide on the best option—the best way to say it in a positive way.* For example:
   - "So, ah, well, are you thinking of going to the home-coming dance?"

- "Hey, Tara, want to go out with me sometime—like maybe the homecoming dance?"
- "Tara, I'd like to ask you to go with me to the homecoming dance."

THE BEST THING FOR ME TO SAY TO TARA: *"Tara, I'd like to ask you to go with me to the homecoming dance."*

4. *Rehearse all the possible things she could say.*
   - She could say, "Oh, I'd love to! Yes!"
   - She could say, "Oh, I'd love to—but I've already promised someone I'd go with him" (or her—maybe she has already made plans to attend with a girlfriend).

5. *Think of how you should best respond to what you think she will say.* This will help you sound cool with whatever she says—whether it's "yes" or "no"—and possibly, to overcome any objections. For example:
   She says: *"Oh, I'd love to! Yes!"*
   You say: *"Cool! Let's (and then clarify arrangements) . . ."*
   She says: *"Oh, I'd love to—but I've already promised I'd go with Connie."*
   You say: *"I see. Well, then I'll see you there—and you can count on my asking you to dance!"* or you say, *"I know that my friend Juan has been wanting to ask Connie out. Do you think Connie would like to double-date with Juan and the four of us could go to the dance together?"*
   She says: *"Oh, I'd love to—but I've already promised another boy I'd go with him."*
   You say: *"I knew I shouldn't have waited so long to ask you. By the way, I've got soccer practice tomorrow after school. Maybe you and your friends can stop by again. It was really great seeing you there!"*

6. *Decide when is the best time to make your request.* "Tara is usually alone at her locker after school while putting her

books away. This is a good time for me to go up to her and ask her to the homecoming dance."

Of course, there are other possible things that could be said, but you get the idea. The goal of "self" dialogue is to give yourself a heads-up on possible ways the conversation could go, and to be prepared for what you might say in each instance. Doing this can help you feel confident in handling the stress you will no doubt feel, and therefore, give you the continued courage to see yourself through the situation of asking. Preparing yourself in advance makes sense in that it also helps you avoid becoming flustered, tongue-tied, or saying something really dumb or inappropriate.

I wish you the best of luck, Brian. And remember, Tara can't say "yes" or "no" unless and until you ask. And here's something to keep in mind, Brian. Just in case the very worst thing in all the world should happen—Tara says "no" to going to the dance with such a swell guy as you—you might consider asking her for a date to something else, perhaps a movie in the next week or so. If she says "no"—and gives you two "lame" excuses in a row (or you see—or hear—that she "likes" someone else)—you might want to take another count on how many other girls in your school are still without boyfriends. There just may be another girl who would also be fun to go with to that dance—or movie. Just as you are wishing and hoping Tara will go with you, you just never know when another special someone in your school is feeling that way about you. Just checking! And remember, if you wait too long to ask Tara, it may be your only next best option!

❤ *Taste berries to you, Dr. Bettie B. Youngs*

A Hurting Heart

Dear Dr. Youngs,

I had just become friends with a boy in one of my classes at school—Alex Perez. He seemed like a cool guy—we both liked baseball, collected cards and were computer "geeks." I'd noticed him around but it wasn't until we worked on a class project together that we hit it off. I had a feeling he and I were going to become very good friends, and we did. Then, a couple of months later, I got some terrible news.

I got to my first period class and noticed right away that there wasn't any "today's assignment" on the blackboard—which is something the teacher *always* posts every single day. Something else was different, too. Usually the teacher starts teaching the minute the bell rings, but on this day she sat at her desk, sorting through papers. She even let us talk amongst ourselves *after* the bell rang. Then, within a few minutes, the principal, along with several people in suits and carrying clipboards, walked in. Our teacher must have been expecting them, because at that point, while they stood in the front of the room near her desk, she stood up and told us: "Class, I'm sorry to have to tell you of the unexpected death of one of your classmates." Instantly, we all looked around to see who was missing. I already knew that Alex's chair was empty. The teacher continued saying, "Your friend and classmate, Alex Perez, passed away this morning after collapsing in his driveway."

Alex, dead? I was shocked. I had never heard of anyone so young "collapsing" and dying. Why did he collapse? As the teacher's words sank in, I could feel my heart sink. Alex was only thirteen.

No one in our class said anything; we just sat there staring at the teacher, our eyes wide and mouths open. The adults in the room looked at each other, and then at us, and then at each other.

I was looking at the teacher but thinking about Alex. It was just two days ago that we'd worked together on a really big class project, and just last night—at 7:30 to be exact—he called me to ask if I knew the steps to retrieve a lost file on his new Samsung SyncMaster 770 computer. (It was just like mine.) Just twelve hours from that phone call, he was dead. It didn't seem possible. Or true.

The rest of that entire class period, we talked about how we would always have memories of Alex and how we could cope with grief. We each talked about what a nice person Alex was, and how he said and did nice things so we should remember all the good times. Two boys told the class that they had been mean to him and said how sorry they were. So then the counselors talked about how we could "get beyond" those kinds of thoughts. That got me to remembering how once he'd asked me to loan him thirty-five cents for a library fine, and I told him I didn't have thirty-five cents, but I did. I just didn't want to give it to him because I was saving it to buy candy at the store on my way home. Now, I wished I'd given him the money. Then the adults in the room told us we had the option of eating in the classroom with our teacher, or in the cafeteria, sitting in groups of ten at a table with an individual counselor assigned to that particular table. Then, my class was given cookies and told we could get up and walk around and talk with our friends.

My mom took a friend and me to the funeral. Everybody cried. I couldn't. Then, at the burial service we were all handed a purple balloon and told that right after the pastor said, "Ashes to ashes, dust to dust," we all were to release the balloons. Everyone did, except me. It seemed to me that letting go of the balloon meant I had to let go of Alex, so I handed it to the boy next to me. I'm wondering if what I did—not letting go of the balloon—was wrong. I've got another question, too. I can't stop thinking about Alex, and it seems to me like they've forgotten him—like when they released their balloons, they released the memories of Alex, too. How can I feel so different? Is it because I didn't release the balloon?

Daniel Greteman, 13

Dear Daniel,

My heart goes out to you. To lose a friend so young is difficult for anyone to understand. It will help that your school has made available to you and your classmates those trained professionals who can help you understand and cope with the loss of someone you cared about. Also, check to see if your school offers Peer Counseling, which is a group of teens trained to talk with other teens and help them cope with their feelings.

I'd like to tell you a little bit about the nature of grief itself. *Grief is our body's way of telling us how beautifully human it is that our hearts can care about another human being so much that we actually hurt when we are without the fellowship and companionship of that special person.* The friendship you had with Alex was special, and now all the expectations you held for the two of you to share time together are no longer. While you are sorry that Alex is no longer living, you are understandably sorry *for yourself,* too—sorry that you have to give up spending time together. It's a big loss.

Sudden death of a friend can also be a fearful experience, one that is difficult to understand. So, in addition to continuing the grief counseling provided by your school, here are some other things you can do.

1. *You can still have "talks" with your friend.* Just as you sometimes talk to yourself, you can also have "talks" with Alex. Do this when you are thinking of him. You can do this when sitting alone, when you have private moments. Your "talks" can be out loud or simply moments of silence. Tell Alex that you miss him and that you're sad he's not here,

and thank him for all the good times. The point to all this
is to express your feelings.

2. *Do things in honor of your friend.* Consider all the ways you
can remember Alex. Whether you vow that you will be kind
and more thoughtful to those around you, or while up to
bat say, "Alex, this grand slam is for you, buddy!," all can
be done in the name of honoring your good friend, Alex.

3. *Give yourself all the time you need to grieve.* Grieving knows
no time line. Expect that you will feel many different emotions in the year ahead, and allow yourself the freedom of
expressing these feelings without judging them. Think
back to how you felt at the service when everyone expected
you to release your balloon, but you couldn't—because
you weren't ready to. You were right in doing what you
did.

4. *Celebrate the passing of your pain.* You will always remember
Alex, which is why it is said that memories are another
chance at happiness. In time, and with the love and support and understanding of family and friends, your feelings of pain will subside, and the wonderful and positive
memories of the friendship you shared will be the ones you
remember the most. So, *when you are ready,* get a new balloon, take it to a special place—and let go of the balloon.
And remember, letting go of the balloon is only a symbol.
It doesn't ever mean you let go of all the ways you and
Alex shared the journey of a boyhood friendship, nor that
you will ever forget him. Grieving is not about forgetting.
It is about expressing your being human—which includes
the gift to *feel* all of the things you do. You're in our hearts
and prayers.

❤ *Taste berries to you, Dr. Bettie B. Youngs*

Ultimatums

Dear Dr. Youngs,

My girlfriend, Stella Anne Harding, has given me an ultimatum: Either I pick her up in a car and take her out on dates—or she finds a new boyfriend! Right now, our dating depends on double-dating with friends who have cars, or having our parents drop us off at the movies, school events or other places we're going. But Stella Anne doesn't like this setup and constantly reminds me that she knows plenty of guys—with cars—who are just dying to take her out. I know it's true. Stella Anne could look at a guy and he'd be drooling. If she decided she wanted to go out with that guy, he'd be there in a heartbeat!

This ultimatum, my entire quality of life—everything—depends on passing my driver's license test and being able to use the family car. Added to this stress is that passing the driver's test is not as easy as it sounds; my friend Tom Jennings has failed it twice so far! Plus, my parents have tied my using the car to getting good grades. So now I'm not only practicing for my driver's test, I'm also spending all kinds of extra time studying for all my classes so none of my grades fall. Any slip-up, whether it's grades, or being late for class or curfew could end up meaning not having a car even when I've finally gotten my license. All this is really stressing me out right now—most especially when I see guys who have wheels flirt with Stella Anne. My question is, how do I get Stella Anne to cut me some slack with the ultimatum thing?

Zach Shields, 16
(excerpted from A Taste-Berry Teen's Guide
to Managing the Stress and Pressures of Life*)*

Dear Zach,

No one likes to be under the pressure of an ultimatum. When the stakes are "too high," an ultimatum creates stress and pressure that can actually prevent you from being at your best and doing your best. In handling your girlfriend's ultimatum, here's what you should do:

1. *Talk to Stella Anne.* Tell her that you'd like to be her boyfriend, and then reassure her that you are doing your best working toward getting your driver's license (and that it's your goal, too). In the meantime, it's important for you to stay committed to getting good grades so as to earn the use of the family car once you have your license.
2. *Ask her to turn down the pressure.* Then, tell your girlfriend that you would like her to be more understanding about things and not turn up the pressure (any more than it is).

Should Stella Anne not be understanding and supportive of you as you work toward getting your license and earning the use of the family car, and should she continue to "threaten" to go out with others, then you might want to let her make good on that. You must decide not to be treated in this way (bullied via threats).

There's something else you must consider, too, Zach. As you mentioned, you're under a lot of stress: What are you doing to relieve the stress and pressure you feel from all this? I hope you're taking good care of yourself—eating nutritiously, getting adequate rest and exercise, and surrounding yourself with family and friends and others who like you just the way you are—without ultimatums.

❤ *Taste berries to you, Dr. Bettie B. Youngs*

Are You the One for Me?

Dear Dr. Youngs,

I just knew that when I had a boyfriend, life would be great—especially if that boy was Sean Harrison. Every single day I'd read my horoscope (his, too) to see what the universe had in mind for us. Always it said stuff like, "Follow your heart!" or "Take charge! Get what you want out of life!" I especially liked the assurance of the one that read, "Love is waiting in the wings!" I even clipped all three out and hung them on my mirror.

Becoming Sean's girlfriend wasn't a piece of cake! You can't believe the lengths I went to, to make it happen: At lunchtime I'd search for the table he and his friends were sitting at and then get as close to it as I could; I'd walk past his locker every chance I got and sometimes, I'd get a hall pass and walk by a class in which his seat was near the door. Sometimes, like when he was doing his work and didn't look up (once I purposely dropped a notebook so he would!) I even walked by twice—which was a little embarrassing, because I knew a couple of the students sitting around him caught on as to what I was doing. All in all, it was pretty stressful, but in an exciting sort of way.

Then one day, just as destiny had in mind, Sean asked me out. Little did I know it was only the beginning of my stress. He asked me out on a Tuesday for the following Friday. I was stressed the whole time, waiting for Friday to arrive. We went to a movie and then met up with some friends for a pizza, so it was a fun first date. But then, starting the very moment I got home, a new stress set in: Would he ask me out again?

Well, he did. You'd think that would have ended my anxiety, but it didn't. The following week, I wondered all week long what he was going to do on the weekend, and whether or not I was included in those plans. Even after we'd been dating three weeks, I stressed out over whether or not we'd be "a couple"—

and when! After a month of dating, he told me he was "serious" about me. You'd think that would have made me relax, but it only brought new worries. Whenever I see a girl talk with him, I get jealous and wonder if she's trying to steal him away from me. So now I keep tabs on him—which basically has me behaving like I did when I was first wanting him to notice me (not to mention that I'm accumulating a lot of "tardy" passes).

Though now I feel secure that he's "my guy," I have a whole new issue: He's too possessive and demanding. I'm not kidding. I just don't seem to have any time for my friends anymore. And when I do spend time with them, I feel like I have to answer to Sean and apologize for being with them and not with him. I don't like it that I don't get to decide how I spend my time without explaining myself. And, he expects me to be in the bleachers at practically every one of his practices (he plays football and baseball)—which I find very boring. I mean, I want to be with him, but not spend an hour (and sometimes an hour and a half) every day after school while he's out on the field. I'm getting so behind in my homework. I tried taking it with me, but the wind blows my papers around half the time—it's just not working. (And that's the daily stuff; I'm way behind in the big term papers, too.) And though this may sound stupid, I'm not sure I want to French kiss either. All my friends do, but to me, exchanging saliva with someone is not cool. See, I worry about things like that, too, because maybe that I don't want to French kiss (I love regular kissing!) means I don't really love him as much as I think I do.

Here's the thing: I'm very surprised at my feelings. I mean, for such a long time I wanted Sean to be my boyfriend, and now that he is, I have problems I never expected. I want to have a boyfriend, and I'm pretty sure I want Sean, but how I feel makes me question if I want to be as "steady" as he expects. But I don't want to break up, because trust me, Trina Durrant would be with him the very next day. So for now, I've been reluctant to "make waves"—meaning, I haven't said anything to him.

I'm so confused. One day I'm crazy in love and just want to be with him even if that means my homework isn't done. The next day, I'd rather get my homework done on time and then go hang out with my friends. One day I feel secure knowing he loves me as much as he does, but the next, I'm checking up on him (well actually, I'm mostly keeping an eye on Trina Durrant) just to be sure. It seems to me that I'm always stressed out about something! What does it all mean? Why are my feelings all over the map like this?

Sierra Sherman, 16

Dear Sierra,

Why are your feelings "all over the map"? It sounds like you're letting Sean rule the relationship: Are you?

Sierra, a relationship is a two-way thing. As you've learned, a relationship is about *discovering* what another person is like—his (or her) personality, likes and dislikes and so on. For example, when you were at the stage of trying to get Sean's attention, perhaps it didn't dawn on you that there could even be such a thing as Sean wanting to be around "too much." But now you're finding that Sean takes up more time than you'd like. Have you told him?

Sierra, having a special someone in your life shouldn't mean that you have to give up being you, or stop enjoying time with your friends. Nor does it mean that you should stop leading *your* life—attending to your homework and things. *Why are you doing that?* You have friends with whom you want to spend time, and homework that needs to get done. That you have a special someone in your life doesn't mean other things in your life come to a halt. But, it may not be Sean's entire fault. If you haven't told your boyfriend about your likes and dislikes, then how does he *know* what they are? For example, have you told Sean that you simply can't afford—nor do you especially enjoy—the time spent in the bleachers at his practice times? You have to. If you don't, then expect him to continue making his demands—and do not be upset with him for doing so.

You have to be willing to set *boundaries*—the sooner, the better. Boundaries (where you draw the line for what happens) are about you knowing what you want and need, and standing your ground in bringing these about. Ask yourself questions such as:

- Does my special someone treat me fairly (where my feelings count as much as his own)?
- Does he respect my needs (such as time with friends, homework, family demands and curfew)?
- Does he comfort me when I'm going through a rough time?
- Does he cheer me on and encourage me?
- Is he a good listener?
- Does he offer congratulations when I'm a winning, shining star?
- What are the rules for flirting with others? How far is "too far"?
- Do I want to French kiss, or not?

Talk with Sean. Once he knows how you feel about these things—if he's "a keeper"—he'll revise his demands. If he doesn't, then just as the horoscope clippings on your mirror suggest, "Take charge!" and set your heart on a "win-win" relationship. "Get what you want out of life." If Sean balks, rest assured that, as your horoscope suggests, "Love is waiting in the wings!"

So stop stressing out and take action. And speaking of stress, stop worrying about Trina Durrant. Sean has chosen to be with you. And, I'd like to encourage you to discuss your feelings with someone you feel you can confide in. Having a sounding board is always a good thing and can help you make up your own mind about what is best for you to do—whether or not it's supported by your daily horoscope.

❤ *Taste berries to you, Dr. Bettie B. Youngs*

The Rumor Going Around

Dear Dr. Youngs,

I'm devastated! I've just heard a nasty rumor circulating around school about me. It feels as though everyone just sort of stares at me, like I've come down with the plague or something. It's so unfair: No one in school has a clue if I prefer cheese or pepperoni pizza, but they say things about me as though they *know* me. I'm so upset; I just want to go live in another country! What do I do now?

Dana Jennings, 17

Dear Dana,

A rumor, true or not, is a violation of our private self, and therefore, is painful. But, even if you'd like to go live in another country, unless you have a passport, going abroad is out of the question. So, you'll have to hang tough, go to your classes and keep up your regular schedule. You haven't said what the rumor is, but here are some options:

1. *Think things over before taking action.* This can help you keep your cool—and feel less vulnerable, less like a target, and more in control. Take stock of the situation: What exactly is being said? Who is doing the talking. (Is it a disgruntled "ex" or everyone in the entire universe?)

2. *Decide on a game plan.* Go ahead, get out your pencil and paper and write down (so you can see your thinking) what you feel are possible options. For example:

   • "It had to be Brenda! I'm going to start a juicy rumor about her! That'll teach her!" *(This is a bad idea because Brenda will probably say other things, making your life even more miserable and, of course, maybe it wasn't Brenda who started the rumor.)*

- "I'm going to do and say nothing until I have an opportunity to talk with my good friend about this. That will
  give me a better read on this." *(A good idea.)*
- "I'm going to talk over this whole matter with my counselor." *(A great idea!)*

3. *If the rumor isn't going to change your life, be gracious and do
   nothing.* The good news is that rumors eventually die out
   and life goes on (just think back to what you've learned
   about rumors from elementary years to date). So if you feel
   the rumor is a silly one, or so preposterous only a fool would
   believe it, do nothing. Sometimes you can attract unwanted
   attention if you respond (and the rumor will persist—maybe
   even grow). So if you feel that trying to counter it will only
   exacerbate the issue (this is assuming, of course, the rumor
   is not slanderous or dangerous), then leave it alone and do
   nothing.

   A special warning to all readers: *If what you hear going
   around is slanderous, sounds like a threat or is potentially dangerous, report it at once. For example, if you hear that someone
   has brought a weapon to school or that someone is suicidal, report
   it to the principal, a teacher or counselor, or tell your parents
   immediately. Rumors (and most especially those that even
   remotely sound like a threat of any kind toward others) are not to
   be joked about or taken lightly. Confide in an adult, discussing
   what you've heard, even who said it. And don't worry about
   "being a snitch"; you may be saving someone's life.*

4. *Confront the person who started the rumor.* If you know who
   started the rumor (or is spreading it), go to that person and
   say something such as, "The word is out that you are saying XXX about me. Is there a reason you find it necessary to
   do this?" If what is being said hurts your feelings, tell that
   person so: "I feel hurt that this rumor is going around, and
   I'd like you to please stop spreading it."

5. *Enlist the help of an "influential friend."* Can you get your most influential friends to dispel the notion of any "heavy top-secret" stuff? Often, a classmate who is admired and looked up to by others can go a long way toward helping classmates dispel the rumor or realize such gossip is not welcomed.

6. *Share your feelings with someone whom you trust.* Even though you may not want to explain yourself, or feel embarrassed about what you have to disclose (the rumor), confide in someone with whom you trust—a teacher, counselor, school nurse, principal, your mom or dad, or clergy. Regardless of whether or not the rumor is a nasty one (and sometimes they all feel this way), or not necessarily true, don't feel you have to cope with it alone, nor that it's yours to resolve on your own. Don't feel guilty or "wimpy" for reaching out. When left unchecked, behavior such as a rumor can make everyone feel vulnerable and unprotected. If the rumor is being circulated at school, the principal will want to know. It is his or her job to see to it that the schoolplace not be an environment where students take potshots at other students.

Rumors hurt. Even so, don't fight back unfairly. Getting back can be temping, but "taking the high road"—being a taste berry—means not putting others in a position *you* find uncomfortable to be in. And here's something else to think about, Dana. Would your reputation benefit from classmates knowing you better? Because if you'd like for your classmates to know you so well that they even know your pizza preference, you may have to be the one who makes sure they do. Are you open and courteous and friendly with your classmates? Do you smile? Are you a good listener? Maybe you are, I'm just checking, because usually it's the little things that win friends. I'm sorry you've had this happen to you. Friends, true friends, don't hurt others via thoughtless and cruel comments that can only serve to diminish their self-esteem.

Hang tough, Dana. Be on your side and be yourself. Remember, the best friend is the face you see in your mirror, and it's her reputation with you that matters the most. And, if you feel you simply cannot bear facing your classmates one day longer, then you may want to ask your parents if you can apply to be a foreign exchange student (you'll still need a passport)!

❤ *Taste berries to you, Dr. Bettie B. Youngs*

Bad Choice of Words

Dear Dr. Youngs,

I play on my school's basketball team. I love playing (I even love going to practice!) and I'm a pretty good ballplayer. I'm usually one of the first team members to get to the lockers, change my clothes and hit the practice floor. Some of my team members hang out with their friends or boyfriends until the last minute to get to practice, and I think that's cool, too. My problem is that while I love basketball, I'm humiliated by the taunts and jeers—aimed at me—coming from the bleachers during the game.

Believe it or not, these "comments" come from my mother! She'll say things like, "Take the shot—NOW! I said 'NOW!'" or goad, "Get up there! Hustle that butt of yours!" I really get embarrassed when she says that—which she does a lot. "You can do better than that!" is another one of her "encouraging" lines, as is "Make me proud, baby!" or "Don't disappoint your school!"

Just two weeks ago, our team was one point behind our opponents, and there were only six seconds to go in the game. I had possession of the ball and then, because I'd been fouled, was awarded a free throw. So there I was, standing at the free throw line, nervous as all get-out because our team winning the game depended on my scoring these critical points. The crowd was going wild: "Take it easy!" "You can do it, Angie!" "Concentrate!" So I'm standing there, bouncing the ball a couple of times, trying to regain my concentration, when suddenly I hear my mom yell, "If you miss this shot, you'll be *walking* home!" It was so humiliating.

I took the shot. The ball missed the hoop, and the buzzer let everyone know the visiting team won.

Mom didn't make me walk home, but the ride home with her was silent. We pulled in to the drive, and just as I was getting out of the car I said, "Why do you always act like my playing is all about you?"

"I just want to be proud of you, that's all," came her reply.

I wanted to say, "Does my missing a shot or even having an off-game once in a while mean you're not proud of me?" But I didn't because I knew she'd have another "zinger" ready to toss my way, and I was exhausted—and bummed that we'd lost the game. But I was still upset and so I slammed the car door extra hard. Then, as I was heading off to my room I said sarcastically, "Gee, I'm sorry I don't live up to the daughter you had in mind!" I timed my comment so that I'd reached my room, and because it felt good, I slammed the door to my room extra hard, too.

I couldn't hear all of her words, but she was yelling at me for slamming the doors—and probably saying other things, too. The thing is, I just detest the tension that arises between my mother and me during and especially after my games. From my standpoint, it begins with her comments during the game—I don't understand why she says the negative things she says. I mean, does she think her comments mean I'll play better or feel less nervous? There's always a lot of pressure when you're on the court and trying your best to stay focused and play well. Does she think the things she says won't hurt my feelings? Does she really care if my team wins? I'm beginning to question it. I want to know what I can do to get her to stop.

Angie Tyson, 17

Dear Angie,

You certainly have a right to feel upset and hurt by the comments coming your way from your mother in the bleachers. You're not alone in wishing a parent (or a stepparent) were more understanding and supportive of your feelings in a given situation.

What you really want your mother to know is that her

comments hurt and embarrass you; they make you feel self-conscious and distract you from doing your best while playing. Your mother needs to hear this from you—and not just as a jab as you get out of the car or head off to your room. *You* need to communicate more clearly—effectively—with your mother. In short, the change must begin with you (which is good news, because it puts you in a leadership position—not a helpless one).

Here's what you can do:

1. *Get clear on the goal you have in mind.* For example, rather than sending your mother the "I'm mad about this" message, your goal is to send a message that says, "I need you to be supportive of me and show good sportsmanship at the game."

2. *Change the way you deliver your words to your mother.* The "You'd-better-interpret-my-slamming-doors-as-'I'm-mad-at-you'" reaction isn't really all that effective in changing things for the better. Instead, communicate clearly what you wish to have happen. Say, "Mom, I need you to be on *my* side. When you say things like 'Hustle that butt of yours' or 'If you don't make this point, you'll be walking home,' it embarrasses me in front of my team, the coach and everyone watching. Saying those things only makes me feel down on myself and doesn't help me play better. I'd like you to be more positive. When you encourage me with positive statements I feel encouragement to do my best. Please root *for* me. When you do, I play better, and I feel closer to you. And that's important to me."

3. *Choose a "good time" to deliver the message.* If it's possible, hold this conversation with your mom at a time when you're both in a "good space," when there is goodwill going on between you. That way, your mother is sure to hear your words as constructive criticism and not as an

attack on her. If you don't see a good opening, try setting one up. Say, "Mom, I'd like to talk to you about something really important. Do you think we can have a nice talk over dinner tonight?"

Try this and see for yourself the difference it makes. I'm betting that it helps your mother take a good look at what she's been doing, apologize and turn in a better performance at your next game. If at the next game she continues to heckle you in ways that you've asked her to forgo, then you should talk with your coach and explain things (it must embarrass him or her as well). Your coach probably already has an idea about what's going on, and it's very likely he or she would be most agreeable to discuss with your mother the importance of positive support.

And, if that fails, then tell your mother you prefer it if she not attend your games. We're wishing you the best in your discussion with your mother and rooting for a "win" at your next ballgame!

❤ *Taste berries to you, Dr. Bettie B. Youngs*

When a Friend Gets Involved . . .

Dear Dr. Youngs,

My older sister started hanging out with Lindsey Conrad who is a year older than she is. Lindsey is really outgoing and has a lot of friends, many of whom are already out of school (some have graduated, others dropped out). My sister told me that she thought Lindsey was really cool, and liked hanging out with her—even though Lindsey was always in trouble with her parents over something. Lindsey told my sister that her parents were simply too strict, and since practically every teenager thinks their parents are too strict, I didn't think Lindsey's always being in trouble with her parents meant she was a bad person or anything.

My sister had been hanging around with Lindsey for almost two months when she discovered her new friend was doing some pretty awful things (like stealing from clothing stores). My sister told me what she had found out about Lindsey, and told me not to say a word about it to anyone. I could tell my sister was getting concerned, but I don't think she knew what to do about it. Then, about a week after my sister had told me about Lindsey's stealing clothes from stores, I told my mother about it. My mom found a shoebox filled with clothing tags.

Of course, my mother asked my sister about this box of clothing tags. My sister told her that she was keeping them for Lindsey—so her parents wouldn't find them. She also came clean with my mom about what was going on. She told Mom that she was pretty sure that Lindsey was stealing clothes from local stores and selling or exchanging them for money so she could buy beer and pot. She said that once Lindsey stole a miniskirt when my sister was with her, and made her swear not to tell anyone, "or else." That was also when Lindsey told my sister to keep the tags for her.

My sister told Mom how frightened she was for Lindsey—but didn't know what to do. My mom told my sister she should no longer be Lindsey's friend. My sister said she'd already told Lindsey she didn't want to be her friend any longer, but that Lindsey threatened that if my sister didn't stay "loyal," she'd tell everyone terrible stories about her, including that she was stealing, too (which she wasn't).

I'm frightened for my sister and want to know how to help her.

Kristin Maas, 14

Dear Kristin,

Probably the best thing that could have happened is that your mother discovered the clothing tags. Now your sister no longer has to harbor the secret of the theft and has a trusted adult in her camp. Your mother will know how to help your sister withdraw from a "friend" who is breaking the law and in need of help to get free of her drug use (and stealing). Rather than being frightened for your sister, feel relieved knowing that your mom is on board.

Both you and your sister would be wise to depend on your mother's advice now. Ask your mother what she plans to do (for example, is she going to contact Lindsey's parents?). Since you two sisters and Lindsey attend the same school, she may also wish to get the school counselor involved in knowing what's going on. It's doubtful that Lindsey will remain at school (she may end up in juvenile hall), but if she does, you need not fear harassment or threats from Lindsey in "keeping quiet, or else." Your principal and teachers see it as their responsibility to do everything they can to make sure students do not suffer emotional stress and duress—as well as physical threats—inflicted by other students.

And don't feel guilty about Lindsey's being found out. While

Lindsey may get in trouble for now, in the end you will have done her a favor. Drug use and thieving can lead to nowhere but even bigger trouble than she is already in.

And stay close to your sister right now. Just as this whole thing was frightening to you, you can imagine that it was for your sister, too. Tell her you're proud that she leveled with your mom, and that you feel it was the right thing for her to have done.

Good for you for having the courage to confront this scary situation, and for your efforts in supporting your sister. You are a real taste berry—which brings us to something else you can do. You've been through a lot right now, too. Now that your sister is getting the help and support she needs, you need to go about life with your friends, too.

♥ *Taste berries to you, Dr. Bettie B. Youngs*

How Do I Stop?

Dear Dr. Youngs,

I've got a problem I hope you can help me with. I started drinking every once in awhile with my friends. We don't drink all of the time, just when we get together on the weekends. Now many of my friends have started smoking pot, too. Well, I don't know how most of my friends are able to take or it or leave it, but I'm afraid I've become addicted, because I can't stop on my own. In fact, I think my problem is getting worse. Sometimes I use pot during school hours, and I'm beginning to drink and smoke pot every day as soon as I get home from school. So far no one has caught me, but I can tell it's affecting me. I'm having a lot of trouble staying awake in school, and in the last month, I've been suspended for truancy three times. Plus, I'm losing some of my friends because I owe practically everybody money, and I have no way to pay it back. And I think friends are beginning to suspect that I'm stealing liquor from their homes—because several have confronted me about it. (My parents haven't questioned me on using theirs, but it's because they rarely drink and I'm pretty sure they just haven't discovered it yet.) I know everything's going to get worse for me if I don't stop. What can I do so I don't get any worse?

Byron McReilly, 16

Dear Byron,

Here are some things you must do to break free of your alcohol and chemical dependency.

1. *Tell your parents.* Even if you think they will be upset, even if you feel you have let your parents down, tell them anyway. Yes, at first they will be upset because they'll be frightened for you and disappointed that this problem has

befallen their child. Just as you have to sort out your feelings, they will, too. They may even feel guilty—like they've let you down in some way—and it might be the reason you're using. But, your well-being is their number-one concern, so brave their reaction and know that your parents will do all they can to get you the help you need. (They will need some help, too, and luckily, it's available.)

2. *Get into a treatment program.* With or without your parents' help or support, this step is crucial. But do begin with your parents. They may have insurance benefits to help cover the cost of the treatment and care you need. (Another option is to ask your family doctor, clergyperson, school nurse or counselor where to go for treatment.)

The treatment program will depend upon its availability to you, and what you and a professional feel is best for you in breaking your addictions. You may need to go to a center that offers an "in-house" program—meaning you live within the treatment facility anywhere from seven to twenty-eight days. Or, maybe you need only go through a "detox" program, where a professional medical staff helps you through the period of cleansing your bloodstream from immediate dependency (this is usually a four- to seven-day process). This will then be followed by a prescribed treatment program. And, you may be able to break your addiction by attending weekly meetings with a trained "recovery" professional. You may need all of these. A trained professional can help you decide which is best for you.

3. *Join a support group.* Even if you go to an in-house treatment program, once out, don't stop there. You'll need help staying sober. It's a day-by-day process. Whether teens helping teens or adults helping teens, sharing your situation with others helps you stay committed to your goal of being drug- and alcohol-free. If you're choosing professional

help, they'll help you find these groups. But if you're doing it alone, look in the yellow pages for the hotline numbers of the various agencies that assist teens—such as Alcoholics Anonymous or Narcotics Anonymous—to find out when and where there are meetings near you. Also, do check to see if your school provides "Peer Counseling," a program where teens in schools are trained to support teens going through tough times.

I'm rooting for you! You can do it! You've already taken the first and most important step—recognizing you have a problem and not wanting it to continue. Stay in touch. We'd like to know how you're doing and share your progress with other teens so if they're facing a problem similar to yours, they'll better understand the "journey" of battling an addiction.

❤ *Taste berries to you, Dr. Bettie B. Youngs*

What Is an "Intervention"?

Dear Dr. Youngs,

My best friend told me her family held an "intervention" for her brother who has a serious problem with drugs. My friend didn't say anything else about it, because she said she'd "rather not talk about it." I think I have an idea of what an intervention means, but I'm not totally sure. I keep hearing other kids at school talking about someone they know who has had it happen to them. I really want to know what it is, but I can't ask my friend, and if it's something really serious or embarrassing, I'd rather not ask anyone I know. Could you explain it better to me?

Keri Brunner, 13

Dear Keri,

Alcohol and drugs are very addictive. Once you've started using, it's hard to stop without help. Often the person using doesn't even realize he or she has a problem: That person thinks he can stop whenever he "chooses." To admit how serious his using has become would mean he needs to stop using—except he can't. It's a vicious cycle. To help someone confront his or her problem and to accept help in quitting, an "intervention" takes place.

An intervention is where family members, friends and others who care about the person using—along with a trained professional—come together to confront the person using drugs with the facts about his or her behavior and how it is affecting each of them. Let's say it's decided that the intervention will be held within the teen's home. With the "addict"—the person who uses—in the room, each member who has gathered takes his turn to share with the addict how they love and care and are concerned for him. Taking turns, each one reports the facts about the hurtful actions ("I miss the close friendship we used to have" or, "I am so worried about your health and hope you will get the help you need") caused by his or her drug use. This helps prevent the addict from being able to deny that he or she has a problem. Then, that person is offered some treatment options so he or she can get help.

Intervention can be a very powerful process for freeing the addict from his or her denial of how much help is needed—which is a crucial first step on the road to recovery. And, it also shows that person how much he or she is loved and supported in getting free of drugs and staying clean. Hopefully, your friend's family experienced a successful intervention with their family member—and he is ready to accept help.

You say that your friend doesn't want to talk about this. Chances are, your friend (and the entire family) has been through a lot. Usually, by the time a family gets around to doing an intervention, drug (or alcohol) use has been wrecking havoc on all members of the family for some time. It's understandable that your friend is hesitant to talk about the intervention. These events are sometimes painful and very personal to the family, and information not easily shared for conversation outside the group. The best thing you can do for your friend is wait for her to feel comfortable in talking about it. She may never want to. Your thoughtfulness and concern are what really matters. It's exactly the meaning of being a taste berry.

❤ *Taste berries to you, Dr. Bettie B. Youngs*

Part 9

Who Is "Binky Poodleclip"? and Other Tantalizing Trivia Tidbits

Life is a jest, and all things show it;
I thought so once, but now I know it.

—John Gay

If you can't find the truth right where you are,
where else do you think you will find it?

—Jack Kornfield

A Word
from the Authors

What do the letters "S-O-S" (as in help!) stand for? The answer: Nothing, although some interpret them to mean "save our souls." The letters were chosen in Morse code as a distress signal because of their simplicity—three dots, three dashes and three dots. And speaking of tapping sounds, did you know that rabbits talk to each other by thumping their feet? Of course, when really distressed, they simply hightail it out of here! And speaking of "tailwinds" to get you from one place to the next, did you know that if the headwind is greater than a plane's maximum speed, the aircraft will fly backwards? It's true, and yet, no matter how low or high it flies, an airplane's shadow always appears the same size.

Speaking of flying, did you know that the only mammal that can fly is the bat? It can, and it's pretty fast, too, although who knows just exactly who, among all the creatures of the world, would win if there was a contest to see who could make a trip around the world in the best time! Consider this: A pig can run a 7.5-minute mile; a kangaroo can hop along at a clip of forty miles an hour; and a tuna swims at nine miles per hour! While nine miles an hour may not seem fast, a tuna never, ever, stops swimming! Now that's quite a feat, don't you think? Almost as amazing as the fact that a flea can jump more than a foot in a given bound (and in case you're wondering, that's comparable to a human leaping over the Washington Monument with plenty to spare)! Not to be left out of the "running" is the duck, who swims even when sleeping! Oh, and don't forget about the snail. Though it takes this little creature 115 days to travel one mile, consider the outcome of the race in the famed fable "The Hare and the Tortoise"!

Though we don't know how fast the average person walks a mile, we do know that the average person walks the equivalent of three times around the world in his or her lifetime! So, does that mean that President George Washington—who wore a size-thirteen shoe—would make the journey faster than say, General Robert E. Lee, who wore shoe size 4½? It depends if they make the journey the long way, or "as the crow flies." What route does the crow fly? It's a term that means "shortest distance." So if the crow (or you) were to travel "as the crow flies" from the East Coast to the West Coast in the United States, in what city should you begin, and in what city would you end up? The answer: You would start in Jacksonville, Florida, and travel a straight line to San Diego, California. And just in case you're wondering, that would be for a total of 2,092 miles. Of course, it might just be quicker to call: a telephone signal travels 100,000 miles a second!

Speaking of feet, did you know that a hummingbird cannot stand on its own two feet? The reason: Its feet are not strong enough to hold up the bird on a flat surface, which was pretty much the case of the tallest man in the world, Robert Wadlow, who was reported to be eight feet, eleven inches. He was just twenty-two years old when he died in 1949 (which was from an infection caused by leg braces he needed to keep him on his feet). And speaking of wings being better than feet to keep you upright, did you know that hummingbirds flap their wings eight hundred times per second, while bees flap their wings three hundred times a second? And speaking of flapping, did you know that the buzzing sound bees make comes from the rapid up-and-down movement of their wings? Buzz has it that the honeybee is the *only* bee that dies after stinging. And not to be trivialized is the fact that the bee is the only insect that produces food eaten by people!

Speaking of being eaten, did you know that sharks are ten times more likely to attack a male (person) than a female? And, while it sounds "fishy," it's true that fish become seasick if kept on board a boat or ship for longer than a couple of hours! And speaking of water creatures, did you know that the sound you hear in the seashell when you hold it up to your ear is not from the shell, but rather, it is the echo of the blood pulsing in your ear? Don't be disappointed: At least we can hear (did you know that your hearing is *not* as sharp on a full stomach?), which is not the case for turtles; they are stone-deaf—even with an empty stomach!

Being able to hear is a good thing, even if we have to put up with our ears being attached to our heads! Grasshoppers and crickets have their hearing organs on their legs! At least we have ears! Did you know that worms have no ears whatsoever (nor eyes)? As for hearing things, did you know that in Hawaii, when you hear the word "Aloha," it means both "hello" and "good-bye"! Not that you want to say "good-bye," in any language, but did you know that because of the reflux action of a rattlesnake, it can bite you up to a half an hour after it's dead? Sort of makes you want to stay out of the desert—speaking of which, did you know that only one-fifth of the Sahara Desert is sand? (The rest of the world's largest desert is barren rock and rubble!) And by the way, if someone is afraid of snakes, they are said to suffer from *ophidiophobia*. So now when someone appears squirmish at the sight of that snake in your science class, with your usual cool you can say, "What an ophidiophobic! It's only a snake for goodness sake."

If hearing the word *snakes* makes you shiver, you may want to go to the North Pole (because there are no snakes there), but if you do, don't expect to see any penguins (they reside south of the equator, *not* at the North Pole). You'll probably see some bears, though. Speaking of which, did you know that all polar bears are lefties? Not that it matters too much. Right hand or left hand, you'd be dinner just the same! Did you know that a flamingo can eat only when its head is upside-down, or that a snake has to close its eyes in order to swallow?

Speaking of being swallowed, did you know that the average person swallows 295 times when eating a meal? So how many swallows will it take for you to down a bag of M&M's? Only you have the answer to that one, but we can tell you that there are more brown M&M's than any other color in a package of that candy! Candy: Mmmm! Poor kitty cats—did you know their taste buds do not taste sweet things? What a loss, because who doesn't like candy? Just thinking of sweets can get the taste buds salivating—and by the way, did you know that the human produces more than 25,000 quarts of saliva in his or her lifetime! Speaking of which, did you know that a fly's taste buds are in its feet? Don't laugh, it's true—but if you do laugh, you'll burn up three and a half calories. No joking—though if you're planning a trip to outer space any time soon, it won't be necessary to watch your weight! Astronauts on the moon weigh only one-sixth of what they do on Earth! Even so, it's unlikely that NASA has plans to send clams—who can weigh almost five hundred pounds—up to space any time soon!

Five hundred pounds! That's a lot of eating! Speaking of which, did you know that the strongest muscle in the human body is the tongue (it's also the only muscle in your body that's attached at only one end). So if the tongue is the strongest muscle, which animal has the longest tongue? The answer: A giraffe wins with its seventeen-inch tongue—though it won't do them much good in the water, because giraffes cannot swim! And speaking of "tongue muscles," did you know that the bee uses twenty-two muscles to sting someone? Gosh, no wonder a honey bee dies after stinging. You'd think the bee would have a little more heart! Speaking of hearts, did you know that an elephant's heart weights about forty-five pounds; that earthworms have five hearts; and that the heart of man's best friend (the dog) beats forty times a minute faster than a human's?

Did you know that the average person sheds forty pounds of skin in a lifetime, and on the average will catch 140 colds in a lifetime? And speaking of colds, should you come down with one, the National Health Foundation suggests you wait six days before kissing someone—or else that person will be infected with your cold germs. And speaking of kisses, we call it the "French kiss," but did you know that in the French language it's called the "English kiss"? Did you know that the two well-known kissers, Montague and Capulet, were better known by their first names—Romeo and Juliet? And speaking of love, who doesn't love superstar Elton John, who travels under aliases that include Sir Tarquin Budgerigar, Bobo Latrine, Jr. and Binky Poodleclip.

Binky Poodleclip? Yes, and now that you know, the next time he's in your town and you're trying to call him at his hotel to personally ask him for a backstage pass, you'll know who to ask for. Backstage passes—wow! It just goes to show you what useful information *trivia* can be!

It has other uses, too, of course, like getting others to see you as witty and cool. Have there been times when you wished you could spew out an enticing and tantalizing tidbit of trivia, a juicy "quick" fact that would captivate everyone's attention, hold them spellbound—and impress them with your astounding intelligence and great mind? Of course you have. Teens everywhere tell us of that time when "I needed something interesting to say that would break the ice, or be able to say something catchy so as to capture—and own—the moment. Like in that moment, everyone is looking at *me*. I'm the focus of attention. I get to shine. It's my 'fifteen minutes of fame' and I love it!"

We understand. It's cool to be cool. It's a natural desire to want to stand out among your friends. We're here to help! As you've guessed by the title, the next pages are jam-packed with fun, interesting, rare and juicy trivia facts. In this unit you'll get to beef up on a broad base of information: everything from music, sports, animals, movies, famous books, love, languages, religions of the world—even how to use your zodiac sign to find your perfect mate for a date! Whether you use this information to spice up a conversation or fill a lull in a boring one or use it as a way to surprise someone with your wit and intelligence, you'll find trivia is a great way to impress your friends—and teachers and parents, too, and stand out among your friends and fans.

Okay, so we've convinced you to become a spermologer (a collector of trivia). But you better get reading! Books not printed on acid-proof stock disintegrate in a certain period of time. How long is that? You'll find the answer buried in this unit!

Enjoy! And don't forget to try out your newfound knowledge on your friends—or for that matter, any other taste berry.

♥ *Taste berries to you, Bettie and Jennifer Youngs*

Do Bees Have Knees?
Facts on Furry, Feathered and
Creepy-Crawly Friends

Question: Can insects shiver?
Answer: *Yes.*

Question: Can a rattlesnake bite if it's dead?
Answer: *Yes. Because of a reflux action, it can bite you up to a half an hour after it dies.*

Question: How many legs does the average caterpillar have?
Answer: *Sixteen.*

Question: Do toads have teeth?
Answer: *No.*

Question: Do earthworms have eyes?
Answer: *No.*

Question: Can cats taste sweets?
Answer: *No. Cats cannot taste sweet things.*

Question: What is the only bird that has nostrils?
Answer: *The kiwi bird.*

Question: What is the only mammal that can fly?
Answer: *The bat.*

Question: Do spiders have blood?
Answer: *Yes. It is transparent in color, but it's blood.*

Question: Do all mosquitoes bite?
 Answer: *No. Only the male bites.*

Question: What animal lives longer than any other?
 Answer: *The six-hundred-pound tortoise of the Galapagos Islands lives up to two hundred years.*

Question: Can eels live in saltwater?
 Answer: *No. If put in saltwater, it will short-circuit itself.*

Question: Why is the Tokyo Zoo closed two months out of the year?
 Answer: *To give the animals a vacation from visitors.*

Question: In which city in the United States is it against the law for a frog to croak after 11:00 P.M.?
 Answer: *Memphis, Tennessee.*

Question: How many offspring do armadillos have?
 Answer: *Exactly four at a time (and always the same sex: either all males or all females).*

Question: What animal can look forward with one eye, and back with the other?
 Answer: *A horse.*

Question: Where are the taste buds located on a fly?
 Answer: *In its feet.*

Question: Can a duck swim while asleep?
 Answer: *Yes. Ducks often swim while sound asleep.*

Question: How many times can a woodpecker peck per second?
Answer: *Twenty times per second.*

Question: Where are a cow's sweat glands located?
Answer: *In its nose.*

Question: Why can't a hummingbird stand on its feet?
Answer: *They aren't strong enough to hold up the bird.*

Question: Can giraffes swim?
Answer: *No.*

Question: Are polar bears right-handed or left-handed?
Answer: *Left-handed.*

Question: Do birds have sweat glands?
Answer: *No.*

Question: Is the "wise" owl smarter than other birds?
Answer: *No. The owl is known as "wise" because of its scholarly appearance.*

Question: How long can a snake go without eating?
Answer: *A year.*

Question: How long does a termite live?
Answer: *Up to thirty years.*

Question: What is the only animal that will eat a skunk?
Answer: *The great horned owl.*

Question: Do fish have eyelids?
Answer: *No. Their eyes are perpetually open.*

Question: How many muscles does a bee use to sting someone?
Answer: *Twenty-two.*

Question: How much does a newborn panda weigh?
Answer: *Less than a mouse.*

Question: What do adult moths eat?
Answer: *Adult moths do not eat.*

Question: How much does a hummingbird weigh?
Answer: *Less than a penny.*

Question: A male peacock is called peacock. What is a female peacock called?
Answer: *Peahen.*

Question: How fast can a kangaroo hop?
Answer: *Forty miles per hour.*

Question: A person can be identified by her fingerprint. How about a lost cow?
Answer: *Nose print.*

Should You Date a Leo or a Capricorn? Astrology Knowledge

According to its Greek origin, the word "zodiac" means "lore of the stars." Astronomers say that as we look from our globe at the starry hosts that surround us, we see that the axis of the earth traces out a huge circle about every twenty-six thousand years. This circle, known as the zodiac, falls into twelve distinct parts. Each part, or "sign" as the ancients called it, marks a passage of time.

Knowledge of the zodiac can be found in most all civilizations the world over. From the forgotten islands in the Pacific to the excavations among the most ancient ruins in Asia; be it engraved upon the temples of Greece and Rome or found in oldest Chinese records, all possessed a great knowledge of the zodiac. The Egyptians understood it well; the Chaldeans were masters on the subject, and the American aborigines in Mexico and Peru were well-acquainted with it. Not only was the zodiac common knowledge, but all believed it to be the key to understanding the nature of mankind, even our destiny.

In our modern era, we popularized this knowledge. For example, have you ever been asked, "What *sign* are you?" Astrologers believe that the astrological sign you are born under (determined by your birth date) can help explain your personality, reveal what's in store for your future, even help you determine—based on the "sign" of another—who are likely to be those with whom you are most compatible. Do you think it's that simple—or is that why some relationships seem as complicated as they do? Check it out! You might want to check the birth date of someone before asking that person out on a date!

Match the astrological sign with the time period in which it coincides.

January 20–February 18	Aquarius
February 19–March 20	Aries
March 21–April 20	Cancer
April 21–May 20	Capricorn
May 21–June 20	Gemini
June 21–July 21	Leo
July 22–August 21	Libra
August 22–September 21	Pisces
September 22–October 22	Sagittarius
October 23–November 21	Scorpio
November 22–December 20	Taurus
December 21–January 19	Virgo

Correct Match-Ups:

January 20–February 18	Aquarius
February 19–March 20	Pisces
March 21–April 20	Aries
April 21–May 20	Taurus
May 21–June 20	Gemini
June 21–July 21	Cancer
July 22–August 21	Leo
August 22–September 21	Virgo
September 22–October 22	Libra
October 23–November 21	Scorpio
November 22–December 20	Sagittarius
December 21–January 19	Capricorn

While the zodiac has sometimes been treated as a decoration, or regarded as superstition, even used in fortune-telling, some say the real significance of the twelve "signs" is that each represents a particular way to better know God, and that the sign we were born under designates our own particular path to follow in doing this. Therefore, each "sign" of the zodiac is given a symbol. While some believe the symbols refer to the physical shape of the constellations as seen in the sky—such as the shape of a bull or lion or fish—others say each symbol refers to the nature of the lesson we each must learn at a particular time.

Interesting! And definitely something to read up on! What symbol are you? How about your parents and brothers or sisters? How about your friends, and that special someone?

Match the symbol associated with each sign.

Capricorn	goat
Aquarius	ram
Pisces	fish
Aries	virgin
Taurus	scales
Gemini	twins
Cancer	water-bearer
Leo	archer
Virgo	bull
Libra	scorpion
Scorpio	crab
Sagittarius	lion

Correct Match-Ups:

Capricorn	goat
Aquarius	water-bearer
Pisces	fish
Aries	ram
Taurus	bull
Gemini	twins
Cancer	crab
Leo	lion
Virgo	virgin
Libra	scales
Scorpio	scorpion
Sagittarius	archer

What Stone Will Be in Your Class Ring? Trivia Gems

So special is our birth date that one of the loveliest of Mother Nature's works—precious stones—is assigned to the month in which we were born. Mankind has been wearing "rocks" since the beginning of time—and we still do! When you order your class ring, no doubt you'll have it set with your birthstone. And if you want to buy your mother a ring for Mother's Day with the birthstone of each member of the family in it, you'll need to know each of their birthstones. And someday, you just might want to buy a special someone a pin or ring with his or her (or your) birthstone in it! If you do, you'll need to know two things—that person's birth date, and the birthstone associated with it.

Check out your gem IQ: Match the following birthstones to the month each represents.

January	turquoise
February	amethyst
March	emerald
April	diamond
May	sapphire
June	pearl
July	opal
August	garnet
September	aquamarine
October	topaz
November	ruby
December	peridot

Correct Match-Ups:

January...garnet
February ....amethyst
March ....aquamarine
April ....diamond
May ....emerald
June...pearl
July ....ruby
August...peridot
September..sapphire
October ....opal
November ....topaz
December ....turquoise

Shooting Stars Are Not Stars: Corny Contradictions

A horned toad is not a toad. *It is a lizard.*

Shooting stars are not stars. *They are meteors.*

The onion is not an onion. *It is a lily.*

The banana tree is not a tree. *It is an herb.*

A prairie dog is not a dog. *It is a rodent.*

A ladybird is not a bird. *It is a beetle.*

A guinea pig is not a pig. *It is a rodent.*

The kangaroo rat is not a rat. *It is a gopher.*

The silkworm is not a worm. *It is a caterpillar.*

A peanut is not a nut. *It is a legume.*

A camel-hair brush is not made from a camel's hair. *It is made of squirrel fur.*

Catgut string does not come from a cat. *It is from a sheep's intestines.*

Black-eyed peas are not peas. *They are beans.*

The flying fox is not a fox. *It is a bat.*

Blackboard chalk is not chalk. *It is plaster of Paris.*

The pineapple is not pine, and it's not an apple. *It is a berry.*

The Douglas fir is not a fir. *It is a pine tree.*

The Canary Islands were not named after canaries. *They were named after a breed of dogs* (Canarniae insulae).

Boston College is not in Boston. *It is in Chestnut Hill, Massachusetts.*

Kilts did not originate in Scotland. *They had their beginning in France.*

The Dallas Cowboys are not in Dallas. *The team "resides" in Irving, Texas.*

What Did These Famous Stars Do Before Their Orbit to Center Stage?

You know that your favorite stars weren't always "famous," but do you know what they did before they made it big? Match what each did as they began their orbit to center stage before finally joining the galaxy of stars.

Jennifer Lopez	Mouseketeer: Mickey Mouse Club
Justin Timberlake	Mouseketeer: Mickey Mouse Club
Britney Spears	dancer for Janet Jackson
Paula Abdul	maid
Chris Isaak	waitress
Tina Turner	tour guide in Japan
Madonna	hairdresser
Chuck Berry	jewel thief
Ice-T	lifeguard
Jon Bon Jovi	elementary music teacher
Sheryl Crow	teen model
Whitney Houston	Burger King employee
George Michael	ice-cream vendor
Mick Jagger	chicken plucker
Chubby Checker	movie usher
Sting	ditch digger
Garth Brooks	truck driver
Elvis Presley	nightclub bouncer

Correct Match-Ups:

Jennifer Lopez ....dancer for Janet Jackson
Justin Timberlake...Mouseketeer: Mickey Mouse Club
Britney Spears ....Mouseketeer: Mickey Mouse Club

Paula Abdul..waitress
Chris Isaak ....tour guide in Japan
Tina Turner ....maid

Madonna..lifeguard
Chuck Berry..hairdresser
Ice-T..jewel thief

Jon Bon Jovi.................................Burger King employee
Sheryl Crow ....elementary music teacher
Whitney Houston ....teen model

George Michael...movie usher
Mick Jagger...ice-cream vendor
Chubby Checker....................................chicken plucker

Sting..ditch digger
Garth Brooks.....................................nightclub bouncer
Elvis Presley...truck driver

Wanted: Young, Skinny Fellow
Not Over Eighteen: People Personals

Question: In the mid-1800s, if you saw the following help-wanted ad, the company would be trying to hire a person for what position? "Wanted: Young, skinny fellow not over eighteen. Must be expert rider, willing to risk death on a daily basis. Orphans preferred."

Answer: *Pony Express.*

Question: Who was Pablo Diego Jose Francisco do Paula Juan Nepomuceno Cipriano de la Santissima Trinidad?

Answer: *Picasso.*

Question: Famous lovers Montague and Capulet are better known by these names.

Answer: *Romeo and Juliet.*

Question: "La Giaconda" is the actual title of what famous piece of art?

Answer: *Mona Lisa.*

Question: Saint Nicholas, as in "Ho Ho Ho!" fame, is the patron saint of _____?

Answer: *Pawnbrokers.*

Question: What hero is honored with a statue in Crystal City, Texas?

Answer: *Popeye.*

Question: Everyone knows Neil Armstrong was the first
person to walk on the moon. Who was the
second man to walk on the moon?
Answer: *Edwin "Buzz" Aldrin.*

Question: What was Annie Oakley's nickname?
Answer: *Little Sure Shot.*

Question: In the year 2000, Kim Dae Jung, President of South
Korea, won the Nobel Prize for _____?
Answer: *His work for democracy and human rights in South
Korea and East Asia.*

Question: Why was General Robert E. Lee buried barefoot?
Answer: *He was too tall for the coffin.*

Question: Superstar Luciano Pavarotti keeps this in his pocket
for good luck when he performs.
Answer: *A bent nail.*

Question: How did the practice of honking horns at weddings
begin?
Answer: *It was done as a gesture to ward off evil spirits.*

Question: How did the practice of a handshake come about?
Answer: *Strangers shook hands to show that they were
unarmed.*

Question: Who is the only American to have a bust at
Westminster Abbey in London?
Answer: *Henry Wadsworth Longfellow.*

Who Is Buried in Grant's Tomb?
Presidential Pundits

Question: What King became president of the
United States?

Answer: *Leslie King. When his parents*
divorced, he was adopted by his step-
father and given a new name: Gerald Ford. Gerald
Ford became the thirty-eighth president of the United
States.

Question: How many presidents of the United States are not
buried in America?

Answer: *Any president or ex-president who is still alive!*

Question: What president did not have a middle name?

Answer: *Abraham Lincoln.*

Question: How long must a person be a resident of the United
States in order to become president?

Answer: *Fourteen years.*

Question: What does the *S* stand for in Harry S. Truman's
name?

Answer: *Nothing. His parents could not decide on a middle*
name, so simply gave him the initial S.

Question: Besides being known as a great president, Theodore
Roosevelt was also notorious for what?

Answer: *Snoring.*

Question: Everyone knows that President Clinton plays the
saxophone. President Thomas Jefferson was known
to play what instrument?

Answer: *The fiddle.*

Question: Name the three presidents who died in the same
year.

Answer: *Martin Van Buren, William Henry Harrison and John
Tyler all died in 1841.*

Question: What president and first lady were fifth cousins?

Answer: *Franklin Delano Roosevelt and Eleanor Roosevelt.*

Question: What president never voted in a presidential
election, not even his own?

Answer: *Zachary Taylor, the twelfth president of the United
States.*

Question: Name the only president of the United States who
was a bachelor during his office.

Answer: *James Buchanan.*

Question: What president was sworn into office by his father?

Answer: *Calvin Coolidge.*

Question: What president was a tailor prior to his taking
office?

Answer: *Andrew Johnson.*

Question: What president is famous for keeping a gun under
his pillow?

Answer: *Franklin Delano Roosevelt.*

Question: Who was the only president to hold an earned Ph.D.?

Answer: *Woodrow Wilson.*

Question: Who is the only president ever to run for office without opposition?

Answer: *John Adams.*

Question: Name the only person to be both vice president and president, yet never elected to either office.

Answer: *Gerald Ford.*

Question: Which president had four sons, three of whom were killed serving their country?

Answer: *Theodore Roosevelt.*

We Call It the French Kiss:
What Do the French Call It?
Literary Lingo

Question: If ten people were each handed a pen and a piece of paper and told to write down any one word, what would be the word nine out of ten would write?

Answer: *Their own name.*

Question: We call it the "French kiss." What do the French call it?

Answer: *English kiss.*

Question: In the English language, more words begin with this letter than any other.

Answer: *S.*

Question: How far do you have to count before the letter *a* is used in spelling a number?

Answer: *One thousand.*

Question: What is the only letter *not* used in the spelling of any of the fifty states?

Answer: *Q.*

Question: The letter *e* is a commonly used letter in the English language. What is the name of the book in which the author wrote a fifty-thousand-word novel without using the letter *e* at all?

Answer: *Gadsby, by Ernest Vincent Wright.*

Question: How many languages spell the word "taxi" the same way?

Answer: *Five: English, German, French, Swedish and Portuguese.*

Question: What is the correct name for the dot over the letter *i?*

Answer: *Tittle.*

Question: The TID often found on a doctor's prescription stands for *ter in die,* a Latin term meaning what?

Answer: *Three times per day.*

Question: What is the name of this symbol "&"?

Answer: *The ampersand (which is common in hundreds of languages).*

Question: The Finnish term *saippuakauppias* means "soap seller" in English. If you spell the Finnish term backwards, what word do you get?

Answer: *The same one: saippuakauppias.*

Question: The plural of scampi (as in shrimp) is scampi. If you are referring to only one, what is the singular?

Answer: *Scampo.*

Question: Writer Washington Irving gave New York this famous name.

Answer: *Gotham City.*

Question: What is the name of mega-talented talk show host Oprah Winfrey's monthly magazine?

Answer: *O.*

Question: What does the Japanese term *kamikaze* mean?

Answer: *The Divine Wind.*

Question: In ancient Greece, athletes played sports *sans* clothes—in the buff, naked. What American word stems from that practice?

Answer: *Gymnasium, from the Greek word gymnos, which means "naked."*

Question: The literal translation for the French term "pot pourri" is?

Answer: *Putrid pot.*

Question: What is the only number in the English language which, when spelled out, has all its letters in alphabetical order?

Answer: *Forty.*

Question: Unless books are printed on acid-proof paper, how long will it take before they disintegrate?

Answer: *Fifty years.*

Question: How can you tell where a coin was minted?

Answer: *If a coin has the letter "S" printed on it, it was minted in San Francisco. If it has the letter "D," it was made in Denver. No letter at all denotes that it was minted in Philadelphia.*

Question: How do you say "no" in Japanese?
Answer: *There is no single word to say no (or yes) in Japanese.*

Question: How many letters are there in the Hawaiian alphabet?
Answer: *Twelve: a, e, h, i, k, l, m, n, o, p, u and w.*

Question: What does the abbreviation EPCOT (as in the amusement park) stand for?
Answer: *Experimental Prototype Community of Tomorrow.*

Question: What does the abbreviation A.M. (morning hours) and P.M. (afternoon hours) stand for?
Answer: *Ante meridiem, Latin for "before midday," and post meridiem, Latin for "after midday."*

Question: Before Edison suggested that everyone answer the telephone with the word, "Hello," what was the common greeting used by almost everyone?
Answer: *"Ahoy."*

Question: Why does dirty snow melt faster than white snow?
Answer: *Because it's darker and absorbs more heat.*

Question: What is the name of the square-topped cap worn at graduation ceremonies?
Answer: *Mortarboard.*

Everyone Knows Who Wrote
Frankenstein, Right? Famous Books

 Everyone knows who wrote *Frankenstein,* right? Wait a minute, who did write that much-adored popular literary piece anyway? Or, how about the wildly popular *Harry Potter* series? The following will help you brush up on famous brilliant authors—a surefire way to make you sound like a well-read person, which is always impressive!

Set I

Frankenstein
Romeo and Juliet
Huckleberry Finn

Mark Twain
Mary Shelley
William Shakespeare

Correct Match-Ups:

Frankenstein..Mary Shelley
Romeo and Juliet ....William Shakespeare
Huckleberry Finn..Mark Twain

Set II

The Grapes of Wrath
A Tale of Two Cities
The Great Gatsby

Charles Dickens
John Steinbeck
F. Scott Fitzgerald

Correct Match-Ups:

The Grapes of Wrath ....John Steinbeck
A Tale of Two Cities...Charles Dickens
The Great Gatsby...F. Scott Fitzgerald

Set III

20,000 Leagues Under the Sea	Jules Verne
War and Peace	Nathaniel Hawthorne
The Scarlet Letter	Leo Tolstoy

Correct Match-Ups:

20,000 Leagues Under the Sea ....Jules Verne
War and Peace..Leo Tolstoy
The Scarlet Letter ....Nathaniel Hawthorne

Set IV

Moby Dick	J. K. Rowling
Harry Potter	Herman Melville
Robinson Crusoe	Daniel Defoe

Correct Match-Ups:

Moby Dick..Herman Melville
Harry Potter..J. K. Rowling
Robinson Crusoe ....Daniel Defoe

Who Is "Hot Foot Teddy"?
Those Who Changed Their Names

Did you know that Smokey the Bear's original name was Hot Foot Teddy and that legendary pianist, Liberace, went by the stage name Walter Busterkeys? We're not sure about Busterkeys, but Hot Foot Teddy is pretty cute!

How about you? Have you ever wanted to change your name? Some people do. Singer Ray Charles dropped his real last name, Robinson, because he didn't want to be confused with boxing great Sugar Ray Robinson (whose real name is Walker Smith)! Below are some famous bands that have changed their names. See if you can identify which name each group left behind.

The Beach Boys	Feedback
The Beatles	The Screaming Abdabs
The Cranberries	Carl and the Passions
Green Day	The Cranberry-Saw-Us
Pearl Jam	The High Numbers
Pink Floyd	Johnny and the Moondogs
U2	Reenk Roink
The Who	Sweet Children

Correct Match-Ups:

The Beach Boys...Carl and the Passions
The Beatles...Johnny and the Moondogs
The Cranberries...The Cranberry-Saw-Us
Green Day...Sweet Children
Pearl Jam ....Reenk Roink
Pink Floyd...The Screaming Abdabs
U2 ....Feedback
The Who ....The High Numbers

Are You Astraphobic?
Who's Who in Phobia Facts

Franklin Delano Roosevelt popularized this quote: "The only thing we have to fear is fear itself." Easy to say, if you aren't afraid of anything! How about you? Are you afraid of snakes, closed-in spaces or semester finals? Whatever your fear, your phobia (FO-be-uh), there's a name for it. Check out these phobia facts! Match them up, if you can!

Claustrophobia (cl-stra-FO-bee-uh)	fear of water
Acrophobia (ak-ruh-FO-bee-uh)	fear of cats
Agoraphobia (ag-ur-uh-FO-bee-uh)	fear of dogs
Ailurophobia (eye-loor-uh-FO-bee-uh)	fear of horses
Astraphobia (as-truh-FO-bee-uh)	fear of fog
Cynophobia (sy-no-FO-bee-uh)	fear of thunder
Hydrophobia (hi-druh-FO-bee-uh)	fear of snakes
Monophobia (mon-uh-Fo-bee-uh)	fear of looking into mirrors
Ochlophobia (ok-luh-FO-bee-uh)	fear of closed-in spaces
Hippophobia (hi-po-FO-bee-uh)	fear of books
Keraunophobia (ke-ran-o-FO-bee-uh)	fear of fire
Homichlophobia (ho-mitch-la-FO-bee-uh)	fear of light
Ophidiophobia (o-FID-ee-o-bee-uh)	fear of crowds
Photophobia (fo-tuh-FO-bee-uh)	fear of being alone
Eisoptrophobia (i-so-tro-FO-bee-uh)	fear of great heights
Pyrophobia (pi-ruh-FO-bee-uh)	fear of wide-open spaces
Bibliophobia (bib-li-o-FO-bee-uh)	fear of lightning

Correct Match-Ups:

Claustrophobia...fear of closed-in spaces
Acrophobia...fear of great heights
Agoraphobia...fear of wide-open spaces
Ailurophobia ....fear of cats
Astraphobia ....fear of lightning
Cynophobia ....fear of dogs
Hydrophobia ....fear of water
Monophobia ....fear of being alone
Ochlophobia...fear of crowds
Hippophobia ....fear of horses
Keraunophobia..fear of thunder
Homichlophobia ....fear of fog
Ophidiophobia...fear of snakes
Photophobia...fear of light
Eisoptrophobia...................................fear of looking into mirrors
Pyrophobia ....fear of fire
Bibliophobia ....fear of books

Who Else Believes as You Do?
Religions of the World

Believing in a force greater than ourselves is the foundation of faith. Our religious beliefs can provide us with leadership and strength, drawing upon sources that inspire and uplift us, as they tie us to the timeless truths. While not all religions are the same, some of the doctrines upon which they are based have similar tenets. How "worldly" are your beliefs? See for yourself! What is the "spiritual principle" shared by each of these different faiths?

- "Hurt not others with that which pains yourself."

  Buddhism

- "What is hurtful to yourself do not to your fellow man. That is the whole of the Torah and the remainder is but commentary."

  Judaism

- "What you do not yourself desire, do not put before others.'"

  Confucianism

- "Do unto all men as you would wish to have done unto you; and reject for others what you would reject for yourselves."

  Islam

- "This is the sum of all true righteousness—treat others, as thou wouldst thyself be treated. Do nothing to thy neighbor, which hereafter thou wouldst not have thy neighbor do to thee."

  Hinduism

- "Do unto others as you would have them do unto you, for this is the law and the prophets."

  Christianity

Answer: The Golden Rule

Match each faith to its "sacred" scriptures or text:

Hinduism	Koran
Christianity	Bible
Judaism	Torah
Islam	Veda

Correct Match-Ups:

Hinduism ....Veda
Christianity ....Bible
Judaism ....Torah
Islam ....Koran

In Sikhism it is said, "Whatever a man soweth, that shall he reap. If he soweth trouble, trouble shall be his harvest." This same principle is also shared in other faiths. Match each quote to the faith to which it belongs:

a. Hinduism   b. Christianity   c. Confucianism
d. Buddhism   e. Judaism

1. "It is nature's rule that as we sow, we shall reap."
2. "What proceeds from you will return to you."
3. "Whatever a man sows, that will he also reap."
4. "A liberal man shall himself be enriched, and one who waters will himself be watered."
5. "Thou canst not gather what thou dost not sow; as thou dost plant the tree so it will grow."

Correct Match-Ups:

1. d, 2. c, 3. b, 4. e, 5. a

"The Thrill of Victory, The Agony of Defeat": All Sorts of Sports Trivia

Do you remember hearing the phrase, "The thrill of victory, the agony of defeat"? If you've ever tested your endurance and stamina by pushing yourself to the limits in competitive endeavors, you know that phrase says it best. Here are some phrases and facts to get you to first base!

Question: How deep is a golf hole?
Answer: *Four inches.*

Question: What is the biggest playing field in sports?
Answer: *A polo field (12.4 acres).*

Question: Name three sports that are won by going in a backwards motion.
Answer: *Rowing, tug-of-war, and swimming the backstroke.*

Question: A name given to a racehorse must not be longer than how many letters?
Answer: *Eighteen.*

Question: The score of a forfeited baseball game is 9–0. What is the score of a forfeited softball game?
Answer: *7–0.*

Question: Name the two men who have nothing to do with baseball, but are in the Hall of Fame in Cooperstown, New York, just the same.

Answer: *Abbott and Costello for their "Who's on First" routine.*

Question: This man used a six-iron golf club and drove a golf ball some four hundred yards. Who did this, and where was he playing?

Answer: *Astronaut Alan Shepard, on the moon!*

Question: What famous doctor was a member of the U.S. rowing team in the 1924 Olympics?

Answer: *Benjamin Spock.*

Question: "Small bowls," a popular game for centuries, is better known as:

Answer: *Marbles.*

Question: What is the distance from home plate to second base on a baseball diamond?

Answer: *127 feet, 3⅜ inches.*

Question: This sport was originally called "Poona."

Answer: *Badminton.*

Question: Why are only right-handed players allowed to play polo?

Answer: *This ruling was set by the U.S. Polo Association to cut down on collisions between left- and right-handed players as they ride horses to hit a wooden ball with their sticks.*

Question: A basketball hoop is how many inches in diameter?
Answer: *Eighteen inches.*

Question: In tennis, the term "love" represents what score?
Answer: *Zero, which by the way, comes from the French l'oeuf, which is an egg—hence, the shape of "zero."*

Question: In the 2001 Olympics, Marion Jones set out to win five gold medals for the U.S. Team. How did she do?
Answer: *Three gold medals; two bronze.*

Question: In the game of golf, what is a birdie?
Answer: *One under par.*

Question: In what sport would you use a putter?
Answer: *Golf.*

Question: In women's basketball, how many players, total, are on the court at one time?
Answer: *Eight.*

Question: In basketball, why would a player be awarded a free throw?
      a. player was fouled in the act of shooting
      b. player was fouled when the opposing team already had seven fouls
      c. a member of the other team got a "technical," or extreme personal foul
      d. a, b, and c.
Answer: *d.*

Question: Which is not one of the four tennis tournaments that make up the "Grand Slam"?

a. The Australian Open
b. The Canadian Open
c. Wimbledon
d. The French Open
e. The U.S. Open

Answer: *b.*

Question: What is the name of the silver bowl given to the National Hockey League champion each year?

Answer: *Stanley Cup.*

Question: How long is a regulation football field, including the end zones?

a. 100 yards   c. 120 yards
b. 110 yards   d. 140 yards

Answer: *c.*

Question: What is a running play in which the quarterback fakes a pass and then hands the ball to a running-back?

a. Draw   c. Option
b. Rollout   d. Sweep

Answer: *a.*

Question: Who won the Super Bowl in 2001?

a. San Francisco 49ers   c. Green Bay Packers
b. Baltimore Ravens   d. Dallas Cowboys

Answer: *b. (Baltimore Ravens defeated the New York Giants.)*

Question: What team won the very first Super Bowl?

      a. Kansas City   c. Green Bay

      b. New York   d. Miami

Answer: *c. (Green Bay defeated Kansas City in 1969.)*

Question: Who invented men's basketball?

      a. Chuck Cooper   c. John Havlicek

      b. James Naismith   d. Oscar Robertson

Answer: *b.*

Question: Who is credited with "inventing" baseball?

      a. Alexander Cartwright   c. Joe DiMaggio

      b. Alexander Spalding   d. Abner Doubleday

Answer: *d.*

Question: How many players, besides the batter, are there on a baseball field at one time?

      a. 8   b. 9   c. 10   d. 11

Answer: *b.*

Question: How many umpires are used in major league football games?

      a. 5   b. 4   c. 3   d. 2

Answer: *b.*

Question: Which team won the first World Series in 1903?

      a. Chicago White Sox   c. New York Yankees

      b. Boston Red Sox   d. Brooklyn Dodgers

Answer: *b.*

On What Part of Your Body Would You Find Your Pons? Buffing Up Your Body Knowledge

Question: On what part of your body would you find your "phalanges"?

a. your wrist
b. your legs
c. your face
d. your fingers

Answer: *d.*

Question: How many total bones are there in the adult human body?

a. 176   b. 194   c. 206   d. 227

Answer: *c.*

Question: How many total bones are there in a newborn's body?

a. 176   b. 300   c. 206   d. 227

Answer: *b.*

Question: What is the strongest muscle in the human body?

Answer: *The tongue.*

Question: If beauty is only skin deep, how deep is a person's beauty?

Answer: *Your skin is three-sixteenths of an inch deep.*

Question: What is the only muscle in the human body connected at only one end?

Answer: *The tongue.*

Question: Everyone knows that we shed skin. How much skin
does the average person shed in a lifetime?

Answer: *Forty pounds.*

Question: On what part of your body would you find the
most sweat glands?

Answer: *The soles of your feet.*

Question: How much air do your lungs take in on a daily
basis?

Answer: *12,500 quarts each day.*

Question: How cold does it have to be before your breath will
freeze in midair and fall to the ground?

Answer: *Ninety degrees (F) below zero.*

Question: On an average, how much do your fingernails
grow in one year?

Answer: *Two inches.*

Question: During biology, your science teacher says there is a
student in class sporting a keratoma. This means
your classmate has a:

a. freckle   b. wart   c. mole   d. callus

Answer: *d.*

Question: Another name for dandruff is:

a. dermatitis b. pityriasis c. psoriasis d. gingivitis

Answer: *b.*

Question: Which of the following is a cause of bad breath?

a. dermatitis b. pityriasis c. psoriasis d. gingivitis

Answer: *d.*

Question: How much does your hair grow each month?

a. It depends on what conditioner you use.
b. It depends on which phase of its growth cycle your hair is in.
c. Two inches if you trim it every month.
d. It all depends on your genetics.

Answer: *b. It depends on which phase of its growth cycle your hair is in: If it's in the growing phase (which is roughly two to five years for healthy hair), it will grow ½ inch to 1 inch per month; if it is in the resting phase (believed to be a three- to four-week cycle) or in the falling-out phase (which lasts between two and five months), it grows much slower, or not at all.*

Question: How much of your body weight is water?

a. 25%   b. 50%   c. 65%   d. 85%

Answer: *c.*

Question: How many individual muscles are there in the
human body?

a. 250   b. 475   c. 550   d. 600

Answer: *d.*

Question: Approximately how many times does the typical
human heart beat in a day's time?

a. 70,000   b. 100,000   c. 150,000   d. 225,000

Answer: *b.*

Question: In what part of your body would you find your
"pons"?

a. your brain
b. your feet
c. your eyes
d. your torso

Answer: *a.*

Question: In what part of your body would you find your
"zygomatic bone"?

a. your ribcage
b. your skull
c. your cheek
d. your foot

Answer: *c.*

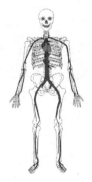

Question: What color is the brain?
> a. grey
> b. reddish-white
> c. pinkish-grey
> d. brownish-yellow

Answer: *a.*

Question: How much does an adult's brain weigh?

| a. about 3 pounds | c. 8.25 pounds |
| b. 5 to 6 pounds | d. about 10 pounds |

Answer: *a.*

Color-Coded: What "Color" Is Love?

1. What is color?

 a. the way our eyes see light
 b. the visual hues that each object in the world was
 made or born with
 c. a system devised to make art more interesting
 d. the way each person views the world differently

2. What is a "hue"?

 a. another name for "color"
 b. the value of a color
 c. the lightness of a color
 d. the darkness of a color

3. What is a "shade"?

 a. a dark color, such as black
 b. another word for "hue"
 c. a color mixed with black
 d. a blend of primary colors

4. What is a "tint"?

 a. pure white
 b. a color mixed with white
 c. a mixture of two colors that are next to each other on
 the color wheel
 d. a mixture of complementary colors

5. True or False: Animals do not see color.

Answers: *1. a, 2. a, 3. c, 4. b, 5. False (Some animals, such as monkeys and some kinds of birds, can see color— though most do not.)*

If David Is Eight Years Older than Theo, and Theo Is Five Years . . . : Nimble Numbers and Things

We live in a world of numbers. From figuring out how much you need to save for a down payment on a car to how much you'll need to save if you want to go on spring break with friends, number knowledge is a good thing! Go figure!

Question: The year 1961 reads the same upside-down. In what year will that happen again?

Answer: *6009.*

Question: Your parents have agreed to sell you their second car for $800. Your payments are $40 a month. How long will it take you to pay off your "new" car?

Answer: *One year and eight months.*

Question: What is the number of steps to the top of the Empire State Building?

Answer: *1,860 steps.*

Question: How much does the Oscar weigh?

Answer: *The Academy Awards Oscar trophy weighs eight pounds, thirteen ounces.*

Question: If David is eight years older than Theo, and Theo is five years younger than Karen, how much older is David than Karen?

Answer: *Two years.*

Question: How long is a "moment"?
  Answer: *According to an old English time unit, one moment is 1.5 minutes.*

Question: You have agreed to care for your neighbor's nine-year-old son at your home from Saturday at noon until Sunday at 6:00 P.M. They have agreed to pay you $2 an hour. How much money will you earn?
  Answer: *$60.*

Question: How fast is a "jiffy," as in "I'll be there in a jiffy"?
  Answer: *Lexicographers say it is equal to one hundred thousand billionths of a second.*

Question: How many keys are there on a piano?
  Answer: *Eighty-eight (fifty-two white and thirty-six black).*

Question: Mike lives three miles away from school. He walks to and from school every weekday. In four weeks, how far has Mike walked?
  Answer: *One hundred twenty miles.*

Question: How did the term "buck"—as in, I've got three bucks in my wallet—come about?
  Answer: *In the early days, a trapper could sell the deerskin of a buck for one dollar, hence the term, "buck."*

Question: You and two of your friends want to go to the lake
this coming Saturday. The lake is thirty-six miles
away. Gas is $1.50 a gallon and your car gets
eighteen miles to the gallon. How much money
will each of you have to pitch in to cover the cost
of gas for the trip?

Answer: *$1.00.*

Question: How long did the Hundred Years War last?

Answer: *116 years.*

Question: How many pounds of potatoes does it take to make
a pound of potato chips?

Answer: *Four pounds.*

In What City Is It Illegal to Ride an Ugly Horse? Spaces and Places Trivia

Question: In what U.S. city is it illegal to ride an "ugly" horse?
Answer: *Wilbur, Washington.*

Question: The traditional color for brides in the United States is white. What color is it in China?
Answer: *Red.*

Question: What state has no counties?
Answer: *Alaska.*

Question: What is the circumference of the Earth at the equator?
Answer: *24,896 miles.*

Question: If all the oceans evaporated, what would be the tallest mountain in the world?
Answer: *Hawaii.*

Question: What city in what state has the highest zip code?
Answer: *Wrangall, Alaska (Agawan, Massachusetts, has the lowest).*

Question: Where would you find 0 degrees longitude, 0 degrees latitude?
Answer: *In the Atlantic Ocean.*

Question: If someone told you to meet her for a picnic on the left side of the river, how would you know where to go?

Answer: *The left bank of a river is the left side, as you look downstream.*

Question: What is the only state in the United States that has only one syllable?

Answer: *Maine.*

Question: What country celebrates Thanksgiving on the second Monday of October?

Answer: *Canada.*

Question: Hawaii was the fiftieth state of the United States. Arizona was the forty-eighth. Which state is the forty-ninth?

Answer: *Alaska.*

Question: Where is the only place in the world where you can see the sun rise on the Pacific and set on the Atlantic?

Answer: *The Panama Canal—where the Pacific is east of the Atlantic.*

Question: What is the only country that does not have a rectangular flag?

Answer: *Nepal. It has two triangular pennants, one on top of the other.*

Question: How much of the earth is covered in water?
      a. 35%   b. 50%   c. 75%   d. 90%

Answer: *c.*

Question: What is the largest island in the world?
      a. Greenland
      b. Ireland
      c. Great Britain
      d. New Guinea

Answer: *a.*

Question: Which city sets the basis for standard time for most
      of the world?
      a. New York, United States
      b. Hong Kong, China
      c. Paris, France
      d. Greenwich, England

Answer: *d.*

Question: What is the lowest point on the planet?
      a. Death Valley in California
      b. Cape Wrangell, Alaska
      c. The Great Plains
      d. the surface of the Dead Sea

Answer: *d.*

Question: Why can't fish live in the Dead Sea?
      a. it's too salty
      b. it's too polluted
      c. there is no outlet
      d. it is too shallow

Answer: *c.*

Question: What is the highest mountain in the world?
a. Mt. McKinley
b. Mt. Kilimanjaro
c. Cerro Aconcagua
d. Mt. Everest

Answer: *b.*

Question: How long is the Earth's diameter?
a. about 2,500 miles
b. about 8,000 miles
c. about 16,200 miles
d. about 29,700 miles

Answer: *b.*

Question: This chunk of Jurassic limestone has been the focus of conflict for millennia and is still the subject of international dispute. Where and what is it?

Answers: *The Rock of Gibraltar is one of the Pillars of Hercules that guard the entrance to the Mediterranean. It's a remnant of an ancient geological collision between Africa and Europe, and the sight of many human collisions as well. It was named for a Moorish conqueror. The heavily fortified Rock is owned by Great Britain but claimed by Spain.*

About the Authors

Bettie B. Youngs, Ph.D., Ed.D., is a Pulitzer Prize–nominated author of twenty books translated into thirty-one languages. She is a former Teacher-of-the-Year, university professor and executive director of Instruction and Professional Development, Inc. A long-acknowledged expert on teen issues, Dr. Youngs has frequently appeared on *The Good Morning Show; NBC Nightly News; CNN; Oprah* and *Geraldo. USA Today,* the *Washington Post, Redbook, McCall's, U.S. News & World Report, Working Woman, Family Circle, Parents Magazine, Better Homes & Gardens, Woman's Day* and the National Association for Secondary School Principals (NASSP) have all recognized her work. Her acclaimed books include: *Taste Berries for Teens: Inspirational Short Stories and Encouragement on Life, Love, Friendship and Tough Issues; Safeguarding Your Teenager from the Dragons of Life; How to Develop Self-Esteem in Your Child; You and Self-Esteem: A Book for Young People; Taste-Berry Tales;* the Pulitzer Prize–nominated *Gifts of the Heart;* and the award-winning *Values from the Heartland.* Dr. Youngs is the author of a number of videocassette programs and is the coauthor of the nationally acclaimed Parents on Board, a video-based training program to help schools and parents work together to increase student achievement.

Jennifer Leigh Youngs, twenty-seven, is a speaker and workshop presenter for teens and parents nationwide. She is the author of *Feeling Great, Looking Hot & Loving Yourself! Health, Fitness and Beauty for Teens;* and coauthor of *Taste Berries for Teens: Inspirational Short Stories and Encouragement on Life, Love, Friendship and Tough Issues; Taste Berries for Teens Journal; More*

Taste Berries for Teens; and *A Taste-Berry Teen's Guide to Managing the Stress and Pressures of Life.* Jennifer is a former Miss Teen California finalist and Rotary International Goodwill Ambassador and Exchange Scholar. She serves on a number of advisory boards for teens and is a Youth Coordinator for Airline Ambassadors, an International organization affiliated with the United Nations that involves youth in programs to build cross-cultural friendships; escorts children to hospitals for medical care and orphans to new homes; and delivers humanitarian aid to those in need worldwide.

To contact Bettie B. Youngs or Jennifer Leigh Youngs, write to:

Youngs, Youngs & Associates
3060 Racetrack View Drive
Del Mar, CA 92014

Also from Bettie and Jennifer Leigh Youngs

Code #6692 • $12.95

Code #7680 • $12.95

Find the encouragement and support you need in this innovative collection of inspirational short stories on life, love and friendship. The journal has been created as an excellent companion giving you plenty of space for writing about your feelings and experiences.

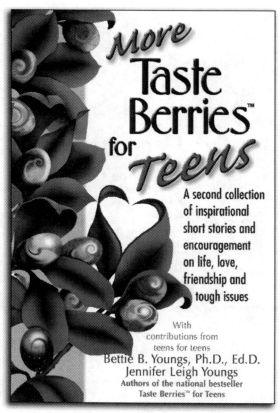

More Taste Berries™ *for* Teens

A second collection of inspirational short stories and encouragement on life, love, friendship and tough issues

With contributions from teens for teens

Bettie B. Youngs, Ph.D., Ed.D.
Jennifer Leigh Youngs
Authors of the national bestseller
Taste Berries™ for Teens

Code #813X • $12.95

More Taste Berries for Teens offers you an excellent way to discover how other teens have survived their experiences with life, love, friendship and tough issues. Their stories will bring you insight and encouragement and help you through your life experiences.

Available wherever books are sold.
To order direct: Phone 800.441.5569 • Online www.hci-online.com
Prices do not include shipping and handling. Your response code is BKS.

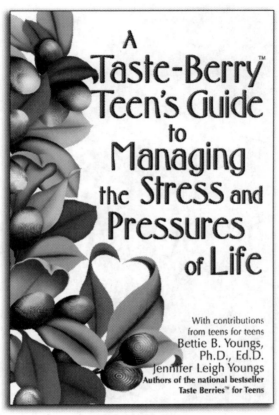

Code #9322 • $12.95

Have you ever had a day when you felt overwhelmed, down-and-out or simply "at wit's end"? On the days when stress sets in, pressures mount and anxiety lingers this book is yours. *A Taste-Berry Teen's Guide to Managing the Stress and Pressures of Life* will help you.

Beautiful–
Inside and Out!

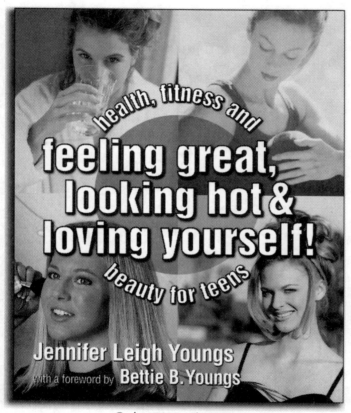